KU-215-340

Susan Jonusas attended the University of St Andrews and holds a Masters in Science, Technology and Medicine in History from Kings College London. During her Masters she focused on the intersection between crime and technology in the 19th Century. She was a bookseller, but now spends her free time on the archery range. This is her first book.

Praise for *Hell's Half Acre*

'Very good at painting a picture of hardscrabble life on the prairie. The thousands of European settlers who headed West for a better life may have been dirt poor, but they were also enterprising, hopeful and committed to doing the right thing. Jonusas is also very good at describing the creepy behaviour of the family, who lured travellers to their inn with the promise of a meal and a bed, before whacking them over the head with a hammer and cutting their throats' *Daily Mail*

'A compelling and lively thriller that chronicles the story of a serial-killer family in 19th Century Kansas' *New Statesman*

'Spending hours combing archives for new clues is one thing; fashioning that work into a vivid narrative is quite another. Jonusas excels at both' *The New York Times Book Review*'s 'The Best True Crime of 2022'

'Expertly told ... [A] gripping true crime narrative' *Slate*

'Rich in historical perspective and graced by novelistic touches, grips the reader from first to last ... Jonusas discovered several further leads in official archives and correspondence, enough to transform *Hell's Half-Acre*, at the halfway point, from a gothic popular history into a Wild West chase full of extraordinary developments' *Wall Street Journal*

'Jonusas, who parsed archival records in order to craft this riveting reconstruction, is especially good at dismantling some of the most salacious rumours surrounding the Bender daughter, Kate' *The New York Times*

'An impressive and deeply unsettling account of the Benders ... Radiant prose enhances the page-turning narrative. The combination of true crime and a vivid depiction of frontier life earn this a spot on the shelf next to David Grann's *Killers of the Flower Moon*' **Publishers Weekly**

'[Jonusas] ably captures the dangers involved in the westward trek that so many of the Benders' victims did not live to see through ... it's a story that, grisly and unsolved, fascinates ... ' *Kirkus Reviews*

'*Hell's Half-Acre* is a mesmerizing combination of gory mass murder and frantic pursuit of diabolical perpetrators, presented in some of the best, most atmospheric context I have ever read in any narrative nonfiction about the American frontier. This saga of the "Bloody Benders" will keep you reading – and flinching – until the last page is turned. Then you'll want to read it all over again' **Jeff Guinn**

HELL'S HALF ACRE

Four Killers, One Family
and the Crimes that
Shocked a Nation

Susan Jonusas

SCRIBNER

LONDON NEW YORK SYDNEY TORONTO NEW DELHI

First published in the United States by Viking,
an imprint of Penguin Random House LLC

First published in Great Britain by Scribner,
an imprint of Simon & Schuster UK Ltd, 2022

This edition published in Great Britain by Scribner,
an imprint of Simon & Schuster UK Ltd, 2023

1 3 5 7 9 10 8 6 4 2

Simon & Schuster UK Ltd
1st Floor
222 Gray's Inn Road
London WC1X 8HB

www.simonandschuster.co.uk
www.simonandschuster.com.au
www.simonandschuster.co.in

Simon & Schuster Australia, Sydney
Simon & Schuster India, New Delhi

A CIP catalogue record for this book is available from the British Library

Paperback ISBN: 978-1-4711-9032-2
eBook ISBN: 978-1-4711-9031-5

Book design by Daniel Lagin
Printed and Bound in the UK using 100% Renewable
Electricity at CPI Group (UK) Ltd

For the victims

James Feerick, William Jones, Henry McKenzie,
Benjamin Brown, William McCrotty, Johnny Boyle, George Longcor,
Mary Ann Longcor, John Phipps, William York

and those who remain unknown

Evil is unspectacular and always human,
And shares our bed and eats at our own table.

—W. H. AUDEN

Contents

Introduction

In the history of the American West, few historical figures have captured the public imagination like the outlaw. During the nineteenth and early twentieth centuries, the exploits of Jesse James, Pearl Starr, Billy the Kid, and numerous others filled newspapers and spilled over into cheap "dime" novels. Their legacy continues to this day, cemented by Hollywood's Technicolor Westerns and the grittier reimaginings of more recent years. In these stories, outlaws who cut a swath of violence across the high plains are struck down by the hand of justice. Alternatively, if the narrative suits, they are permitted a last-minute escape or tragic end defending others, perhaps against crooked lawmen or a greedy railway tycoon. The outlaw, like its more law-abiding relative, the cowboy, is one of the most universally recognisable figures in American history. The word itself evokes nonconformity, the promise of freedom, the choice to carve out your own path against the status quo. It's a much beloved part of country music, a stock character whose reach spans nearly all genres. But it is also a central part of the mythologisation of the West, a colonial narrative that obscures the reality of life on the frontier, sacrificing the more unpalatable history in favour of the overarching theme of progress.

The foundation for this narrative was laid over several centuries but came fully into being in the second half of the 1800s as America grappled with its identity in the aftermath of the Civil War. Stories of outlaws, gunslingers, Indians, sex workers—known colloquially as soiled doves—regulators, gamblers, prospectors, and pioneers entertained children and adults alike, solidifying their place in the fabric of the nation. A gunfight at the O.K. Corral in Tombstone, Arizona, exploded on to the newspapers and garnered those involved a notoriety that Wyatt Earp, a law enforcement officer at the scene, succeeded in transforming into celebrity later in his life. In 1883, Belle Starr, a wily female outlaw who harboured bandits at her ranch in Indian Territory, finally stood trial for horse thievery and found herself in a Detroit prison. The same year, William Cody, more recognisable by his nickname Buffalo Bill, founded Buffalo Bill's Wild West. The touring attraction of actors, dancers, and popular frontier figures recreating famous events from frontier history was a roaring success. Several rival productions emerged, but none could boast a cast list that included sharpshooter Annie Oakley, Hunkpapa Lakota leader Sitting Bull, and frontierswoman Calamity Jane. Buffalo Bill took his show all over the world. It was a glittering spectacle of gunpowder and horsemanship fundamental in shaping the international perception of the West and America as a whole at a time when the young country was still finding its place on the global stage. But it was also a PR stunt that allowed Americans to believe in a world that did not really exist—one where people did not stray into unknown moral territory or ask difficult questions about the state of the country.

IF THE WILD WEST SHOWS PRESENTED A ROMANTICISED VISION OF the frontier, the numerous publications focused on the period's nastier individuals sought to capitalise on humanity's long-standing fascination with villains. A book entitled *History, Romance and Philosophy of Great American Crimes and Criminals of the Various Eras of Our Country* promised readers 161 "superb engravings of the celebrated criminals." In its pages lurk familiar and unfamiliar faces. Some, like Cullen Baker—an unpredictable outlaw with ties to the Ku Klux Klan—barely made it out of the nineteenth century, their crimes too unpalatable for even the more lurid writers. Others, like Jesse James, became staples of cinema and literature for decades, reinvented as folk heroes despite their violent behaviour and unwavering support for the Confederacy. Then there are the Benders— the "Kansas fiends," a family of murderers whose crimes sent the newspapers and the nation into a frenzy. Their case is a stark reminder that buried beneath the myth of the outlaw are very real criminals whose violence left an indelible imprint on communities across the frontier.

I FIRST CAME ACROSS THE STORY OF THE BENDER FAMILY IN A LARGE, ghoulish book entitled *More Infamous Crimes That Shocked the World*. The book was from a local charity shop, its blood red cover held together by decades-old tape. Within its pages, a chapter called "The Bloody Benders" introduced me to the family who committed a series of murders in southeast Kansas that caught the attention of the entire United States. At the heart of the case was Kate Bender, an enigmatic young woman whose involvement in the crimes catapulted them into notoriety. I was fascinated by her role in the story, having focused a large part of my studies on the treatment of the female criminal during the nineteenth century. Aligned with my work on criminal history is an enduring interest in America, imbued in me by my grandmother whose photo albums packed with images of the West enthralled me as a child. *More Infamous Crimes* presented me with a case that drew these existing interests together, but the chapter on the murders was vague and offered virtually no details about the victims or the historical context of the crimes. Tantalisingly, it also revealed what came to be the defining feature of the Bender murders: the culprits had simply disappeared.

Since the discovery of their crimes nearly 150 ago, the Benders have rarely left the newspapers. For decades they served as the benchmark in human cruelty, and notorious serial killers H. H. Holmes and Belle Gunness would both find themselves compared with the Benders. When Hollywood turned its attention to Westerns during the 1940s, a reporter for the *St. Louis Globe-Democrat* offered up the story of the Benders as an "obvious possibility" for dramatic interpretation. During the 1950s, lavishly illustrated articles that paid little attention to the known facts of the case appeared in the *Brooklyn Daily* and *The Odessa American*. Even Laura Ingalls Wilder, celebrated author of the *Little House on the Prairie* series, enthralled audiences with a claim that her family had a connection to the case.

IN MORE RECENT YEARS THE BENDERS HAVE APPEARED SPORADIcally as the focus of true crime podcasts, blog posts, and top ten lists—where they routinely secure the top spot above other murderous families. I read and listened to most of these, but none ventured far beyond the year 1873, when the crimes were first discovered; elements were missing, and I wanted to know what they were. My own research began with the most readily available source on the Bender murders—the thousands of words printed in newspapers in the direct aftermath of the crimes. But nineteenth-century newspapers can be unreliable, as proven by the wild variations in the number of victims attributed to the Benders, with some claiming the number as high as 150. Along with embellished figures come misspelled names, seemingly random locations, and widely varied physical descriptions of the Benders themselves. The newspaper reports also suffer from another significant problem as sources: they are full of the age-old impulse to exaggerate in the name of a good story and better sales. In spite of these hazards, the basics of the case as reported remain largely consistent—a family of four committed a series of murders, then fled the state upon realising it was only a matter of time before their atrocities were discovered. The newspapers alone were not enough to get the full story, but their role in immortalising and popularising the Bender murders is undeniable. As such, they lend their words to the section titles and chapters of this book, though they are not the heart of its history.

AT THE KANSAS HISTORICAL SOCIETY STATE ARCHIVES ARE A WEALTH of primary sources dated from the months before the Benders fled Kansas right up until the late twentieth century, and it is these materials that

I relied on to reconstruct what actually happened. Some resemble documents you might find in cases today, such as official government correspondence. Others fill in the details between the broad strokes of the story—expense sheets filled with telegrams, wagon hire fees, and train fares to places that are now little more than ghost towns. All have been instrumental in the process of separating fact from fiction and in determining the day by day unfolding of events in this book.

The later archival sources, written many years and decades after the murders, provide an important role in understanding the continuing impact of the crimes on the community. They include personal recollections written by those who knew the Benders, those with friends or relatives with knowledge of the family, and people who have been exposed to the rich vein of folklore surrounding the crimes that still exists today. I approached these with caution, as many come from accounts collected by journalist Beverley Baumer for the Kansas State Centenary in 1961, and people's memories fade with time and successive retellings. Among those who contributed to this collection were Lucille Newland and George C. Cunningham, both of whom recount their father's experiences with the Benders—Newland in an interview with Baumer herself, and Cunningham in a short article. Theirs are typical of such recollections, informed partly by the first-hand experience of their relatives, partly by local knowledge of the crimes.

One of the more complicated examples of later sources is *The Bender Hills Mystery*, a serialised account of the crimes written by Jean McEwen from interviews with Leroy Dick, the township trustee at the time of the murders. McEwen was a pseudonym used by Jean Bailey, a local resident who had written poems and magazine stories in between raising her three children. Published over the course of 1934 in *The Parsons Sun*, the account places Dick at the centre of events, couching his interview in evocative prose and presenting verifiable facts alongside information that is provably false. Dick's role in the lead up to and discovery of the crimes in 1873 is well documented and, as such, appears throughout the first part of this book. But his claim that he hunted the Benders across the high plains in the direct aftermath of the crimes is almost certainly fictitious.

He makes no appearance in the correspondence between the detectives sent after the family and the governor of Kansas, nor in any of the expenses filed by those involved in the search. Dick also professes to know the true fate of the Benders, something which Jean McEwen makes no effort to question, despite his theory having been largely proven wrong several decades before the piece appeared.

It is always necessary to look at sources in conjunction with one another, to understand who they were created by and for what purpose, to place them on the sliding scale of reliability. Sources such as *The Bender Hills Mystery* are most useful in providing us with local voices through which we have access to the events on an emotional level. My work with the archival material, combined with sources such as transcripts from various United States District Courts and Federal and State Census data is what allowed me to break new ground in my research and open the story up beyond its previous boundaries.

THEORIES ABOUT THE FATE OF THE BENDER FAMILY HAVE CIRCU-lated for nearly 150 years. At first glance, and even after quite a lot of digging, there appeared to be no tangible information about where they might have gone beyond ill-informed speculation in the newspapers. Victims' families moved on and few were willing to share their thoughts on the fate of the Benders with the newspapers. Kansas authorities appeared hapless at best; the reward money offered for the family futile. Detectives followed increasingly wild leads and considered possibilities that seemed far-fetched even for reporters. The search continued into the twilight of the nineteenth century when new characters found themselves caught up in the community's desperate search for closure. But as I made my way through hundreds of letters written to the authorities about the Benders, a very different picture about their fate began to emerge. It became clear that far more was known about the movements of the family than was ever divulged to the general public, and the detectives were not quite as incompetent as they seemed. Caught up in the allure of an unsolved mystery, I tracked the Benders as far as these new leads allowed me.

REAL LIFE DOES NOT ALWAYS FOLLOW A SMOOTH DRAMATIC PATH and the story of the Bender murders is no exception. When I began writing, I knew that constructing a narrative out of such a wide variety of sources would be a challenging task. But in drawing the materials together and weighing the evidence concerning their reliability available to me, I was able to build a narrative firmly rooted in the verifiable facts of the case. I also knew that it was important not to lose the more atmospheric elements of the story, as part of the enduring fascination with the Bender murders comes from the location in which they took place. To convey the peculiar terror which the Benders inflicted on their victims and the community, I collected a series of different and often bizarre accounts of time spent at the Bender cabin. These experiences, which form the early part of this book, appear across multiple, separate sources. Where appropriate, descriptions of the landscape, wildlife, and weather have been informed by the time I spent in Kansas. Alongside this are several first-hand accounts of life in frontier Kansas written by homesteaders in the aftermath of the Civil War.

Labette County, Kansas

———

In a valley fourteen miles east of Independence, a party of seventy-five men on horseback pick their way through the mud. Mist not yet burned off by the sun moves adrift on the breeze, clinging to them like a second skin. For weeks they have been searching for Dr William York, a beloved local doctor who disappeared on the trail around the time the first signs of spring broke through the winter-hardened landscape. They steer their horses towards a cabin less than ten feet (three metres) from the trail, where they are greeted by Leroy Dick, the local official in charge of the search party whose cousin is also missing. Dick tells the men that the property has been abandoned. Billy Tole, the wiry farmhand who alerted Dick to the desertion of the cabin, shuffles uneasily in his saddle. He looks to the stable, where two men are busy removing a dead calf to make space for their own animals. Beyond the stable is a small, well-kept orchard. The ground is clogged with weeks of relentlessly bad weather and the scent of rain-soaked wood fills the air. Beneath it lies a second smell. Like the other members of the party who are veterans of the Civil War, Leroy Dick knows that it is the smell of death.

THE MEN SPLIT INTO GROUPS AND THE HUNT FOR THE SOURCE OF the smell begins. Some head to the stable, others to the cabin. The cabin is a modest one-storey structure, sixteen feet by twenty-four feet and wholly unremarkable. Inside, a single room is divided by the canvas sheet from a wagon. Dick yanks the makeshift curtain aside and is engulfed in a cloud of filth. It settles to reveal a sparsely furnished living space inhabited by insects that retreat into crevices at the fall of heavy boots. The cabin has been empty for some time, but it is clear that the occupants left quickly, taking only the essentials needed for travel. Towards the back of the room the scent of decay is stronger. A Bible with a cracked spine lies discarded near a straw mattress pulled aside to reveal a trapdoor. Grasping the leather strap nailed to the wood as a handle, Dick throws the door open and the smell leaks into the cabin. It sticks in the throats of the search party. Beneath the men a dark void opens.

Silas Tole, Billy's older brother, volunteers to descend. He is a rancher and used to the smell of animal carcasses, but down in the cellar he struggles to breathe. The floor is a slab of sandstone, reddened by unnatural stains. When Silas crouches to investigate further, he finds that the soil surrounding the slab is damp. Hoisting himself from the pit, he tells the group that they will have to move the cabin to gain better access to the cellar; that there is definitely something buried beneath the slab. Pale faced, the men vacate the building with expressions that send a murmur of disquiet through the others waiting outside. Dick gives the instruction for the cabin to be moved.

Men tie ropes to horses and pulleys, dislodging the cabin from its foundation and exposing the rancid contents of the pit to daylight. Excavation of the site corrupts the spring afternoon with the smell of earth and sweat. As they dig, the men discard layers of clothing and wipe dirt across their brows. News of the events unfolding reaches local towns, and the afternoon brings with it curious spectators who arrive on foot and by wagon. Beneath the slab the soil reeks of human decay and the men take turns shovelling the dirt. There is still no sign of a body.

When Billy Tole points to a team of horses pulling a buggy at full gallop, Leroy Dick recognises the man behind the reins as William York's younger brother, Edward. Ed York is a bright but volatile man whose gruelling search of the landscape has left him desperate. Beside him is Thomas Beers, a private detective hired by the York family, eager to make a name for himself. Beers knows the area well; he has been investigating William's disappearance for the preceding month and has come to a grim conclusion. The two men climb down from the buggy and join the proceedings.

DURING THE HOURS THAT PASS, ED TEETERS AT THE EDGE OF DE-lirium, vexed by the imprint of slaughter without any answers. He has walked the orchard, checked the stable, stared into the empty pit. Beers watches him closely, worried that the young man's desperation might slip into violent rage like it has before. Ed disappears inside the cabin, away from the eyes of the detective and the crowd. Though its contents have already been riffled through by inquisitive hands, Ed decides to search for himself. It is not long before he discovers a bridle wedged haphazardly behind the grocery counter and recognises it as belonging to his brother. He thinks of William's pregnant wife, Mary, and her three little children who wait back home in Independence, anxiously waiting for news of their missing loved one. Tucking the bridle into his overcoat, he surveys the rest of the room and notices that the clock on the counter has stopped. It has not been wound for three weeks.

OUTSIDE, THE LAST OF THE DAYLIGHT DISSOLVES ACROSS THE PRAI-rie. Leroy Dick chews with agitation on the end of his pipe and listens to the mundane chatter of the search party. He looks to the cabin. When Ed emerges, he extinguishes the pipe. Ed has his gaze fixed on the orchard, where evening shadows fall on irregularities in the surface of the soil. Walking slowly to the spot with the disturbance, Ed calls for the detective. He indicates the area at his feet. Around them the chatter gives way to silence as a small congregation forms in the orchard. Detective Beers slides the ramrod from his rifle and passes it to Ed.

Taking a deep breath, Ed plunges the ramrod into the soil until its downward path encounters matter too soft to be soil. Grasping the rod with white knuckles and a rising nausea, he feels it dislodge from something not quite solid buried roughly four feet (120 centimetres) below the surface. Ed knows he is shaking and wishes that his eldest brother, Alexander, who is also eager for news of William, had come to the cabin in his place. Steadied by the firm hand of the detective on his shoulder, Ed draws the rod from the earth. With it comes the sharp, pungent odour whose source has plagued the search party all day. In the last of the light, Beers can make out five more areas among the saplings where the ground is disturbed.

Ed stares at the base of the rod. It is slick with human viscera.

Part I

THE THEATRE OF A
NATION'S STRUGGLE

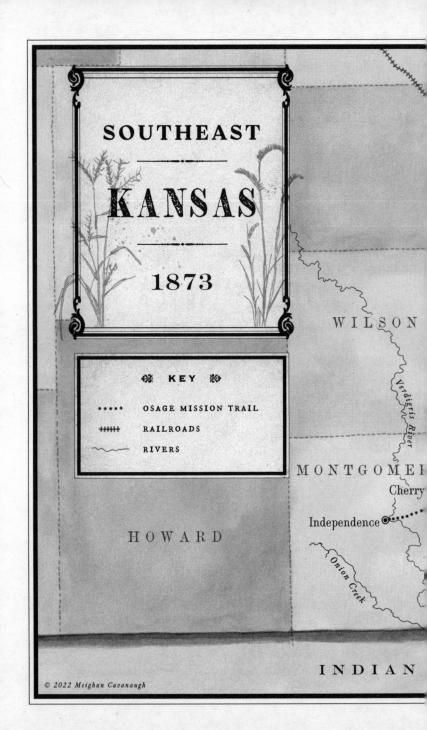

SOUTHEAST

KANSAS

1873

❊ KEY ❊

••••• OSAGE MISSION TRAIL
╫╫╫╫╫ RAILROADS
～～～ RIVERS

WILSON

Verdigris River

MONTGOMERY

Cherry

Independence

Onion Creek

HOWARD

INDIAN

© 2022 Meighan Cavanaugh

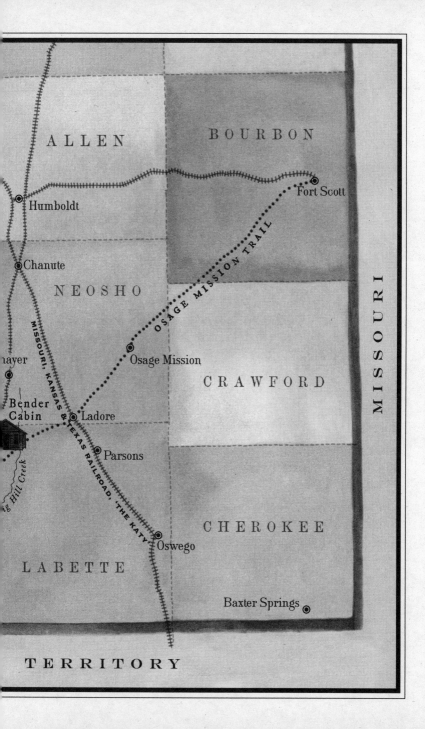

A State Birthed in Violence

In the spring of 1854, nearly three decades before the grisly discovery in Labette County, a steady stream of settlers headed west from Missouri into the newly created Kansas Territory. Some came alone to find their place among new communities. Others packed entire families into wagons and drove livestock hundreds of miles towards land ripe for farming. They were met by a land of open prairie vaulted by an endless sky. Water was readily available, and plentiful forests provided a steady source of timber. But many of the new arrivals harboured an agenda they held above the dream of life on the prairies. On 24 June, at a committee meeting of the Settlers of Kansas Territory, the group passed a resolution recognising slavery as a legitimate institution within the territory. It was a cause they were willing to fight for.

Since its formation in 1776, the United States had struggled with the issue of slavery within its borders. In 1850, when California was admitted to the Union as a free state, tensions escalated, with free states now outnumbering their slaveholding counterparts. As the railway moved further west and territories were incorporated into the Union as new states, each side grew increasingly desperate to hold the advantage in Congress. In May 1854, the U. S. Congress passed the Kansas–Nebraska Act, placing the decision over whether the territories of Kansas and Nebraska would be free or slave states when they entered the Union in the hands of the people who lived there. With Nebraska considered certain to declare itself a free state, abolitionists and their opponents turned their attention to Kansas—and it seemed that the pro-slavery faction already had a head start.

AS THE YEAR UNFOLDED, ABOLITIONIST PARTIES FROM THE NORTH arrived on the prairies of Kansas Territory to establish rival communities, hoping to turn the tide. The pro-slavery settlers from Missouri were dubbed "border ruffians" for their tendency to move back and forth across the border. The abolitionists referred to themselves as "free-staters." By December, hostility between the two factions spilled over into violence, and the rest of the nation watched with growing unease. "It is the fate of the young territory of Kansas to be the scene of unceasing strife and agitation," observed one newspaper in Washington, D.C.

As Kansas neared the date of its first election for the territorial legislature, it became clear to people across the nation that the election was about far more than the land within its boundaries. It was about the future of the United States at large. The elected legislature would determine whether the state would allow slavery. Both sides turned to intimidation as a means of securing victory, bolstered by newspapers that printed sensationalist stories about the opposition. When settlers from Missouri with no intention of remaining in Kansas crossed into the territory and swamped the vote in favour of pro-slavery candidates, the region erupted into chaos amid accusations of voter fraud. In Leavenworth alone ballot counters recorded nearly five times the amount of votes as known residents in the town. Sensing violence on the horizon, *The Kansas Herald of Freedom* declared, "Kansas will probably be the first field of bloody struggle with the slave power." The turbulent period that followed became known as "Bleeding Kansas," and the events that unfolded between 1854 and 1861 continued to shape the state and its people long into the latter half of the century.

CIVILIANS FOUND THEMSELVES TARGETED BY CAMPAIGNS OF TER-
ror that sought to force them out of the state and obstruct local elections.
The violence was physical, psychological, and highly localised. Bordered
by the fiercely pro-slavery Missouri, eastern Kansas was subjected to
some of the worst guerrilla warfare before and during the Civil War.
Counties along the border both produced and suffered at the hands of
guerrilla fighters as groups of raiders formed to protect their communities while wreaking havoc on others. Pro-slavery bands hailing from
Missouri were referred to as Bushwhackers; their abolitionist, Kansan
counterparts as Jayhawkers. Settlers who wanted nothing to do with either
side were dragged into an existence punctuated with violence that continued to escalate.

FOR TOWNS LIKE FORT SCOTT IN SOUTH-EAST KANSAS, WHERE THE
two factions lived alongside each other, violence became a part of every-
day life. In December 1858, its citizens awoke in a panic to the thunder
of hooves. James Montgomery, a hard-line abolitionist and soon to be
colonel in the Union Army, was leading a band of Jayhawkers on a rescue
mission to free a man imprisoned in one of the town's hotels. While
Montgomery headed to the hotel with a smaller group, the others rounded
up the town's pro-slavery citizens and held them in a prisoner circle at
gunpoint. Those sympathetic to the anti-slavery cause stayed inside to
avoid confusion. Montgomery freed his prisoner with little resistance, but
the situation escalated when John Little, a zealous pro-slavery activist,
decided to make a stand from his general store. Upstairs, his fiancée,
Sene Campbell, concealed herself in the bedroom with the two Black
children the couple kept as slaves. Little opened fire on the Jayhawkers,
but when he risked a look through a narrow window, he was shot through
the head. When Little was confirmed dead, the Jayhawkers plundered
the building and abandoned the town.

A month later, still filled with rage, Sene wrote to Montgomery after hearing he had publicly declared that he did not regret the murder of her fiancé. She signed off with a warning:

"Remember this. I am a girl, but I can fire a pistol. And if ever the time comes, I will send some of you to the place where there is weeping and gnashing of teeth."

IN 1861, KANSAS DECLARED ITSELF A FREE STATE AND THE COUN-try descended into civil war. In Kansas, the guerrilla violence that had plagued the state for years continued long into the war, with devastating consequences. In the early hours of 21 August 1863, 450 Confederate Bushwhackers led by William Quantrill attacked the Union-sympathising town of Lawrence. The attack was relentless in its brutality. Over 150 civilians were killed and a quarter of the buildings in the town burned to the ground. The wounded crawled into the undergrowth to hide. Un-armed men fled and were shot down as they ran. Children were sepa-rated from their parents, lost amid the screaming stampede of horses and debris. The Bushwhackers systematically sought out and executed spe-cific individuals, but many of the towns' key abolitionist figures escaped. In a fury, the group turned to executing as many men as possible, includ-ing the elderly and young sons of anti-slavery parents. By nine o'clock in the morning the raiders had vanished, leaving the town and the nation traumatised. Papers across America raged against Quantrill and his men, branding them vipers and their actions a fiendish atrocity. But they also condemned the guerrilla warfare in the area in its entirety, for nei-ther side could claim freedom from a legacy of slaughter.

When on 9 April 1865, Robert E. Lee surrendered to future president Ulysses S. Grant and ended the war, an exhausted nation began the slow process of rebuilding itself. Though the conflict was over, the people of Kansas were left with the residue of nearly a decade of sporadic violence, where there had been no clear border between home and the battlefield. The experience imbued communities with a strong sense of localised jus-tice and a tendency to take matters into their own hands, especially on those

The Raid on Lawrence, Kansas. *Harper's Weekly*, September 5, 1863.

who escaped the law. Towns and families who had fought against each other coexisted with a certain level of peace by avoiding questions that had difficult answers. Young men who had once burned off energy riding with the Bushwhackers or Jayhawkers settled in to farming or travelled further west. Those who could not shake the itch of violence became listless and dangerous, turning the skills they had garnered under men like Montgomery and Quantrill to horse thievery and the saloons. No longer restricted by the border wars, pioneers from the East flooded in with the spring rain. They came by horse and wagon and then by railway. Families settled on homesteads, the land grew rich with wheat, and frontier towns blossomed into thriving communities. Men with gold on their minds and greed in their hearts raced through on their way to mountains out West that promised riches. On their tails came astute businessmen and -women who would reap the benefits of the prospectors' misfortunes. Families that did not settle bought and traded goods for the long, perilous journeys that lay ahead. The railway thundered through the landscape like an iron horse, carrying all manner of passengers into the boom-and-bust cycle of pioneer living. All who came to Kansas were united by the most powerful of dreams: life on the American frontier.

BUT WHEN WHITE SETTLERS ARRIVED IN THE STATE FROM THE EAST Coast and parts of Europe, they did so at a devastating cost to its Indigenous peoples. To the south of Kansas lay Indian Territory, the outcome of more than a century of forced removal of Native Americans from their lands in order to make room for white settlers seeking to hunt and set up homesteads. In 1834, the Trade and Intercourse Act had defined Indian Territory as the part of the United States west of the Mississippi and "not within the states of Missouri and Louisiana, or the Territory of Arkansas."* Almost immediately the area of land allotted to the tribes began to shrink, its borders closing in around Indigenous communities as the U.S. government and local authorities ignored treaties in favour of white settlers. During the aftermath of the Civil War, tribes who had sided with the Confederacy had their allotted reservations restricted even further.

By 1870, Indian Territory encompassed much of what is today the state of Oklahoma. Within its limits the tribes struggled against railway companies that had been granted right of way through the area in the Reconstruction treaties of 1866. The Missouri-Kansas-Texas Railway cut through land allocated to the Cherokee, Creek, Choctaw, and Chickasaw Nations and was quickly joined by the St. Louis and San Francisco line that crossed through the Cherokee Nation at Vinita. Though the nations had been given the right to form tribal governments in the area, corporations sought to penetrate the land and disperse the native population, and the federal government made little effort to stop them. As non-Indians attached to railway companies, oil fields, and coal mines poured into the region, the tribes found themselves locked in yet another battle to protect what small amount of land they had left.

---

* A land roughly encompassing present-day Kansas and Oklahoma.

AMONG THOSE WHO HEADED TO THE PLAINS TO BUILD NEW LIVES
were newly freed African Americans. After Congress passed the Thir-
teenth Amendment in the winter of 1865, formerly enslaved people hoped
for land, freedom of movement, and the chance to reunite with loved ones
from whom they had been separated. But in the immediate aftermath of
the Civil War, Southern states enacted Black Codes, laws that varied
from state to state but focused on continuing to restrict the rights of African Americans. Designed to provide former slaveholders with a steady
supply of cheap labour to revive the Southern economy, the codes ex-
cluded freed people from leasing land and owning businesses. Many also
broadened vagrancy laws, allowing authorities to round up and arrest
Black people perceived to be out of work, who would then be forced into
unpaid labour as a sentence.

The implementation of the Fourteenth and Fifteenth Amendments
sought to overrule the codes, but in 1877, when the last of the federal
troops left the Southern states, local legislatures immediately set about
circumventing protections afforded to Black people by the amendments.
White supremacist organisations terrorised fledgling and successful Black
communities. Land held by the federal government was returned to its
white owners and former slaves found themselves locked in poverty, with
little alternative but to return to plantations, where they could work for
wages or as sharecroppers. Looking to escape the poverty and intoler-
ance of the South, some Black communities turned their gaze north and
westwards, where the vast expanse of open prairie held the possibility of
self-sufficient settlements. In the decades following the Civil War, twelve
all-Black agricultural colonies sprang up on the plains of Kansas alone.

SOUTH-EAST KANSAS, THE NEXUS POINT OF SO MUCH CONFLICT DURING THE
war, experienced a lively post-bellum boom ("post-bellum" refers to the
years after the American Civil War). Free from the presence of unruly

militia, Fort Scott became an agricultural and commercial hub. Lawyers, farmers, and bankers full of ambition walked the streets. They bought land, established businesses, and then sent for their young families. Fresh paint glistened in the sun on new shopfronts nearly every day of the week. During 1869, when railway workers began to lay tracks south of the town, squatters who were living on the proposed route became violent, staging protests until construction became impossible. The army returned to the town and crushed the protests in the interest of big business. For the local officials, a group of disgruntled citizens was worth the prize of the railway. By the early 1870s, Fort Scott was one of the great gateways to the West and the South. A vital artery in the network of American transport, it offered connecting trains as far east as New York and as far west as Sante Fe.

For those travelling on foot, Fort Scott was the entrance to the only marked route into the newly established counties of Labette and Montgomery, via the Osage Mission Trail. The trail had been in use since the settlement of Osage Mission in 1847, a town founded to be the heart of the push to convert the Osage Nation. Now it had a new ending point in Independence, the seat of Montgomery County. Immediately popular with settlers due to its proximity to the Verdigris River and expansive, rolling prairieland, Independence was one of the great successes of the frontier. A journalist for *The Leavenworth Bulletin* wrote a glowing review of the town in May 1870 in which it declared "the giant progress is making rapid strides towards greatness in this famous region." The surrounding area was alive with the sound of sawmills, and though it was still a new town, it already had a newspaper.

The Osage Mission Trail, once reserved for hardy Jesuit priests and fur trappers, became a well-trodden thoroughfare joining a number of rapidly expanding communities. It appeared deceptively safe by frontier standards. Devoid of mountains and canyons, the dirt trail wound its way through grass that shone gold in the early morning light. But it was a stretch of land that claimed many lives in many ways. Lightning struck at anything exposed. Deep, cold nights punctuated warm spring days, freezing unsuspecting travellers in their tents. Great floods burst riverbanks and swept ill-prepared pioneers into the churning water.

If travellers were lucky enough to escape death at the hands of the natural world, there were myriad bizarre accidents to fall foul of. People sliced their feet open chopping wood, fell beneath the feet of angry horses, and maimed one another with unreliable firearms. And out on the prairie another danger was soon to manifest itself in the landscape, one uniquely positioned to take advantage of the transitory nature of frontier life.

The Benders Come to Kansas

Labette County, Kansas

AUTUMN 1870

Nestled in the south-east corner of Kansas, Labette County is a land of whistling grass and mirrored waters. Creeks, dancing and clear, divide vast expanses of prairieland rolling towards the sky. In the days before white settlers, when mountain men and fur trappers were among the few to venture west, a group of French trappers passing through the region encountered a skunk so large near the banks of a creek that they named the water *La Bette* in honour of the animal's size. When land boundaries were drawn, the river in turn passed its name to the county.

Established in 1867, Labette passed a whole year before its first recorded murder trial. It did not take long for others to follow. Less settled than other parts of the state, Labette proved a haven for those on the run from the law or seeking to make a living outside it. Citizens beat one another to death in land disputes and stabbed one another in drunken knife fights. As the railway grew, so did the number of train robberies. Outlaws exploited the proximity of the county to Indian Territory to the south, disappearing across the border to fence stolen goods. Men and women from all walks of life swindled, bribed, and stole as they moved through the county and continued further west. Newspapers professed horror at the amount of criminal activity in the area but reported every story with the gleeful sensationalism of tabloids. Along with crime, the press reported on accidents, sandwiching them in the Town and City news section between advertisements for clothing and dry goods. A column in *The Fort Scott Daily Monitor* ran separate adverts for watches and men's dress shirts; between them was a brief announcement that two men had been killed when a loaded musket accidentally discharged after being dropped on the floor. They had been delivering goods to a general store.

ON A BRIGHT OCTOBER MORNING IN 1870, TWO MEN ARRIVED AT Osage Township in the north-west corner of the county. From their crudely built trading post, Edward Ern and Rudolph Brockman watched them approach. The post sold a selection of dry goods to settlements in the area and those passing through. Ern disliked visitors and regretted letting Brockman talk him into a business venture that forced him to talk to so many people. He went inside to avoid conversation. The sun hung cold and distant above the clouds. Beside the wagon ran a wiry dog of no distinct breed. It yipped and snapped at the team and then at Brockman. The younger of the two men jumped from the wagon, shaking the grime of a fifteen-mile journey from his clothes. He turned his face to the sun and gave a weird laugh. He introduced himself to Brockman as John Gebhardt and the man in the wagon as John Bender. John, or Pa Bender, as the townsfolk would eventually refer to him, wore his sixty years on his face in a perpetual look of contempt for his surroundings. Though the two men did not share a surname, a natural assumption existed that they were related either by blood or by marriage. Neither man ever elaborated on the matter.

BROCKMAN HEARD THE GERMAN IN GEBHARDT'S ACCENT AND REplied in their shared language. Gebhardt laughed again. It was a tic that punctuated his sentences and his thoughts. Brockman thought he might be simple. Gebhardt had a narrow, handsome face, but his eyes were pinched slightly too close together, flint grey and restless.

"Lookin' for a claim," he said cheerily. Brockman offered the two men lunch and lodging. On the wagon the older man grunted, scratching a head of hair as coarse as that of the dog that now rolled in the dirt beneath the porch. He climbed down with an ease that didn't belong to a man his age, but next to Gebhardt, Pa was stooped and rangy. Hitching the team to the side of the trading post, the men followed their host inside.

Ern, hearing that their visitors were also German, decided his misanthropy didn't extend to people who spoke his native tongue and joined them for lunch. At the time Pa Bender and Gebhardt arrived in Kansas, people who spoke Germanic languages made up the majority of the European demographic in the state. Lumped under the collective term "Dutch," they included recent immigrants as well as second- and third-generation Americans from the East—in large part Pennsylvania. Mostly for better but sometimes for worse, a natural association formed between those who shared a language on the frontier.

Over lunch the two men were vague about everything except their enthusiasm for locating a claim. Like many settlers who had drifted in across the plains, they were eager to take advantage of the 1862 Homestead Act. Designed to encourage westward expansion, the act offered 160 acres of land to whoever could afford the eighteen-dollar claimant fee. If the settlers could prove that they had worked on and improved the land over a five-year period, they were entitled to keep it. Homesteads were most commonly comprised of a cabin or farmhouse and several outbuildings containing livestock or harvested produce. Surrounding the buildings were acres of open prairieland used to grow a variety of crops and graze the animals. But the act was also another tool designed to facilitate displacement of Native Americans. Gebhardt, Bender, Brockman, and Ern ate their lunch and chewed tobacco on land that had once belonged to the people of the Osage Nation.

On 10 September 1870, the same year the two Bender men arrived in Labette County, the Osage signed the Drum Creek Treaty after years of struggling to control the flood of white settlers on to their land. Years before, in the mid-1860s, the tribe appealed to the federal government for help turning the more aggressive settlers back. After a series of treaties disliked by everyone except the railway companies that stood to benefit, the government promised to buy the Osage lands for $1.25 an acre. Removed south on to a reservation in Indian Territory, the tribe watched as the 8 million acres on which they had lived freely for centuries became overrun by white settlers. They did not receive their payment until 1879. During the interim they were exploited by traders and many starved, unable to afford goods they had been promised. Writing in the *Labette Sentinel* in 1870, an anonymous member of the tribe expressed doubt that the Osage would be allowed to remain on their newly allocated land for long.

"As long as grass grows and water runs are doubtful terms nowadays, for the winter of covetousness and oppression will wither the grass, and the drought of broken faith will dry up the waters."

AT THE TRADING POST, GEBHARDT TALKED SO INCESSANTLY THAT it took him over an hour to finish the meagre meal of bread and beans in front of him. Pa Bender muttered when it suited him and didn't seem to care whether he was audible or not. Lunch transitioned to cards and the light softened into dusk outside the window. Gebhardt threw his hand down on the table and exclaimed that they had better get out to view the claims. The two tradesmen exchanged a glance. Ern offered to drive Gebhardt and Pa Bender through the available claims in the area the following day. He had promised to assist, but the erratic demeanour of the younger man made him uneasy. Ern had no desire to camp on the prairie with strangers he did not trust when he could sleep in his own home with several guns within reach of his bed. Gebhardt surprised the little group by acquiescing and disappearing into the fold of the night. Grumbling, the old man followed him. He nodded his thanks to the two men as he left.

THE FOLLOWING DAY, BILLY TOLE WAS DRIVING CATTLE ACROSS his claim when he noticed the trading post's wagon jostling its occupants along the trail. Up top sat Ern in unusually good form, gesturing to various features in the landscape. Squashed in beside him was an older man whose only reaction to Ern's babbling was to spit occasionally, push the brim of his hat up, and squint at the land. Billy watched this continue for a good half a mile before calling out a hearty good morning. Ern raised a big hand in greeting. The older man stared. When Billy returned to the cabin for dinner, he told his brother Silas that it looked like they were getting new neighbours, but that he wasn't sure whether they ought to be pleased or not. Silas shrugged; so long as they left the cattle alone he didn't think it was any of his business what they were like.

THE BENDER MEN WERE QUICK IN MAKING A DECISION ABOUT THE location of their claim. When Ern drove the wagon between two small hills into a vale that dipped below the line of the horizon, Gebhardt had immediately inquired whether the claim was available. The land with the mounds was owned by a Mr Hieronymus, Ern explained, but the land immediately to the east was free and well served by Drum Creek. Pa Bender grunted his approval. Gebhardt jumped from the back of the wagon, placed a felt hat with a sun-bleached brim on his head, and looked out across the prairie. He judged the visibility as a mile, perhaps further on a particularly clear day. He asked about the neighbours.

"Tyack's to the south, Tole brothers' ranch on the north-east, we're on the other side of the hills," Ern replied.

Gebhardt picked the Tyack and Tole cabins out of the landscape with relative ease, as they squatted high against the horizon. Though the land appeared weather-beaten and exposed, it was deceptive. Where he stood the prairie sloped into a natural depression. If they built at the lowest point they would be lost against the barren hills unless they chose to light a lamp after dark. Gebhardt's laugh pitched high and shrill in the stillness of the day. By the evening the two men had staked their claim and their campfire burned low and warm below the hills. Pa Bender sucked at a crude stew while the younger man marked out the dimensions of a cabin, pacing the length and breadth of what would become one of the few resting places for travellers making the journey from Fort Scott to Independence. *The History of Labette County* records that the men registered land in section 13, township 31, range 17, Osage Township. Pa registered the usual 160 acres, but Gebhardt's unusual selection of a strip a mile long and an eighth of a mile wide ensured that a portion of Drum Creek shrouded in heavy undergrowth lay north-west of the cabin.

As the population of the area grew, so would the number of travellers eager for food and shelter from the deep Kansas nights. No stranger to the trials of frontier life, Gebhardt knew the value of a glowing oil lamp as dusk fell across the landscape. A steady stream of customers was a certainty, as was the fact that many of them would be carrying money and valuables. He finished pacing out the layout of the cabin, roughly marking where the cellar would be with a shovel from the wagon. On the return journey from the trading post they had stopped at the homestead of Mr Hieronymus and haggled over a slab of sandstone to act as the floor for the space. Gebhardt paced the dimensions again for good measure, then threw down the shovel, patted the two horses affectionately on the flank, and lay down beside the campfire. The old man had finished his stew and was snoring like a pig in the wagon.

Gebhardt felt the last of the heat from a drawn-out summer in the earth. In the northern sky great pillars of white light reached towards the stars, softening to crimson, then lost amid the dark.

THE AURORA BOREALIS WAS STILL VISIBLE WHEN GEBHARDT RE-turned from Fort Scott in nearby Bourbon County with enough wood to build a cabin, a stable, and a rickety corral. In his absence the old man had laid the foundations for the cabin and begun the construction of a well. Brockman had called intermittently to check he had drinking water but found him gruff and uninterested in any offers of help. John Dienst, the patriarch of one of several families in the area, stopped by the property out of curiosity. Bender had eyeballed the man until the latter apologised for trespassing. He was unwilling to exchange more than a grunt of conversation, even when it was in German. It seemed Pa had reached his social limit the day they arrived. He took no steps to remedy his unflattering reputation.

Frost silvered the landscape and the men worked quickly to break the soil before the cold made it impenetrable. Together they finished the well and excavated the cellar. After digging six feet (180 centimetres) into the earth, the two men hauled the sandstone into the pit where it acted as a crude but effective floor. Next, they set about constructing the cabin around the hole that would become the entrance to the cellar. Gebhardt was kinder to those who passed through and Brockman liked the young man despite his initial misgivings. He was impressed with the speed at which the two were able to work. As the frontier prepared to celebrate Christmas in the small ways its citizens were able, the two men finished the structure. Modest but well put together, it was tight, neat, and symmetrical. Standing at 16 x 24 feet (five by seven metres) with a solid floor and a 9-foot (270-centimetre) ceiling, it was a basic structure, cut from the same wood as many other buildings on the frontier. Cheap glass windows framed a door at each end. Concealed beneath a straw mattress, a trapdoor gave access to the cellar. To the left of the house was a stable, four poles thatched tightly together and roofed with hay and prairie grass. A precarious corral did its best to stand up beside it.

Like all winters in Kansas it was cold and sharp. Children skated on frozen creeks, travellers froze to death and were stumbled upon by unsuspecting farmers, and sleet fell in great sheets that made the fields slick and grey. Gebhardt spent long stretches of time away from the Bender cabin driving stolen horses across the border into Indian Territory and down to Texas, unbeknownst to the people of Labette. Pa Bender occasionally materialised at the trading post, where he spat, quarrelled, and played cards. Nailed to the front of their cabin was a sign reading GROCRYS. They neither realised nor cared that it was spelled incorrectly. The few travellers who stopped to buy dry goods were perturbed to discover that there were none. Even more aggravating was that the old German man who supposedly ran the store pretended that he didn't.

BY THE BEGINNING OF MARCH, THE ROADS WERE A MIX OF DUST AND mud. The sun pushed higher in the sky and warmed the earth. The sign on the cabin now read GROCERYS. In the orchard of the Bender cabin a young woman moved between the saplings. Kate Bender turned at the sound of hooves on the trail. She watched, silent and still. Gebhardt strode out from where he had been repairing the thatch on the stable. Together they waited for the sound to materialise into a rider.

"First proper guest," he grinned, wiping his hands off on a piece of rag tied to his belt. Kate turned eyes that were soon to be the subject of local gossip on her companion.

She almost smiled.

"Find Ma." She set off towards the cabin. "I'm not for cooking."

An Ambitious Town
Just Four Weeks Old

Cherryvale, Kansas

1871

Leroy Dick rode into the fledgling town of Cherryvale on a bright spring morning and was pleased to find the local carpenters already at work. He dismounted, tethered his horse, greeted each man with a warm handshake, and plunged into animated discussion about the day's agenda. As a newly appointed township trustee, Dick was responsible for the welfare of communities in the area, and his friendly demeanour made him well-suited to the role. Born in Indiana, Dick relocated to Kansas in the aftermath of the Civil War in search of land where he and his new wife could raise a family. When they first arrived in 1868, settlement in the area was sparse and they were among the only homesteaders. Now more families were arriving by the day, and Dick was excited at the prospect of the community expanding. A well-presented man with a pointed beard and cheerful eyes, Dick found it easy to ingratiate himself with newcomers. He concluded his discussion with the carpenters and crossed the street to the general store, one of the first buildings to be erected on the town site.

In July, when the railway station opened, Cherryvale experienced the usual trickle of families, businessmen, bankers, and Civil War veterans. In its heyday it boasted a tram, eight grocery shops, and seven thousand inhabitants. But in the spring of 1871, Cherryvale was in the early months of its existence, home only to a hotel, a grocery shop, a post office, and a timber yard. The settlement had been plotted to provide a centre for homesteads in what was a popular area at the corner of four counties: Montgomery, Labette, Neosho, and Wilson. A town like Cherryvale provided a focal point for local communities and the success of a town reflected the success of homesteads in the area. The more settlers, the wealthier the businesses on the town's main street would become. Settlers relied on their towns for transport links, education, religious practice, and gossip.

OUTSIDE THE GENERAL STORE, JACK REED SAT WITH HIS FEET PROPPED up on a barrel. Occasionally he spat chewing tobacco juice into the street. A good-natured layabout in his mid-twenties, Reed preferred loitering in saloons to helping on the family farm. He spent his time travelling between the towns in south-east Kansas to avoid garnering too much of a reputation in one place. Pleased that he would no longer have to ride to Independence to buy a drink, Reed had come to Cherryvale to see who the stagecoach would bring into town. The stagecoach took passengers to and from Independence twice a day, and it was an uneventful trip unless local horse thieves were feeling particularly brazen or the driver overslept. The rattle of the coach drew Reed's attention to the thoroughfare. With a great deal of convincing, the horses came to a stop outside the shop. An older woman whom he had not seen before slapped at the hand of the coach driver when he tried to help her down. Reed guessed she was in her fifties, but her scowl was so off-putting that he couldn't be sure. Her demeanour made his top lip curl.

Behind the older woman came a younger woman he immediately recognised as Kate Bender. Word travelled quickly through the trading posts, and Kate's arrival travelled quickest. The women came down through Ottawa and had been in the area for a week. The Tole brothers saw Kate walking the Bender property and Billy had been finding excuses to call on the family ever since. When the coach driver helped her down, she thanked him with a smile that made Reed reconsider squirting his tobacco juice. She turned the smile on Reed, and he saw the eyes that would waylay many unsuspecting travellers over the coming years. Kate stepped past him and he was left staring directly into the face of the older woman. Her eyes were a little too close together for his liking. She squinted at him and followed her younger companion into the shop.

IN THE TIME THE BENDERS RESIDED IN THE COUNTY, THE TWO OLDER members of the family rarely ventured beyond the Brockman trading post. The community was at best indifferent and at worst goaded by their presence and most were pleased they did not have to worry about running into either in the town. Occasionally a traveller would grumble about being run off the Bender land by the old man brandishing a hammer, but with so many unsavoury types to deal with, townsfolk did not blame him for wanting to protect his land. Ma spoke broken German that only members of the Bender family seemed capable of understanding. When she wasn't sleeping, she cooked and accompanied Kate on visits to neighbouring homesteads. She was so unfriendly that after the family vanished, the county discovered that no one knew her first name.

The relationship between all four members of the Bender family became a source of endless conjecture in the community. Though it seemed certain that Kate and Ma were mother and daughter, no one could be sure how the men were related to the women. Kate and Gebhardt further confused matters by presenting themselves as siblings, but exhibiting a physical closeness that suggested they were husband and wife. More sensational rumours entertained the possibility that they were incestuous half-siblings.

Unlike Pa and Ma Bender, the younger couple worked hard to ingratiate themselves into the local community. Both were fast-talkers, yet there was a warmth to Kate that set people at ease. Maurice Sparks, a resident of the county, later told reporters from *The Topeka State Journal* that she "was not a bad looking girl." By the majority of sensible, contemporary accounts Kate was good-looking enough that the Bender cabin received a steady stream of male travellers, some of whom made it a

regular stop on their journeys across the state. High cheekbones and auburn hair gave her face a pleasingly unified look. Beneath her left eye a
small scar lent an edge to her otherwise delicate features.

The first time she and Gebhardt attended the local Sunday school at
Harmony Grove, Kate arrived with a wide smile and a dress that showed
her calves when she sat in the pew. She sang loudly and chatted to anyone
who wished to speak to her. Run by Leroy Dick, the school provided lessons as well as choir practice. The week after Kate first attended, several
young men whom Dick did not recognise jostled for a position where they
could at least keep an eye fixed on her during the lessons. Though he was
cordial to her face, Dick found the young woman disingenuous. She reminded him of women he had encountered in the bigger cities during his
time in the Civil War, friendly until they needed something and discovered you could not provide it. He was much fonder of Gebhardt, who
impressed him with his knowledge of Scripture and ability to pull precise
passages of the Bible out of the air when they were most appropriate. The
young man's persistent giggle bothered him, but he had met men with
stranger habits, brought on by the trauma of war.

Between them, Gebhardt and Kate did well for the family within the
community. Those who were unsure of Kate felt that Gebhardt must be
a good influence on her, and those disturbed by his demeanour thought
how kind she was to look after her disadvantaged brother. The siblings,
or lovers, became experts at encouraging people to divulge information
without realising they were putting themselves in danger.

IN THE WEEKS FOLLOWING THE ARRIVAL OF THE BENDER FAMILY,
county marriage certificates show that Rudolph Brockman married Mary
Hiltz. A diminutive eighteen-year-old from Germany, Mary had taken
an immediate dislike to Ern and eventually persuaded her husband to
ask him to leave the trading post. Reluctant to lose his business partner
but determined not to lose his wife, Brockman offered Ern the cash equivalent of his share in the business. It was an easy decision for Ern, who,
bitter at how quickly his partner had turned on him, decided he would

set up a rival trading post in the area. Before leaving for America he had promised his foster mother that he would one day have the funds for her and her daughter to join him. Now, making good on his promise, he wrote to the women and asked for the daughter's hand in marriage. She accepted and they arrived in America a little over a month later. It was a cheerful reunion, and Ern had arranged for the women to stay with the Benders while he decided on a final location for the new shop. Like many others making the journey to a new life, the two women carried everything they had with them. Among their possessions was a small metal box packed carefully with the few items of jewellery they had inherited. Before travelling, they had sold many of their goods and transferred the value to cashier's cheques amounting to $3,200. The women enjoyed the company of the younger Benders, who were full of anecdotes about life on the frontier and advice about how best to set up a homestead.

On a bright, unseasonably warm afternoon, the family suggested a walk to explore the local area. Keen to understand the environment they were now to call home, the women agreed and the group set off towards the mounds. Though the terrain was easily walkable, the distance began to exhaust Ma Bender, who made a great show of panting and hacking up bile. Pa took her by the arm and steered her back towards the house. Brushing off concern for her mother, Kate asked the women to help her look for what she called Indian relics. It was a popular pastime on the frontier, where remnants of Indigenous cultures lay scattered across a land they had once called home. Settlers collected arrowheads, beads, and other items, displaying them in their homes, where they sat like victory markers of a war they had not fought. The group amassed a small collection that delighted their guests, and they headed back to the cabin in the waning of the day.

Ern's foster mother was the happiest she had been in a long time, and she resolved to keep the objects she had found that afternoon safe in order to bring the new family good luck. She decided to put them in the box with the jewellery. After a great deal of searching she discovered the box was gone. So, too, were the cashier's cheques. Furious, she confronted Kate, who put on such a believable show of alarm that had the rest of the family not conveniently disappeared, the woman might have been convinced. But her daughter demanded that they search the house. Kate agreed and the three women searched again. The cabin that once seemed safe now felt squalid. Dust, mud, and insects seemed to coat everything in a moving layer of filth.

The younger woman stopped searching and started packing. Kate did little to stop her, looking instead to Gebhardt, who had appeared out of the quickening darkness.

"Horse thieves," he announced loudly, startling the two frightened women. "I'll take you over to the Dienst place. You don't want to stay here."

Unsure of how to react but certain they wanted to be far away from the cabin, they clutched their remaining belongings close and scurried out to wait for the wagon on the trail. Kate watched them from the porch with an intensity that made the women draw into themselves. From the back of the wagon they stared at her until she became indistinguishable from the cabin. The entire journey was one long sentence from Gebhardt about the prevalence of horse thieves in the area. They had gotten worse in recent months, he explained, too jovially for the older woman's liking.

"Spring weather makes 'em frisky."

His diatribe came to a stop when they reached their destination. The women had barely scrambled from the wagon before he set off back for the cabin. They were left to explain themselves to their confused hosts. After much deliberation it was agreed that John Dienst would set out to look for Ern at first light.

THE NEXT DAY, THE BENDER FAMILY WAS IN THE MIDDLE OF FEEDing a pair of freight haulers when Ern appeared in the cabin, huge and feverish with rage. One of the men spilled hot coffee on himself and swore. Gebhardt laughed awkwardly, swallowing it in a cough when Ern raised a revolver. He pointed it at Kate, then thought better of it, swinging it to land on Pa. The silence pulsed.

"The money," Ern stated. Gebhardt made to stand but sat down again when the gun turned on him. Kate blinked twice, her face open and disbelieving.

"You can't believe it was us? The cabin must have been gone through while we were out walking. I feel very bad about it."

Silence returned to the room. The two freight haulers moved their hands to the six-shooters concealed about their persons. Outnumbered, Ern realised he had made a mistake that would likely cost him any chance of seeing the money and the jewellery again. There was no proof that the Benders had taken the goods, just as there was no proof that they hadn't. Now he had brazenly threatened them in front of witnesses in a rash attempt to force them to confess. Had he the good sense to go first to law enforcement and persuade them to accompany him to the cabin and conduct a search, something might have come of it. Ern stared into the faces of the family he had trusted to look after those he held most dear. In his heart he blamed Brockman for persuading him to set out into the unforgiving land that had now stripped him of his family's belief that he could protect them. Kate looked at him with pity. Pa grunted and kicked a foot towards the door. Bristling with anger, Ern backed his way outside. He spat on the porch as he went and spat again when he rode off.

THE FOLLOWING SUNDAY KATE SPOKE TO EVERYONE AT HARMONY Grove about how terrible she felt for the Ern family. Leroy Dick kept his reservations to himself. Both Ern and the Dienst family had reported the incident to Dick, keen for his opinion on the matter as township trustee. Though he found Kate's behaviour suspicious, Dick also knew there was no tangible evidence to suggest the Benders were involved in the robbery. It seemed perfectly plausible that the cabin had been ransacked while the group was out on the prairies. Plus, Gebhardt had been quick to escort the women to a safer place. To placate Ern, Dick notified the German consul in St. Louis that the cashier's cheques had been stolen. To satisfy his own curiosity, he requested that he be informed if anyone attempted to cash them.

PUTTING THE MATTER BEHIND HIM, ERN MARRIED HIS YOUNG WIFE and along with her mother they moved west, settling on one of the new Texas cattle trails where the sky sparkled and the ground ran red with clay and blood. Despite his former business partner's experience, Brockman maintained his close acquaintance with the Bender family and turned his attention to farming. More families moved into the area surrounding Big Hill Creek. Residents of Cherryvale raised two thousand dollars to build a schoolhouse, and each day the silhouette of the town was different against the sky. The German consul in St. Louis never encountered anyone trying to cash the cheques. Like Ern and his new wife, the incident was forgotten until two years later, when Leroy Dick recalled it to a young man looking for his brother.

Matters Spiritual and Temporal

——

By the end of 1871, the Bender cabin looked the way it would be described in national newspapers just over a year later. A heavy wagon canvas divided the space into two rooms. Upon entering, travellers were greeted by a meagre selection of goods arranged on several shelves above a counter. The quality of the items available was dependent on Kate's mood when she went into town to collect them. In front of the canvas sat the only piece of furniture in the cabin that looked like it was of any value, a crude but sturdy walnut table flanked by two benches of the same wood. Beyond the curtain the family slept on pallet beds or straw mattresses. If the weather was good their guests slept outside. If it was bad, they slept with their possessions in the front room. The cabin had quickly descended into a state of squalor the family barely bothered to disguise. Basic utensils bought in Ottawa grew a second skin of grime, and the whirring of flies made a noble effort to compete with the grasshoppers outside. Despite the unsanitary conditions, travellers and settlers alike were drawn to the little cabin and the young woman who lived there.

As soon as she arrived in Labette County, Kate Bender began to advertise her services as a spiritual healer. First through word of mouth at the Sunday school and then through the publishing of notices in local papers and in shop windows. In addition to healing, she claimed she could talk to the dead, coaxing them into answering questions from the living. The Bender family were spiritualists, and they were not alone in their belief in the importance of talking to the dead. Between 1870 and 1872, at least five families openly practised spiritualism in the area, a source of much debate among those who did not.

ORIGINATING ON A SPRING NIGHT IN 1848, SPIRITUALISM WAS A religious movement born of the unique cultural climate of nineteenth-century America. John D. Fox lived with his wife and two of his daughters in Hydesville, New York, where they began to be pestered by a persistent knocking in the early hours of the morning. Kate Fox, the youngest member of the family, challenged what she suspected to be a ghost to mimic a series of clicks she made with her fingers. When the noise complied, they continued to ask it questions. Each was answered correctly. Over the course of several days the spirit identified itself as Charles B. Rosma, a peddler and victim of a vicious murder who was now buried in the foundations of the building. Curious neighbours and local officials visited the house, and the girls became an overnight sensation. When the Fox sisters relocated to nearby Rochester, the spirits came with them. On 14 November 1849, the spirits followed them onstage in front of a paying audience. It was of little consequence that when the cellar of the original house was excavated, no human remains were found.

Following in the footsteps of the Fox Sisters, many leading spiritualist figures in America became celebrities. Mediums and hypnotists drew large, enraptured audiences by performing séances on stage. Spirit photography fascinated the press and mystified sceptics. Though there were plenty of successful male spiritualists, as the movement developed it became primarily associated with women. The ideal medium was sensitive, impressionable, and passive—all qualities perceived to be feminine in nature. But being a medium also presented women with the opportunity to be a mouthpiece for controversial opinions. Mrs Fannie Allyne, a medium active in Labette County while the Benders lived there, drew large audiences and

Nineteenth-century German woodcut showing a group of people participating in a séance.

was particularly popular with women. Her conversations with the spirit world centred firmly around the necessity of women's suffrage. The fight for women's rights was far more palatable as a voice from the ether than it was from living proponents. It seemed improper to argue with a ghost. As spiritualism became an increasingly powerful cultural movement, it allowed women of a lower social class access to places and positions normally closed to them. Cora L. V. Scott, a striking Pre-Raphaelite beauty whose stage presence enthralled male and female audiences alike, was born into a low-income background in New York and died one of the most famous women in America.

The movement drew its strength and commercial success from being both a public and domestic performance. It promised that any spirit could be contacted at any location. All that was required for communication was the presence of a medium. After the Civil War, spiritualism offered the hundreds of thousands of people who had experienced loss a way of processing their trauma. Families invited dead loved ones back into their homes and cushioned their grief with domestic séances. It was a movement that reached the highest offices in the country. In 1862, Abraham and Mary Todd Lincoln lost their young son William to typhoid fever.

Mary surrounded herself with spiritualists, desperate to feel as though her son had not truly left her. Among them were Charles Colchester, a man who revealed his sleight-of-hand techniques after several glasses of spirits, and Nettie Colburn, who later exaggerated her influence on the family in a memoir about her time spent with the Lincolns. Mary's relationship with the spiritualists embodied the main criticism of the movement—that it was a deeply exploitative con that preyed on emotionally vulnerable individuals.

For every article praising its doctrines there was one attaching it to bizarre and sometimes horrific events. On 28 March 1870, the *Leavenworth Daily Commercial* ran an advertisement featuring the bold claim that if the spiritualists raised the ghost of King Solomon, he would have endorsed Phalon's Vitalia as the best hair tonic for men. A week later it decried spiritualism as the "grossest charlatanism," which preyed on gullible members of the public. In the spring of 1871, it was held directly responsible for two tragedies. Sometime around the end of March, the Walker family of Elgin, Illinois, were found dead in their beds. After drugging their two young children, Mr and Mrs Walker had committed suicide. By their bedside was a letter saying they had chosen to cross over to the spirit world so their children could have a happier existence. *The Longton Weekly Ledger* reported the tragedy with a wry comment that "if the spiritual doctrine works in this manner, we will soon have no more spiritualists." Two months later a man named Mr Tuttle starved himself to death under the supposed orders of a spirit who claimed it was the path to salvation.

IN KANSAS, SPIRITUALISM WAS POPULAR AS A PRACTICE, A CURIOSITY, and a scapegoat. By the time the Benders arrived in the state, it was flourishing. A meeting of the First Society of Spiritualism in 1870 had double the number of attendees than the year before. Out on the prairies, the nature of frontier living allowed spiritualists the space to practise their beliefs relatively free from persecution. It also provided a welcome distraction from the monotony of frontier existence. Kate, already a local curiosity because of her demeanour and appearance, attracted yet more attention through her work as a medium and healer. Highly manipulative, she embodied the traditionally feminine characteristics of a medium when it suited her. In reality, she was far from being a frail, even-tempered waif. Whether she and her family truly believed in the movement is hard to know. But what is certain is that they used spiritualism with criminal intent. Kate frequently went on tours of the local area where she lectured to promote her business, inviting clients out on to the trail in the early hours of the evening with the promise of speaking to the dead. *The Oswego Independent* later recalled her speaking in the town on the subject of women's rights, perhaps inspired by the success of Fannie Allyne. More enticing for male clients were Kate's assertions that she was a supporter of free love. On a practical level, free lovism during the nineteenth century sought to separate the legal and economic structures of the state from sexual and romantic relationships. For Kate, including free love in her lectures bought her a level of notoriety in the region that she relished.

Wrapped within her spiritualist pretensions was another uniquely American belief system, powwow. Taking its name from Native American tradition, powwow originated in Pennsylvania Dutch culture and spread quickly throughout Germanic communities as they moved across America. Kate sold papers on which she had written charms for protection, fertility, and luck. Many came from the book *Pow-Wows: or, Long Lost Friend*, originally written in German by John George Hohman, a healer and practitioner of folk magic. She pressed them, neat and folded, into the hands of travellers and locals alike, promising solace in the unforgiving landscape. The Bender family was not unusual in their mixing of religion and folk magic; all across the West settlers relied on a combination of superstition and faith to offer them a semblance of control over their little lives in a vast land. Kate was also not the only woman in Labette County to advertise spiritual services. Susanna Tyack lived with her family in a cabin a mile south of the Benders and had made a name for herself in the area by claiming she was in possession of magnetic healing powers. The extent of the powers involved her waving her hands over an elderly gentlemen's foot and then proclaiming that he didn't believe in her enough for it to work. Susanna's enthusiasm was not dampened, and she was a frequent visitor to the Bender cabin, where she and Kate would hold circles to talk to the dead. But not everyone was as enamoured with Kate as Susanna.

JULIA HESTLER STUCK OUT AMONG THE OTHER WOMEN WHO WORKED at the Cherryvale Hotel. Standing at a little under six feet (180 centimetres), she loomed over customers and staff alike. Her height made her defensive, imbuing her with a constant desire to prove that she could fend for herself in all aspects of life. She preferred to travel alone and turned down sporadic offers from men who wanted to escort her home in the early hours. When Kate Bender started working as a waitress at the hotel during the late spring of 1871, she was one of the few women Julia found herself drawn to. Julia had long been interested in spiritualism, and Kate talked frequently about her talents as a medium. When the young woman invited her to a séance out at the Bender cabin, Julia was quick to accept.

In the early hours of a warm evening, Julia hitched a ride in the stagecoach that took passengers from Cherryvale to Independence. The earth hummed with signs of life after a bitter winter, and the trail was beginning to descend into its seasonal quagmire brought on by the rain. Intending to stay the night at the cabin, Julia had taken the stagecoach instead of her horse to save the animal the journey. When she arrived at the cabin, she was struck by how decrepit it looked, as though the entire structure was trying to make itself part of the landscape. Upon entering, she was disconcerted to find Kate alone preparing the circle, but the woman reassured her that the fewer the participants, the greater the chance of reaching the spirits. If there were non-believers in the group, the voices might not reveal themselves. As dusk seeped into the cabin, the building seemed to shrink around her. A single candle cast a meagre halo against the canvas dividing the space. Kate sat herself down on the bench and beckoned for Julia to sit across the table. An unpleasant smell lingered at the back of Julia's throat, but not wanting to offend her friend, she sat down with her back to the curtain. They discussed the spirits they wanted to contact, but after the appearance of several plump, glistening flies Julia could not focus. Lifting a finger and glancing behind the curtain, she recoiled at the sight of a cluster of flies. When she turned back, Kate was looking at her. Bathed in the amber glow of the candle, her eyes were deep and oddly vacant. The two women clasped each other's hands and closed their eyes. In a soft voice Kate began to invite the dead to join them. Julia's mind wandered to her horse, and she wished she had ridden him over. The buzzing of the flies whirred in her skull; occasionally one threw itself against the curtain with a grotesque thud. Fear began to make her nauseous. At the hotel, she and Kate had performed several séances, but now the woman's whispers sounded disingenuous. Julia opened her eyes in a panic.

Behind Kate stood the rest of the family. They had crept silently into the cabin, the dim light casting shadows that obscured their eyes. Julia withdrew her hands and stared at the table. She wondered whether she could steal a horse. Leaning forward, she told Kate that she needed to relieve herself. Kate was unresponsive. Sliding out from behind the table, Julia began to move towards the door. She attempted a smile, but her face wouldn't co-operate. The family watched her closely. In his hand Pa Bender gripped something that glinted unnaturally in the light. She excused herself again and felt for the frame of the door.

When Kate moved towards her Julia shot out into the darkness. The long skirt of her dress caught and she fell, her wrist twisting beneath her as she hit the dirt. A sudden noise from the cabin frightened her more than the pain in her arm, and she bundled her skirt in her arms, dragging herself to her feet. The black gulf of the prairie opened up before her as she ran.

A single gunshot tore a hole in the night sky as she fled. Julia dropped to the ground. Behind her there was movement in the tallgrass and another gunshot. A mixture of German and English rang out as the family cursed at one another. She started to crawl, chest tightening against the cold in the waterlogged soil. Rustling in the grass replaced the shouting, and when she checked again, Kate's lamplight danced in the air like an insect. Julia felt for imperfections in the ground where she could hide but she knew she had to run.

Gebhardt stalked the landscape, bemoaning the delight Kate took in frightening people who thought they were her friend. When he found the flattened grass, Julia was already running. The Benders watched in silence as she dissolved into an indistinguishable shadow. They returned to the cabin. Kate smothered the flame of the candle between her fingertips and snapped at the men for not being fast enough. Behind the curtain the flies had found their way beneath the floorboards.

JACK REED EMERGED FROM HIS TENT AT DAYBREAK AND POKED AT the remnants of the previous night's campfire. He cupped his hands, breathed into them, and rubbed them together. The local wildlife thought it was spring, but the mornings were still bitterly cold. On the horizon a thin line of smoke disappeared into the sky. To the south someone was running. He squinted and guessed it was a woman. Her skirt was hitched over her shoulders. Reed shouted but she didn't respond. He glanced briefly at his horse and decided it would be a wasted trip. She would reach Joe Newman's cabin just in time for breakfast.

The First of Many

Baxter Springs, Kansas

AUTUMN 1871

The autumn of 1871 was cool and bracing. Settlers in south-east Kansas read about the battering walls of snow and wind suffered by their western counterparts and thought themselves lucky. On the days when the temperature did drop below zero and the trail was slick with ice, they watched the expansion of the railway and took comfort in the fact that soon they would be able to travel safely in the bowels of the iron horse. Towns sprang up organically around new railway stations, drawing workmen, their families, and all that follows after them. In Cherokee County, east of Labette, one such town was growing. Baxter Springs had been one of the first towns in Kansas to function as an outlet for the Texas cattle trade and was popular with settlers due to its unusually scenic surroundings. Spring River flowed into Spring Creek and the town was verdant in the summer, then golden in the autumn. After it was confirmed that the railway would be coming to the town, tradesmen and speculators arrived with blank cheques for businesses and the community alike. First came twenty-five thousand dollars for schoolhouses, then ten thousand dollars for a courthouse. Of all the burgeoning settlements in Kansas, Baxter Springs held itself to be among the best.

WHEN JAMES FEERICK ARRIVED IN BAXTER SPRINGS WITH HIS WIFE, Mary, and their little boy, they were a happy, busy family. They had made the journey from Ireland, determined to build a richer life alongside thousands of others on the prairies. James quickly found work as a contractor for several of the railway companies operating in the area. At the time of his employment, the Leavenworth, Lawrence & Galveston Railroad Company was laying tracks joining many of the small towns in the south of Kansas, and like many contractors, James travelled frequently and was well acquainted with the area. Though they settled in Baxter Springs, the Feericks also purchased land in Howard County. The Leavenworth, Lawrence & Galveston Railroad Company bought up large swaths of land in order to ensure the passage of the track would be uninterrupted by grumpy settlers as it had been in Fort Scott. In order to continue to turn a profit and boost use of the railways, they then encouraged settlers to purchase the land from them for the purpose of homesteading.

FEERICK AND HIS WIFE DECIDED TO EMBARK ON THE VENTURE AFTER reading one of the many pamphlets advertising railway land. It promised the best timbered and watered sections available in any of the prairie states. Land rich with coal, stone, ochre, and fire clay awaited those brave enough to settle on it—a perfect home for a young family eager to make a living from farming some of the most fertile land available. They neglected to mention horse thieves, freak weather conditions, cholera, and the possibility that the railway company itself might evict you should they decide to alter the route of the tracks. The Feericks chose the land in Howard County for its proximity to the neighbours, so that Mary would have company when her husband was away on business. They planned to relocate there and raise a family as soon as James earned enough money to properly establish the homestead. Their closest neighbours were the Watton family, a couple the census lists as in their thirties with seven children. Mary and Mrs Watton became good friends, and the latter would play a much greater role in Mary's life than either could have imagined upon first meeting.

AS CHRISTMAS APPROACHED, MARY FEERICK WAS INTENDING TO make good on her promise to return to New York to visit her sister. It was a long journey from south-east Kansas, but she was looking forward to introducing their little boy to his aunt. James accompanied them to the station, kissed the little boy and Mary goodbye. and asked that she write to him upon arriving in New York. He made preparations to leave Baxter Springs and spend the remainder of the winter months in Howard County with the Wattons. Though his job with the railway kept him busy, James harboured an ambition to have built a home for his wife and child by the time they returned from the East Coast. When she arrived home they could plant the garden. By summer they would be living successfully on the plot, free from the restrictive and noisy streets of Baxter Springs. Informing his partner at the railway company of his intentions, he set off along the Osage Mission Trail on horseback with the money he had saved for the homestead.

Mary wrote to her husband the evening she arrived in New York City, venturing out into the heavy snow to ensure the letter was received as soon as possible. The days passed, but there was no reply. After Christmas she wrote to their Howard County address but still had no response. Her sister told her not to worry, as frontier post could be unreliable. James could be travelling, she reminded her, and by unlucky accident missed both the letters. Throughout January Mary worked to trace him, too frightened to return to Kansas when there was no answer. She wrote to existing railway stations and new ones as they opened, desperate for news of James. The company was apologetic when it did respond but offered no means of assistance, beyond advising her to hire a private detective. When the family had been in Kansas together, the state lived up to the promises made by the advertisements, but now all Mary came across in the papers were reports of fatal accidents and lawlessness. Sometimes she felt better not knowing. It was easier to think that James might be dead than that he had abandoned her. But when she looked into the face of their little boy, she was overcome with longing for news, regardless of what it was.

Finally, she received a letter from Mrs Watton informing her that James had not been seen since he left Baxter Springs in the first truly bad weather of the season. It would have been impossible to make the journey in a day, even if the elements had been kinder. Somewhere along the Osage Mission Trail he had stopped for shelter and the prairie had swallowed him up.

An Invitation

SUMMER 1872

ROOT OUT ALL SPIRITUALISM—FREE LOVISM—HORSE THIEVES—INCENDIARIES AND RASCALS OF ALL KINDS read a headline in *The Head-light*, a popular newspaper out of Thayer. Cherryvale was still without its own newspaper and its inhabitants relied on neighbouring press to provide them with news. For frontier towns, having a newspaper, or several newspapers, was a vital part of establishing their place in the West. Instrumental in developing a town's identity, newspapers kept readers updated with the day-to-day dramas of life in the region, as well as wider happenings across the world. Businesses posted advertisements, the comings and goings of residents were reported, and most also featured columns dedicated to humour and advice. The best way to understand the daily life of a town was to read the sections entitled "City News" or "Announcements," usually found on the third or fourth pages of the paper. These columns also provided some of the best examples of editors' voices in the Old West. In February 1873, the exasperated editor of *The Osage County Chronicle* started the City, County and State News column, on the third page of the newspaper, with "Money. We want money. Pay us some money. We want money on Subscription." The *Leavenworth Daily Commercial* cheerfully informed its readers that "one or two citizens in Kansas City are boring the earth for water. Most of the others are boring the retailers for whiskey."

Outside the Cherryvale general store where he had first seen Kate Bender, Jack Reed read *The Head-light* and shook his head. Every week regional and national papers accused south-east Kansas of planting horse thieves as quickly as they were planting crops. Occasionally one would be caught in the act, a cause for brief celebration and, in more vengeful areas, a hanging. If horse thieves were in short supply, there were always armed groups of settlers ready to beat railway officials over land disputes. Later in the year, *The Wyandott Herald* reported such an incident in Parsons, a town in Labette County just over twenty miles east of Cherryvale. A band of fifty masked men attempted to kidnap a railway agent from a hotel where he was staying. In the chaos, the commissioner escaped with the aid of a guest who had been playing cards in the hotel's saloon. The masked brigade grumbled and shot into the air before retreating in a state of embarrassment.

With so many conflicting interests driving life on the frontier, the level of day-to-day violence was unsurprising. Disputes between farmers over land boundaries could end amicably or, in one instance, with one drawing a large butcher knife from his boot and planting it directly into the chest of the other. Kansas was a state of expansive, open prairie, yet there never seemed to be quite enough land. But families who focused on their own homesteads looked out for one another, respected boundaries, and offered assistance when it was needed. Newspapers reported on sensationalist crimes, but there were so many other things to worry about that it took a true atrocity to garner more than half a column of coverage.

SINCE THE ARRIVAL OF THE BENDER FAMILY, REED ALTERED HIS route from Cherryvale to Independence, taking a trail that ensured he passed the cabin. Unlike many of the townsfolk, he put no stock in Kate's spiritualist chatter, but he enjoyed her spritely manner and mean sense of humour. On a morning in the midst of an unusually hot July, he was making his way back from Independence to Cherryvale. He picked insects from the folds of his clothes and flicked them into the ringing throng of grasshoppers that surrounded the trail. When he was three hundred yards (275 metres) away from the Bender cabin, Reed hollered good morning and was surprised to see Kate appear from behind the cabin with a metal bucket in her arms and soaking-wet hair. Instead of her usual high-necked shirt she wore a chemise. Reed kicked his horse into a trot and came up beside her.

"Fine weather for hair washing."

Kate walked horse and rider around to the stable.

"Fine weather for bugs," she put the bucket where the animal could reach it, "and minding your own business."

Reed watched her head back to the cabin and groaned when he spotted two other horses in the corral. He grumbled until he sat down and recognised the men as gambling associates. Then he was keen to discuss the card tables. They ate greedily and laughed loudly, arranging to meet in Independence the following evening, then head on through to Dodge City to spend their winnings. Kate listened as she tidied the plates and joined the laughter when she thought they would enjoy it. Gebhardt and the old man were due to return after dark the next day, and it would be easy to persuade Reed to stay the night. She knew if he was intending to gamble, he would be carrying money. She also knew he was laid-back about keeping his word.

Full of high spirits, the three men thanked her, unhitched their horses, confirmed their plans, and steered out in opposite directions. Kate followed Reed on to the trail and touched her fingers to the horse's neck.

"Come by on your way back through and I'll give you good luck."

JACK REED HAD A WIDE GRIN AND A LOOSE TONGUE WHEN HE ARrived in Cherryvale in the afternoon. He awoke late the next day but did not mind, intending to loiter until it would be too late to continue travelling after dinner at the Bender cabin. It was past seven when he arrived at the cabin and the sun was beginning its slow dip out of the sky. At dusk in south-east Kansas, the insects buzz amid the tallgrass, joined by birds the prairie harbours in its thickets. It is a land most alive in the hours before dark, when the evening chorus fills the air before night swallows all into glittering oblivion.

Reed went inside to greet the women and then spent a long time watering his horse and unhitching the saddlebags to bring them inside. When they sat down to eat, Kate was quick to suggest he spend the night and he was quick to agree. They settled into their normal conversational exchange. Reed embellished his gambling achievements and pretended to listen to her talk of spiritualism. When they played cards, Kate let him win. The old woman slept. Every so often she snored herself awake. Outside, the call of a lonely whippoorwill danced above the grasshopper chorus. The sound wound itself in circles in Reed's mind. He picked at the corner of a playing card and waited for Kate to play her hand.

"Reed!"

A voice rang through the cabin and Kate stiffened. Two eager, red-faced young men hung in the doorway. The two had been en route to Independence and recognised Reed's horse in the corral. Kate was frigid with the extra visitors and refused to offer them coffee. She slunk behind the counter and became increasingly sullen. Reed mistook it for a desire to be alone with him and drew out the conversation to tease her. Eventually he wished them a hearty goodbye and good luck, asking them to relay a message to the men already waiting for him in Independence. He would join them for coffee after breakfasting early at the cabin. Kate laughed and told them not to bother with the message.

"Reed doesn't know how to keep his word."

An awkward silence descended on the cabin until one of the younger men doffed his hat to the women and nodded at Reed.

"We'll tell 'em anyway. Won't hurt no one to do so."

They went on their way in a clatter of laughter and horse hooves. Reed turned back to the Bender women and discovered they had both disappeared. Kate returned and lit a candle with a vacant, uninterested expression. She played cards with absent eyes and rolled them when he suggested they turn in. He tried to coax her back into conversation by asking her opinion of a medium he had read about in the paper, but she was so cold that he wished he had continued on to Independence. He gave up and went to bed. In the last of the light he saw a large, plump spider pull itself out from beneath the floorboards. It sat, weightless and still. Reed tried to ignore it and looked at the dividing canvas instead, but it was soiled in a way that made him uneasy. He got up and squashed the spider beneath the heel of his boot and felt better. Putting one of the saddlebags on the pallet bed as a headrest, he lay back down, closed his eyes, and focused on the whirring of the grasshoppers.

The rattling of a wagon shook him from his sleep in the early hours. Several sets of footsteps followed and the snoring of the old woman confirmed that he wasn't dreaming. In the depths of the night he could make out Kate's voice, hushed and soft. Then a heavy blow and an unnatural gurgling. Kate again, pressured and agitated. A male voice he recognised as Gebhardt, and muttering in German he guessed was the old man. The argument went on for several minutes until Reed thought he ought to investigate. Suddenly he decided against it. The snoring had stopped, but he could feel Ma Bender in the room. Overcome with fear, he lay perfectly still and shut his eyes.

IN THE SOFTNESS OF THE EARLY MORNING SUN, REED FELT COWARDLY for not getting up in the night. Kate served bacon and coffee and seemed to have forgotten that she had been cold with him the night before. He made a hasty exit and ignored Gebhardt when he wished him luck in the saloons. When he recounted the story to his friends in Independence, they told him he was a coward. Later, the same story that had him laughed out of saloons would be used in court as evidence of the Benders' criminal behaviour. In the evening he made a small win, not quite big enough to pave his way to Dodge City. He went west regardless.

Not Much Law in the Land

Local attitudes towards the Bender family were beginning to vary by the summer of 1872, but experiences like Jack Reed's seemed outlandish even by frontier standards. Kate stopped her work at the hotel to devote her time completely to her spiritual practice. Her aspirations towards spiritualist fame were bolstered by an invitation from Mr Scroggs, the keeper of a local boarding house, for her to perform as a medium at his establishment. Initially she was popular, as the house's clients were comprised largely of railway workers who enjoyed her flirtatious demeanour. But when Kate threatened to curse those who would not pay up for her services, she became such a nuisance that the manager fired Scroggs and ordered Kate to make herself scarce.

Local doctor G. W. Gabriel knew of the young woman's reputation and was perturbed to encounter her at a number of his patients' houses. Kate was never pleased to see him and bad at concealing the fact. Whenever she left, he warned the patient against paying for her services; they would do just as well to keep their money and follow their own superstitions.

GEBHARDT APPEARED INOFFENSIVE, BUT HIS NERVOUS LAUGHTER unsettled people enough that they began to avoid him. Like many young men on the frontier, he disappeared for extended periods of time to do business, but no one was quite sure what business he did. Pa Bender and his wife were consistent in their dislike of strangers and it seemed odd to many that they had chosen to run a grocery shop, which required them to interact with so many people. The experience of a guest at the Bender cabin depended entirely on what mood Kate was in when they arrived. If local travellers deterred by the family's odd demeanour decided against calling in, the Benders always had those on long journeys on their way out West. For every odd rumour about the Benders there were very real crimes being printed in the newspapers.

It was becoming increasingly fashionable to blame crime in the area on Ladore, a railway town that squatted on the border between Neosho and Labette. Ladore was a natural stopping point for anyone travelling through the area to Osage Mission. It had also become a known hideout for some of the worst characters south-east Kansas had to offer.

From its inception the settlement was destined to have a mixed reputation. When James Roach, a popular but controversial saloon owner from Fort Scott, heard that the railway had plans for Neosho County, he sold his land and relocated. Brash, outspoken, fond of alcohol and throwing his weight around, Roach made a name for himself through anti-slavery political activism and hosting parties that usually ended in brawls. The saloon he kept in Fort Scott had been affectionately dubbed Fort Roach by regulars and the name stuck when he built a similar establishment in Neosho in the summer of 1869. As rumours continued to spread that the Missouri-Kansas-Texas Railway intended to use the settlement as a key connecting station for southbound freight, settlers streamed into the area. Unfortunately for Roach, many of the characters were prone to antisocial behaviour. The railway company used the site as a base for its operations throughout the south-east of the state, and a gulf opened up between hard-working and hard-drinking rail workers and everyone else who lived there. Rougher saloons encouraged all sorts of iniquity and attracted horse thieves looking to fence stolen goods and turn a quick profit. But the town was booming, and the citizens turned a blind eye until a devastating chain of events concluded with a vigilance committee lynching five men and imprisoning a sixth.

Vigilance committees existed in the West as a way of enforcing law and order in regions where there was little to no structured law enforcement. Though their intent was to protect citizens from cattle thieves and desperadoes, the groups preferred to hand out retribution at the end of a noose as opposed to a court of law. In Kansas, the majority of those lynched by vigilance committees were white outlaws, but in the wider United States and particularly in the South, the practice was used as a method of terrorising Black people that continued long into the twentieth century.

ON A MAY EVENING IN 1870, SEVEN MEN IDENTIFIED LATER BY *THE New York Times* as "straggling outlaws from Indian Territory" were drinking heavily on the outskirts of Ladore. Nearly every establishment in the town served whiskey, and if one wouldn't serve you, there was always a saloon owner down the road who would. At nine o'clock in the evening the men stumbled into James Roach's inn and demanded lodgings. Roach, happy to encourage drinking but staunchly against admitting violent guests, told them in no uncertain terms to leave. The gang beat Roach unconscious with the butt of a revolver and left him bleeding at the foot of the stairs as they ransacked the building. It did not take them long to discover Jane and Matilda Talbott, the two girls Roach employed as housekeepers, cowering in a wardrobe. Roach awoke to the sound of blood rushing in his ears and the cries of the girls, but was too frightened to go for help. In the midst of the sexual assault a fight broke out among the outlaws that left one of the men dead. Taking Jane Talbott hostage, the six remaining gang members staggered out into the street. Three set off towards the Osage Mission Trail.

The bandit with the kidnapped girl dragged her out to the Labette Creek Woods, wrapped them both in a blanket, and fell asleep. Roach heaved himself to his feet and sounded the alarm.

TOWNSFOLK WHO WERE MEMBERS OF A PRE-EXISTING VIGILANCE committee organised to protect the community snatched up their guns and headed out after the men with hard eyes and white knuckles. The night came alive with fire, the light from the committee's torches disembodied among the trees. Two members of the gang had stayed in the town. From the window of the Inn, a boarding house neighbouring Roach's establishment, Susanna Abell watched the men with a rising tide of fear. Her husband, Jim Abell, had ridden out with the rest of the committee, leaving Susanna and her teenage daughters alone. Outside, the two outlaws spat and pushed at each other, looking for somewhere to continue drinking. Susanna and her daughters locked the Inn, but when the door rattled on its hinges the youngest began to sob. Clapping a hand over the girl's mouth, Susanna ordered them up to the attic and armed herself with a hatchet. The outlaws broke through the door in time to see Susanna scramble up the ladder after her daughters. The ladder clattered to the floor but the men were quick to set it once again at the entrance to the attic. As soon as a head appeared above the entrance Susanna swung the hatchet and sent the man reeling backwards, where he collapsed on to his companion. Swearing, the second man struggled to his feet and kicked the man on the floor, furious to discover he had knocked himself unconscious. He made his own attempt at the attic but was met once again by the blade of the hatchet. Stooped with alcohol, the man collapsed at a table. In the attic, Susanna and her daughters waited for dawn.

JIM ABELL AND THE REST OF THE VIGILANCE COMMITTEE RETURNED to the Inn to find the two men passed out, caked in blood and vomit. Both were pulled from the building and hog-tied over the saddles of waiting horses. Jim helped his wife and daughters down from the attic and the women made a formal identification of the outlaws as the men who had attacked them. Out in the woods the committee found the man with Jane Talbott and wasted no time in hanging him from a hackberry tree on the banks of the creek. By noon, the group that fled north was captured and beaten into submission. In total, five of the seven men who had terrorised the town were hanged in the tree, where they stayed until the town's coroner gave the order for them to be cut down. The Talbott sisters attested that the seventh man had not taken part in the rape, and he was thrown in the jail as a gesture to legality. In the following days, the coroner and the sheriff declared there was no way of knowing who among the citizens of the town had committed the lynchings. *The Osage Mission Journal* said the outlaws got what they deserved.

FATHER PAUL PONZIGLIONE WAS NO STRANGER TO VIOLENCE, BUT even he had been shaken by the ferocity of the events at Ladore. He decried the outlaws and the vigilance committee, firm in his belief that the law did not belong in the hands of ordinary men. One of the most famous Jesuit priests in the area, Ponziglione moved to Osage Mission in 1851 to work as a missionary to the Osage Nation. A driven, hardy man, he frequently made journeys of over two hundred miles in treacherous weather conditions, a way of life commonplace among frontier missionaries. Ponziglione saw the potential in the railway, but after one of his colleagues was involved in several life-threatening crashes, he pledged only to use it as a last resort. He was glad to see Kansas flourishing under the influx of so many settlers, but on the road he heard of and witnessed so much criminal activity that he worried for the souls of the state and its people.

THE AUGUST AFTER JACK REED'S EXPERIENCE WITH THE BENDERS disturbed him into leaving Kansas, Ponziglione was at the end of a gruelling three-hundred-mile journey. Caked in the dust of a scorching summer, he was eager to spend the night indoors. Heat lightning flickered among clouds slung low over the horizon, and he did not want to be exposed when it twisted itself into great forks to pierce the earth. He passed between the hills and spotted the Benders' cabin, a welcome sign of humanity in the elemental landscape. Riding faster to outpace the brewing storm, the priest stabled his horse as the first lashings of rain darkened the earth. He arrived in the cabin at the same time as Gebhardt and Pa, all eager to avoid the rain. The stove leaked smoke into the small space, where it mingled with the electric heat of the storm. Ponziglione greeted the family with a cheerful remark about the weather and inquired after lodgings. Gebhardt gestured to the bench and nodded his head in respect. The priest shook the water from his wax cloak, pulled out a pipe, and took a seat.

Kate joined them and introduced herself, surprising the man with her eagerness to hear his purpose for stopping in. Ponziglione had been raising funds for the mission and saw no harm in telling the family, thinking that perhaps they would even contribute. At once a feverish excitement filled the young woman's face and she announced she would make coffee. She continued her questions until Ponziglione became apprehensive. The two men were no longer in the cabin and he was struck by the squalor of the family's living quarters. Extinguishing his pipe, he commented on the absence of the men. Kate's reply was vague and laced with something sharp.

The rain wrapped the cabin in a blanket of sound, and he thought suddenly of the rumours that outlaws operated along the part of the trail near Drum Creek. Years spent on the constant precipice of danger had instilled in the priest the importance of being finely tuned to his surroundings. He watched Kate burn the coffee, her eyes never settling, moving constantly between the door and something else behind the canvas dividing the room. Lightning threw unnatural shadows against the walls. Ponziglione fingered the rosary tied into the lining of his cloak. Heavy footsteps belonging to Pa came in from the rain, but the old man did not join them. The fever went out of Kate's movements. She became languid, setting the coffee down in front of him with wide, gleaming eyes that settled and stayed on his face. Gebhardt returned and read a joke aloud from the paper and they both laughed with practised enthusiasm. The priest sipped the burned coffee and grew increasingly uneasy. Thunder rolled in the foundations of the cabin. Kate sat down opposite him and he leaped suddenly to his feet, overcome with panic. Like Julia Hestler, Kate's spiritualist friend from the Cherryvale hotel, Ponziglione muttered an excuse and strode quickly from the cabin. Rain obscured the landscape, but he saddled his horse regardless and rode, frantic, into the storm.

Part II

A NURSERY OF
MORAL MONSTROSITIES

So Foul a Murder

Big Hill Creek, Kansas

OCTOBER 1872

On an autumn morning filled with the promise of a cold winter, two brothers gathered their fishing equipment and set off for Big Hill Creek. The sky was bright and vast and they argued over scones they had for breakfast as they walked. Well trodden and used alike by local townsfolk and those travelling further west, the stretch of the Osage Mission Trail leading to the water was easy to follow and pockmarked with mud. As the boys approached the creek, they diverted from the path and headed for the undergrowth, a dense tangle with enough branches at eye level to dissuade anyone unfamiliar with the area from entering. The older boy pushed the brushwood aside with his fishing rod and disappeared into the thicket. Younger than his brother by several years, the second boy followed, stopping when he noticed rags in the branches of a wild plum tree. Clothing hanging in the bushes was not uncommon on the frontier, but a dark stain on the fabric and the stillness of the morning air frightened him. He could not see his brother. Birds moved in the corner of his vision, skewering insects that had grown fat on the long, hot summer.

Picking his way closer to the rags, the boy could see it was part of a woman's dress. There was a streak of dried blood across the chest. The smell was rusty and sweet. Beyond it, deeper in the brush, was a shirt like the ones he and his brother wore when their mother dressed them for Sunday school at Harmony Grove. Looking down towards the water, he could make out the shape of his brother watching the creek, with his hands gripped tightly around the fishing rod. Calling out, he scrambled past the dress, eager for a reply. The older boy chewed at his lip and stared into the water where the body of a man drifted lazily in the current, bathed in the early morning light. They stood together in silence.

"He's dead?" said the younger boy. He meant it as a statement, but it came out like a question and left him feeling foolish. His brother poked at the body with his fishing rod and a stream of bubbles spilled out from beneath its neck. He poked it again, but the rod wasn't strong enough to roll the body; it just lay in the water gurgling. His little brother screwed up his nose and squatted in the mud, eyes fixed on the dead man's socks.

"We gotta walk back," the older boy announced after several minutes of further contemplation. He figured the man didn't have any valuables on him, so it was best to tell their father and let the sheriff deal with it. He cuffed his little brother on the back of the head as he made his way back up the bank.

"Reckon we should take the dress," the younger boy's voice was shaking. He stopped and turned around. The rags twitched in the breeze.

"So they believe us."

His brother shrugged dismissively.

"I ain't carryin' it."

THE TWO BOYS TRUDGED THE MILE BACK TO THEIR HOMESTEAD IN silence. The younger clutched what was left of the dress against his chest and stared at his brother, whose face was grim and unreadable. It was the same grey expression the boy saw on the faces of the men an hour later when they heaved the body from the creek. He watched from further up the bank as they turned the dead man over and laid him on a sheet. In the water the body had discoloured and bloated. A deep laceration across the throat gaped unappealingly, and the boy spat into the river to stop himself from vomiting.

Crouching to examine the corpse's head, the coroner's top lip curled at the ferocity of the injuries. Fragments of the skull were lodged in a grey-ish pulp that had once been the brain. The man sighed and swallowed with some difficulty, gesturing to his companions. They rolled the body in the sheet, but the smell seeped through the fabric. The boy watched as the men worked quickly to fix the corpse to the back of a horse. His brother collected the remainder of the clothing strewn in the undergrowth and bundled it into a saddlebag. The coroner thanked him with a nod. When the group set off to Independence, the head lolled unpleasantly inside the sheet and the boy wondered if it might fall off before they reached the town. He was proud that he and his brother had found the dead man and, several days later, couldn't hide his disappointment when the clerk of the general store told him they had not even been mentioned in the papers.

THE BRUTAL NATURE OF THE MURDER AND THE UNCEREMONIOUS way the man had been disposed of unsettled the citizens of the surround-ing counties. The newspapers rallied against the "hellish, foul and bar-barous" crime, demanding vengeance be enacted on the as-yet-unknown but "inhuman perpetrators." Both *The Kansas Democrat* and *The Osage Mission Transcript* ran the coroner's report in the hope that someone would recognise the victim and come forward to identify him:

> Five feet eight inches high [173 centimetres], heavy built, light complexion, light hair, small whiskers on his chin, hair sandy mixed with grey, slim long nose, very sharp near the point, eyes close together and about forty years old. Deceased was dressed in common labourer's wear, brown tweed coat, check over shirt, then a black and white flannel undershirt, and then a white undershirt; white flannel trousers, blue jeans, blue socks, without shoes or boots, with nothing of any kind in his pockets or on his person to identify him.

On 8 October, an inquest was held in which it was declared the blow to the head had crushed the right side of the skull, and whatever life the man had left in him leaked out with the blood from the neck wound. It was also supposed that the body had become wedged in the depths of the water, where it remained for six days before the boys made their grisly discovery.

Shortly after the description of the dead man appeared in the papers, Martha Jones paid a visit to the coroner, where, after a short interview, she identified her husband. In the last weeks of September, William Jones had left his young family on their new farm in Montgomery County to continue his work on a schoolhouse in Osage Mission. When he prepared to return home, he had with him $250, $150 of his own savings and another $100 loaned to him by a colleague with the promise that it would be repaid. He intended to stop at the land office en route and pay off the remaining debt, so that he might surprise his family with the news that the farm was secured.

As the days shortened and frost gleamed among the tallgrass, Martha had become concerned that her husband had fallen ill on his homeward journey. She left her children in the care of a neighbour and travelled to Independence; learning that William had never passed through the town, she began to grow increasingly distressed. Martha read the papers and made inquiries, quickly finding that the townspeople were willing to gossip about the mystery but less willing to join her on a physical search. When she opened the paper on 17 October, the small amount of hope that William would return to her alive was extinguished. The coroner's report was an exact description of her missing husband. Left a widow with three children too young to work the land and a homestead on which she owed $250, Martha had made her way to the coroner's office heavy with the pain of loss.

William was a man with a good and honest reputation, and many were touched by the plight Martha and the children had been left in by his murder. The community, at a loss for suspects and eager to exert vengeance on behalf of the family, fixed its eyes on R. M. Bennett, the farmer unfortunate enough to own the land on which the body had been found. Bennett demanded that a committee revisit the site for further investigation. He claimed that he heard the sound of a wagon in the early hours of the morning when it was supposed the body had been dumped. In the days following the identification of the body, a committee returned to the site, where they discovered remnants of a wagon track that doubled back where the undergrowth became impenetrable. Taking the opportunity to reinforce his innocence, Bennett pointed out that the track indicated the wagon had a distinctive feature: one of the back wheels was dished the wrong way from carrying loads that were too heavy. Not only did it set the tracks apart from those of other wagons in the area, it gave the vehicle a discordant rattle. Bennett had taken note of it the night he heard the wagon because the noise it made was so unique. To his relief, Bennett did not own a wagon with this particular trait. Begrudgingly the committee cleared him of involvement and the suspect list once again ran dry.

The winter of 1872 came in bursts of biting cold spells that stilled the waters of the creek, where the boys continued to fish by cracking holes in the ice. In the mornings they walked an extra mile downriver to keep the bend where they had discovered William Jones out of sight. When they passed it, the younger offered the smallest of nods to the soul of the dead man. His brother ignored him.

ON HER HOMESTEAD, MARTHA WORKED TO PREPARE THE CHILDREN for a winter without their father and listened to the growing rumours that other men had disappeared on the Osage Mission Trail. She did not join the conjecture about the vanished travellers that filled saloons and grocery shops. The newspapers did not report the disappearances because there was no explicit evidence of foul play. The death of her husband loomed large in the imagination of the county, but Martha did not have energy to expend on wondering who the perpetrators were. She could only wait. It would be six months until she knew what had really happened.

By Some Persons Unknown

The Osage Mission Trail, Kansas

WINTER 1872

If the newspapers of south-east Kansas were anything to go by, 1872 was a hard year for Labette County. The murder of William Jones reminded citizens of a similarly morbid discovery that had happened back in late March. A party of walkers came upon a campsite a mile and a half south-east of Oswego during an afternoon relic-hunting expedition. Hogs and other prairie life had plundered the site for food, leaving a trail of human debris in their wake. The source of the debris lay under a pile of blood-matted hay. Nearby, a foot in a sock without a leg stuck out of the undergrowth. A mess of clothing, bone, and flesh, the corpse had evidently been in the clearing for some time. Stripped by foragers and missing its lower jaw, the body was beyond identification. The coroner pieced together a description of the man as best he could: five feet eight inches (173 centimetres) tall, slender, wearing a size-six boot. He had died wearing three shirts: a red flannel, a purple net, and a white shirt with a ruffled bosom. The back of his skull had been caved in with a blunt object. Several weeks later, a farmer shot a pair of coyotes locked in a tug of war over a blood-stained blanket.

UNIDENTIFIED, THE MURDERED MAN SLIPPED OUT OF THE PUBLIC eye. Then in the months following the discovery of the body of William Jones in October 1872, three more men disappeared. Whisperers recalled the nameless body from the spring, and rumours grew that the county was in the grip of a murderous epidemic. The section of the trail that passed through the intersection of the four counties had become unsafe to ride, and local townsfolk knew it. Newspapers continued their campaign against Ladore, but it was becoming increasingly clear the problem had its roots in the open country. But still the Benders avoided suspicion, as many believed the likely culprits to be a roving band of horse thieves.

On his homestead, Leroy Dick began to receive letters from concerned family members inquiring after missing relatives. As trustee of the township where the majority of the disappearances occurred, he was a natural point of contact for those looking for answers. Dick knew from gossip at the Harmony Grove schoolhouse that people were frightened, but he was reluctant to acknowledge a pattern and even more reluctant to imagine that anyone in his community could be somehow involved in the disappearances. Even for seasoned travellers the prairie was dangerous in the winter. People frequently went missing, only to reappear several weeks later under dubious circumstances. Some became genuinely lost, sending word to loved ones as soon as they reached a settlement with the facilities to do so. Others simply chose to disappear, and that was none of his business. Dick also considered it likely that if horse thieves were responsible, they would eventually move on. Loath to issue a public warning and draw attention to the issue, he replied to the letters on an individual basis. Then, in the first weeks of November 1872, one of his own family members vanished on the trail.

DICK'S COUSIN HENRY MCKENZIE WAS A TALL, ATHLETICALLY BUILT man nearing thirty, whom Dick found to be obnoxious. A war hero in his home county of Hamilton, Indiana, McKenzie enjoyed boasting of his time fighting at Chickamauga, one of the most devastating battles of the Civil War. He had been wounded but recovered well and was quick to remind anyone within earshot of his bravery. Hank, as the family called him, appeared on the doorstep of Dick's homestead in early November, announcing his intention to call on his sister, who lived in Independence, and then visit the land office. Dick begrudgingly let him inside and he spent the night with the family. The children adored Hank's outlandish stories and fell asleep beneath the expensive chinchilla coat he always wore in the winter months. The following morning, Hank set off from the homestead with thirty-six dollars in his pocket and little fear of horse thieves and vagabonds. Though full of bluster, he was a capable and skilled fighter. An unexpected pocket of dismal weather forced him into the home of J. H. Sperry, where he spent the night drinking and playing cards. Not one to adhere to any kind of schedule, he roused himself at midday and ate lunch with his host. Thanking Sperry, Hank set off on foot towards Independence. Dick never bothered to check whether the man arrived.

BENJAMIN BROWN HAD SET OFF FROM CEDARVILLE IN NEIGHBOUR-ing Howard County with a story that was becoming worryingly familiar. He left behind his wife, Mary, and their two children, with the intent to secure a loan. Now that their family was growing, he wanted to purchase a land claim closer to one of the many towns in the area. Packing the fifty dollars he had saved to improve his case for a loan into his coat pocket, Brown headed for Osage Mission. But at the town he was denied a loan due to insufficient credit. Reluctant to return to his wife empty-handed, he decided to visit the land office regardless and made west for Independence. At Ladore, Brown traded horses with the man who would later identify his body by a sterling silver ring he wore on his forefinger. When Brown failed to return home, his wife knew it was up to her to locate him. She rode by stagecoach along the trail, inquiring after her husband. After the trail ran cold at Ladore, she was forced to give up. On her way home she stopped at the Bender cabin for supper, where she found Kate full of concern for her missing husband. Encouraged by the hospitality of the family, she stayed the night, unaware that her hosts were the last people to see Brown alive.

WILLIAM MCCROTTY, A TOUGH IRISH VETERAN OF THE UNION ARMY, was also on his way to the land office when he vanished. After the war, McCrotty relocated to Kansas from Illinois, drawn by the prospect of a fresh start on the prairie. With a friend named George Burton, McCrotty staked a claim in Howard County. The area was full of settlers vying for land, and conflicts over ownership frequently escalated into violence. At the time Burton had young children and McCrotty, worried for the safety of his friend's family, suggested they return to Parsons while the claim was finalised. Later, when he was in need of a witness to bolster the claim, McCrotty set out for Parsons to enlist Burton's aid. Like Brown before him, McCrotty stopped at Ladore, where a resident named Dan Gardner gave him twenty-five cents to pay for dinner, suggesting the Bender cabin as a place to spend the night.

AS PREPARATIONS FOR CHRISTMAS WERE UNDER WAY, SNOW FELL SO thickly in the county that citizens abandoned their work to rig up sleighs and race them across the prairies. Alongside a cheery announcement that one gentleman had even added bells to his sleigh, *The Head-light* reported the discovery of a body that had been mutilated by wild hogs after being dumped on the prairie south of the town. It was a crime eerily reminiscent of the campsite discovery earlier in the year. The young man was eventually identified as John Phipps by his father, who recognised what was left of his clothing. The elder Phipps supposed that his son had been murdered for the three hundred dollars he had about his person at the time of the murder. In the article detailing the fate of John Phipps, *The Head-light* raged against the lack of organised action by local authorities, apologising for the "deeds of blood" that plagued the road. But travellers could not avoid the trail, and as men and women alike visited relatives over Christmas the Bender cabin was busier than ever.

A Man and a Little Girl

Onion Creek, Kansas

DECEMBER 1872

On a homestead seven miles south of Independence, Kansas, George Longcor was making preparations to travel to Iowa. Longcor watched the first whispers of snow catch in the evening light and wished he had begun the journey the previous week, when the temperature was still unseasonably warm. In the past, the weather made little difference to him. A blacksmith by trade, demand for Longcor's skill in the small settlement of Onion Creek kept him in work regardless of the changing seasons. But now he and his infant daughter were giving up their homestead to head north, and the thought of making the journey in the snow made him nervous.

BACK IN 1870, WHEN LONGCOR FIRST ARRIVED IN ONION CREEK, his wife, Mary Jane, walked the homestead with him, their little son held tight against her chest. A typical family in post-bellum America, they had come to Kansas to build a new life on the plains. Longcor, like so many other young men, had fought long and hard in a war he was desperate to forget. Upwards of seven hundred thousand men lost their lives during the Civil War in unyieldingly brutal conditions. The landscape was riddled with pestilence, prisoners of war languished in squalid camps, and battlefield surgery left an estimated sixty thousand men with amputated limbs. Mental trauma plagued veterans long after their physical wounds healed, and many headed to the West to rebuild their lives as a way of working through past tragedy.

LONGCOR WAS WELCOMED IN THE SMALL COMMUNITY AND MARY JANE found comfort in the daily chores of frontier life. She worked in the garden, where she planted two cycles of crops a year, one in spring and the other during summer. In spring she planted radishes, salad leaves, and peas as their little boy played among the skirts of her dress. When summer came, she would grow potatoes, pumpkins, and squash to provide them with hearty meals throughout the barren winter months. In May, lightning split the sky and the land ran dark with rainwater and mud. The little boy grew pale, except for two rosy patches on his cheeks brought on by coughing. Mary Jane did her best to treat him with herbal remedies, but as his condition worsened, she exhausted herself trying to nurse him back to health. When a doctor was sent for, he diagnosed the little boy with lung disease, then offered his condolences; the boy was beyond assistance. As the month drew to a close, the child became a shadow and succumbed to the illness.

THE LONGCORS WERE FAR FROM BEING ALONE IN LOSING A CHILD. By the 1870s, the infant mortality rate in the United States was so high that one in five children died before they reached their first birthday. Doctors were in high demand on the frontier and did not always have the equipment or drugs needed to treat their young patients. Those in rural areas who had chosen to settle ahead of the towns found that life in isolation could quickly become fatal. Homesteading was a lifestyle that needed as many hands as possible, but rural life was fraught with so many seen and unseen dangers that even if children made it past their first birthday, many did not come out the other side of adolescence. The need for children also took its toll on women who, if they survived childbirth, were often pregnant for consecutive years. Families were large and death was inevitable, but like everything on the frontier, the road to loss was unpredictable.

THE SUMMER FOLLOWING THE DEATH OF THEIR SON HAD BEEN QUIET, and George often watched his wife walking in the garden or the orchard. Mary Jane was pregnant again, and she found solace among the vegetables and the flowers. Crisp autumn evenings gave way to winter nights, and she spent her evenings knitting clothes for her husband and the unborn child. On 12 January 1871, Mary Jane gave birth to a little girl. In the following days they named her Mary Ann. Less than a week later, Mary Jane was dead from complications relating to the birth of her daughter. In the spring following his wife's death, Longcor heard the chatter of children on a nearby homestead. With Mary Ann in his arms, he walked the short distance to investigate and happened upon the family of Dr William York. William was also a veteran of the war, inspired to relocate to southeast Kansas after his father moved to Fort Scott, and was full of praise for the area. Mary York had been reluctant to uproot the family with three very young children. But she softened at the sight of Longcor and his little girl and made a great fuss of introducing the children. The family was lively and William's practice flourished. Mary Ann played with the York children while her father worked and the community welcomed more families to the area.

FOR NEARLY TWO YEARS AFTER THE DEATH OF HIS WIFE, GEORGE Longcor remained in the homestead without her. The business prospered and the settlement was fond of the blacksmith and his daughter. But Mary Jane's parents had written at least once a month since the death of their daughter, urging Longcor to return to Iowa so that they might help raise their grandchild. He did not want to abandon the homestead where he and his wife were supposed to raise a family together, but Mary Ann was now eighteen months old and required constant supervision. She was inquisitive and good-humoured, and Longcor knew she needed to live in a house with other children.

William and Mary York encouraged the idea. Mary was now pregnant with the couple's fourth child and had no extra time to dedicate to the care of Mary Ann. William suggested Longcor purchase a wagon and team of horses from him at a discounted price and the blacksmith agreed. The wagon was basic but hardy and certain to take them as far as Iowa with horses that were much the same. As the weather stayed fair long into December, Longcor had taken his time making arrangements for the journey. But now cold winds descended suddenly on the prairie and he knew he had to leave as soon as possible.

In the early hours of a particularly chilly morning, Longcor fitted his daughter into the wagon. He wrapped her in a quilt, nestling her gently in a wicker basket lined with rabbit fur. The little girl wore a bonnet knitted by her mother and a pair of mittens to protect her against the dry bite of winter. She drifted in and out of sleep to the sound of her father saying his goodbyes to William and promising he would write to the family when he arrived in Iowa. Excited chatter from the York children drew William back inside and, wishing his friend well, he and his wife waved to Longcor as he set off down the track. As he passed through the outskirts of Onion Creek, Mary Ann began to stir. Longcor talked to her about the journey ahead and the grandparents who were waiting for her. The Osage Mission Trail opened up before them, awash with gold and white.

Deeds of Blood

The Bender Cabin

DECEMBER 1872

Two days after George Longcor and his daughter set out for Iowa, John Handley and his colleague pulled their horses to a stop outside the Bender cabin. A large mongrel dog flung itself from the back of the wagon and sniffed in excited circles around the men's boots. They unhitched the horses and led them to the stable. Handley, a local freight hauler, was on familiar terms with the family and called at the cabin on his journeys from Fort Scott to settlements further west than Kansas. The air temperature dropped rapidly as they made their way inside. The ground had been impenetrable for days. Word from Junction City was that the week had been the coldest on record. The mercury had dropped to roughly twenty-eight degrees below zero Celsius and stoically refused to rise above twenty below no matter how much the newspapers implored it to. Frostbite stung the extremities of anyone who was unfortunate enough to have to travel. The dog pawed at the dirt but gave up when the cold singed its paws.

Handley was surprised to find a paltry fire in the stove and the cabin enshrouded in near-total gloom. Kate was not pleased to see him. She was even less pleased to see his companion. She loitered in an odd manner by the dividing canvas, then shot forward when Handley moved to greet her. Guiding the men to the few goods that lined the shelves, she apologised and said that they would not be cooking, instead suggesting they purchase something. When Handley asked why they had picked such a cold evening not to eat hot food she ignored him.

His colleague reached for the stack of firewood by the stove and at once a great commotion erupted in the small room. The dog burst into the cabin, knocked over a rifle propped up against one of the benches, and scrambled beneath the table, where it pawed at the floorboards and slobbered. Pa Bender staggered out from behind the canvas wielding a large stick and hunting for the dog. The animal crouched on its haunches and began to growl. It was obvious Pa had chased it inside and come through the back door of the cabin intending to beat it. With some effort Handley heaved the animal from beneath the table and walked it back to the wagon. When he returned, he found Gebhardt arguing with his colleague over the stove. Kate had vanished behind the curtain and he could hear her in agitated conversation with her mother.

"If you want a fire you buy extra wood," Gebhardt said repeatedly, each time punctuated with his pitching giggle. He darted between the men and the stack of firewood when either one attempted to reach for it.

"No problem paying." Handley's words hung in the air like cold fog. Gebhardt didn't move. Cursing under his breath, the other man suggested they just move on. They weren't welcome and they were wasting time that could be spent somewhere with people who did have a fire and hadn't tried to attack the dog. Handley let a moment pass to see if Kate would reappear. When she didn't, he sighed and agreed. Gebhardt watched the two men closely as they stalked out of the cabin and back to the wagon. Picking the rifle up off the floor, he followed them out as far as the porch.

"You won't get no firewood this side of the hills."

Handley stared at him with contempt. The dog barked furiously as the wagon pulled back out on to the trail, creaking under the strain of the cold. They travelled in silence until the other man let out a deep groan upon realising his toes were blackening with frostbite in his boots. When Handley looked back, he saw that even the light from the stove had been extinguished. If you did not know the cabin was there, it would be impossible to pick it out against the landscape.

The evening after Handley's disturbing visit to the cabin was the first of several warmer nights leading up to Christmas. Winter had driven all life from the prairie, leaving only the hollow ring of the wind in its wake. On a straw mattress in the Bender cabin, Mary Ann Longcor was fast asleep, still wearing the mittens she had been dressed in several days before. Her father was nowhere to be seen. Kate sat listening to the Bender men shovel dirt in the orchard. Pa's curses drifted in through the open door. After the digging came the soft thud of a dead weight hitting the earth. Kate rose, crossed the room, and threw open the trapdoor. The smell of decomposition was not as bad in the winter, but she held her breath regardless.

As the year drew to a close, those who stopped at the Bender cabin found the family accommodating and friendly. John Handley begrudgingly called in to water his horses, prepared for another icy reception. But he found Kate in such high spirits that he wondered if spending too long in the elements had led him to dream her previous hostility.

A Man of Resolution and Nerve

Topeka, Kansas

1873

While south-east Kansas grappled with the growing number of disappearances on the Osage Mission Trail, a different kind of trouble was brewing in the state's corridors of power. In January 1873, Kansas was in the midst of a hotly contested Senate race. Not yet a position elected by direct popular vote, the new U.S. senator would be chosen by the Kansas state legislature. Disenchantment with the small group of men who had dominated politics in the state since its founding in 1861 had reached a tipping point. The era of street brawls and guerrilla violence that defined Bleeding Kansas and the state's experience of the Civil War hung in recent memory, threatening to boil over into the present in the state capital of Topeka and as far as Washington, D.C. Young, ambitious, and emboldened by ranks attained during the war, veterans fought for their rightful places in politics and enterprise. They sought to replace a governing body that was leading the state into stagnation before it had the chance to flourish. Having risked their lives for an America they believed in, they now demanded a central role in the forging of the nation's post-bellum identity.

AMONG THE RISING TIDE OF YOUNG POLITICIANS WAS ALEXANDER Miner York. Thirty-five years old, a former colonel in the Union Army, and an experienced attorney, Alexander became a state senator in 1872. He represented Montgomery County, whose border with Labette was not far from the Bender cabin. The first of nine siblings, Alexander had his father's sharp blue eyes and high cheekbones. Tall and lean, he cut an unmistakable figure during his time in politics. A passage describing Alexander in *The History of Montgomery County* called him "active, zealous and enthusiastic; a man who could not sit down and contentedly wait for anything." He operated with energetic directness on whatever project had currently taken his interest, but he was also a complicated man who abided solely by his own set of principles.

During the war, Alexander was popular with his peers and respected by superiors, proving himself adept at handling both personnel and tactical challenges. In 1863, while he and his regiment were travelling on a steamer down the Cumberland River, Alexander uncovered a plot by the captain and a crew member to sink the boat. Both were Confederate sympathisers. Ordering the two men to the engine room, he informed them that he would not hesitate to shoot them if the boat did not reach its intended destination. The journey passed without further incident and Alexander was promoted to colonel within the year.

In the aftermath of the war, Alexander prospered and by 1873 he was residing in Independence with his wife, Juliette, and three young children. He established a successful legal practice in the town with Lyman Humphrey, a man who would later become governor of Kansas. Along with Alexander, the extended York family had relocated to south-east Kansas after the war. His father resided at Fort Scott, where he ran a plant nursery, and his brother and fellow Civil War veteran Dr William York was comfortably established as a doctor seven miles south-west of Independence. The family was well known and well liked, but Alexander was not satisfied. Plagued by the growing reputation of Kansas as a hotbed of corruption, he turned his attention to politics.

————

THE MAN AT THE CENTRE OF THE CORRUPTION ACCUSATIONS WAS Senator Samuel Pomeroy. A physically commanding, pugnacious man, Pomeroy felt himself to be an irreplaceable cog in the functioning of the state. He was a prominent figure in Kansas politics when the state joined the union in 1861 and became one of Kansas's first federal senators the very same year. At fifty-seven, he was a good deal older than the new generation of politicians birthed by the war and he disliked their company and their ideas. Pomeroy's career had burgeoned during the state's territorial period, when exploiting his political position for commercial gain went largely overlooked. Now the state was full of young families, like the Yorks, who arrived headed by men with political ambition, unafraid of exposing fraudulent behaviour. But Pomeroy was not without his supporters who believed him to be above reproach, an honest man truly dedicated to the state's best interest. On either side the voices grew louder and increasingly polarised.

THE CONTROVERSY SURROUNDING THE ELECTION OF 1873 BEGAN less than a year before. On 11 May 1872, the United States Senate opened an investigation into the accusation that Pomeroy had secured his election victory of 1867 by bribing his opponents. The investigation was handed to the Committee on Privileges and Elections, who found in Pomeroy's favour, citing lack of evidence. But back in Kansas the ruling deepened the split within the senator's party. When an anti-Pomeroy group was formed, Alexander York, the newly minted state senator from Montgomery County, was quick to volunteer as secretary.

BY THE TIME OF THE 1873 ELECTION, THE TWO MEN WERE ALREADY well known to each other, having crossed paths in early 1872. Alexander, for all his condemnation of corruption, had blackmailed the older man into moving a land office to a more advantageous location, his hometown

of Independence. This was politics at a local level. As regional represen-
tations of the federal General Land Office, the buildings were where new
settlers filed claims and purchased land. Officials in burgeoning counties
were willing to fight over the placement of the offices. Not only did they
encourage faster settlement of the land, they provided a steady stream of
travellers willing to spend money in local townships. Independence was
a town at the heart of myriad growing communities, and the local city
council knew that the presence of a land office could make it one of the
most important cities in the region. The council raised money to send
Alexander York to Washington, D.C., tasked with persuading Pomeroy
to agree to the move. They also provided him with the address of a man
to turn to if Pomeroy proved obstructive.

ALEXANDER MADE THE JOURNEY TO WASHINGTON, D.C., IN OPPRES-
sive January weather. After his arrival, Alexander and Pomeroy met
several times to discuss the matter of the land office. On each occasion
Alexander found himself dismissed as an inconvenience. When he tried
to complete the move without Pomeroy's involvement, he was blocked by
parties who viewed his behaviour as dishonest. Out of other options,
Alexander paid a visit to the man whose address he had been given by
the Independence City Council, General McEwan. As a friend of several members of the council, McEwan was sympathetic to the interests
of the town. A resourceful, well-informed man, he kept himself busy after
the war by collecting as much information on public figures as possible.
Luckily for Alexander, this collection included Samuel Pomeroy. McE-
wan produced an affidavit, which Alexander took with enthusiasm.

THE AUTHOR OF THE AFFIDAVIT WAS A YOUNG WOMAN NAMED ALICE
Caton, who had once been an employee of the federal Treasury. In 1868,
she was unemployed and eager to embark on a career as a clerk. Samuel
Pomeroy, seeing an opportunity from which he felt they both would benefit, ensured that she was offered a position. She had been delighted but

quickly became dismayed when she realised he expected her to repay him through sexual favours. When he requested her attendance on a business trip to Maryland, she reluctantly accepted. In her affidavit she stated that she had "slept in bed with him in Room 155 in Barnum's Hotel, and that said Pomeroy did have criminal connections with me during the night of February 29, 1868." Though she had gone with him out of fear that she would lose her job, the assault had left her humiliated and deeply distressed. Caton was willing to testify in court against Pomeroy, but Alexander expected that the threat of legal action would be enough to sway the obstinate senator. The assault had occurred almost five years before and had long passed out of the upper-class rumour mill. But it had never reached the press. Should the document leak to the scandal-hungry Kansas newspapers, it was unlikely that Pomeroy would survive. It was yet more evidence that Pomeroy abused the power his position afforded him. It was also decidedly unchristian behaviour. Alexander finally had the leverage he needed.

With the affidavit in hand, Alexander appeared on Pomeroy's doorstep the following evening. Initially he had pushed past the valet who opened the door, but seeing he had interrupted a dinner party, requested a private audience early the next morning. Pomeroy clapped the younger man on the back and led him into an adjoining room, where he offered him a drink. The two sat opposite each other at a small table. Alexander produced the folded affidavit from his pocket, opened it, and passed it across the table. Pomeroy could feel York's sharp gaze as he read, and his face began to colour. It was clear that moving the land office was no longer a request, it was a demand. When Alexander question him about the legitimacy of the accusation, Pomeroy remained silent. On 26 March 1872, the land office opened its doors in Independence.

Later, when Alexander was asked about the morality of his actions, he replied that "they were questionable but the people of Independence sent me to Washington to get the land office, and I got it." For York, blackmailing a corrupt rival was entirely justifiable if there was no other way to achieve his goal. He simply did not have the patience to embark on a drawn-out war of attrition. In Pomeroy's mind, York had proved himself an opponent willing to engage in unscrupulous behaviour. A man potentially open to bribery. Almost a year later the two men met again under similar circumstances. The fallout cost them both their political careers.

IN JANUARY 1873, KANSAS BURNED WITH ELECTION FEVER. WILLiam S. Blakely, the soon-to-be postmaster of Junction City, wrote to a colleague that "the senatorial race is red hot." The state was a milieu of excitement, indignation, and anticipation. The press argued with politicians, with rival outlets, and with the public. Politicians went public with personal grudges and every day brimmed with the possibility of another scandal breaking. Pomeroy had not yet returned from Washington to start his re-election campaign. By the time his train pulled into Topeka, his name was on the front page of every newspaper, along with that of his opponent, John J. Ingalls. Comfortable in his ability to buy the number of votes needed in the legislature to secure another term in office, Pomeroy expressed little concern about defeat. Then, as the day of the election drew close, his campaign became increasingly plagued by the publication of a letter claiming to provide explicit evidence of corruption. Though the letter had been in circulation for several months, Pomeroy's elaborate attempts to dismiss it had piqued the attention of the press. Though he had just survived a campaign bribery accusation the year before, this time, his accusers had proof. It was a document known as the Ross letter.

W. W. ROSS WORKED AS A FEDERAL AGENT TO THE POTAWATOMI PEOple during the 1860s. As the chief administrator for the tribe in the district, Ross had control over who they were permitted to trade with, as well as the goods they were allowed to receive. In 1862, he received a letter from Pomeroy proposing a scheme in which a trader chosen by the senator was to be given exclusive rights to sell goods to the tribe. A trade monopoly would be a lucrative and consistent source of income. It also put the Potawatomi at a greater disadvantage. The chosen trader would have complete control over the price of goods, regardless of their quality, leaving the tribe vulnerable to further exploitation. Pomeroy promised Ross a quarter of the profits if he agreed, the other three quarters to be paid to the men organising the goods. In reality, Pomeroy would be receiving the largest share of the profit, taking his money from the three quarters paid to his lackeys. It was one of many moneymaking schemes the senator had constructed, but this time it had a paper trail, since Pomeroy had signed the letter personally. When the letter came to light in 1873, Pomeroy tried to save face by claiming that the other man named in the letter, his accomplice Edward Clark, had forged the letter for his own financial benefit.

In the papers there was already rampant conjecture about the authenticity of the letter. *The Fort Scott Daily Monitor*, a longtime critic of Pomeroy, ran an article with the headline PUT UP OR SHUT UP, in which it bet *The Parsons Sun* twenty dollars that Pomeroy was the author of the letter. When reports began to appear that Edward Clark had admitted to being the author of the letter, pro-Pomeroy papers were ecstatic. *The Courier Tribune* reported that the letter was undoubtedly a forgery and that Pomeroy's opponents would soon be forced to "dance or pay the fiddler." For several days it appeared as though Pomeroy was in the clear.

THEN ON 27 JANUARY, TWO DAYS BEFORE THE ELECTION, THE BALance shifted again. Edward Clark stood in front of an anti-Pomeroy rally. Steadying himself, he placed a satchel on the table and read from an affidavit he had signed the night before. He told of how, a week earlier, he had met Pomeroy at Tefft House—a hotel where the senator conducted his business while in Topeka—to discuss the letter. Pomeroy had offered Clark $2,000* to write a confession admitting that he was responsible for the letter. He had also promised that two other men involved in the scandal would bear the brunt of the inevitable investigation. Clark agreed.

---

* The modern equivalent of about $45,000 (£33,000).

But when the confession reached the papers, he realised he had been deceived. Testimony from others involved explicitly named him as the sole perpetrator and accused him of exploiting his connection to the senator. At the end of his testimony, Clark opened the satchel, producing $2,000 in $100 bills. He requested that they be accepted as evidence that Pomeroy had bribed him to confess under false pretenses.

Alexander watched the proceedings from a bench near the front of the hall. Privately he suspected that the Ross letter would not be enough to topple Pomeroy. But he decided he couldn't leave that to chance.

That night he stood in the lobby of Tefft House, looking at the same clock Edward Clark had found himself in front of only a week before. It was a cold night, but by the time Alexander made his way into the heart of the building and reached Pomeroy's office, he was hot. In the room, the two men reached an agreement. Alexander sold his vote for $8,000 and received $2,000 on the spot as down payment. They drank from crystal glasses to toast Pomeroy's success. Alexander returned to his lodgings, where he recounted the money into the early hours of the morning. At daybreak, a young man delivered a valise packed tightly with $100 bills totaling $5,000. The final $1,000 was to be paid after the vote had been cast.

ON THE MORNING OF THE SENATORIAL ELECTION, ALEXANDER SAT completely still in the convention hall as the representatives took their places. The valise was tucked beneath his seat. In each of his jacket pockets was a bundle of ten $100 bills. As the convention was formally opened, Alexander began to compose himself, then rose as the speaker concluded the opening address. The action drew accusatory glances, and an uneasy stillness settled on the room. Alexander did not notice. He made his way to the centre of the hall where the electoral officials sat and then turned, fixing his gaze on the attendees.

Alexander addressed the meeting in a voice that was clear and strong, belying none of the tension that had wracked his mind and body in the months leading up to the election. He reminded the committee of the Ross letter and that Pomeroy had dug himself further into the pit of corruption in his attempts to distance himself from the scandal. When disgruntled murmuring began to brew among pro-Pomeroy representatives, Alexander raised his voice. Recounting his visit to Tefft House, he requested the valise. Upon seeing the case, Pomeroy coloured with a heady combination of humiliation and rage.

Just as Edward Clark had done two days before, Alexander opened the valise to reveal the money he had taken to secure his vote. He took the $100 bills from his pockets and began to count them out. Pomeroy shrank further back into his seat with each stack of money that materialised between the officials. When Alexander finished counting, $7,000 in $100 bills sat in front of the convention. In the seconds following the exposure, Alexander felt an immense sense of relief. The money had weighed heavily on his conscience, even though he felt his motives for accepting it were clean. As muttering dissolved the silence, he requested that the money be put towards expenses for the ongoing legal investigation

Alexander York presenting the $100 bills, given to him by Samuel Pomeroy, in front of the Kansas State Legislature. *Harper's Weekly*, 1 March 1873.

into Pomeroy's behaviour. But by accepting the bribe, Alexander had forfeited his own political career. For many he was now as dishonest as his counterpart. Not content with the reveal of the money, Alexander prefaced a blistering denouncement of his colleague with an acknowledgement of his own now-tainted character.

> I know that there are many present who may feel disposed to impugn my motives in this matter and decry the manner of my unearthing the deep and damning rascality, which has eaten like a plague spot into the fair name of this glorious young state. I am conscious that, standing here as I do a self-convicted bribe taker, I take upon myself vicariously the odium that has made the name of Kansas and Kansas politics a hissing and a byword throughout the land.

It was apparent to all that Alexander's devotion to his principles could not be questioned. In a highly emotional conclusion to his address, he accused Pomeroy of bargaining with men's souls and betraying the trust of people who looked to him for protection and guidance. Alexander then turned his criticism on the entire Republican Party, accusing them of enabling Pomeroy's behaviour and reaching a depth of degradation for which he had no words. The entire structure of Kansas politics had a responsibility to its people to change and Alexander had made himself a political martyr in order to initiate the transformation.

THE EFFECT OF THE SPEECH WAS IMMEDIATE. UNABLE TO RETURN TO his seat in the ensuing chaos, Alexander watched the scene momentarily free of any emotion. The seat went to John J. Ingalls instead, who went on to serve in the Senate for eighteen years. Pomeroy had abandoned the convention in the closing sentences of the address, unwilling to face the barrage of questions that would inevitably come his way. He had few remaining supporters, none of whom joined the fray in his defence. In the following months Pomeroy would claim that he had given Alexander the money in order to finance a banking endeavour in Independence. It was a convincing enough argument that an investigative committee could not reach a definitive conclusion surrounding his guilt. Alexander's trap proved to be yet another corruption charge that failed to stick to Pomeroy. But despite his legal luck, his political career was as good as dead. As the year unfolded, copies of Alice Caton's affidavit appeared in the newspapers, though by then it made little difference. Pomeroy had been buried in a grave of his own making.

No Traveller Is Safe

———

MARCH 1873

As the fallout from the election continued, Alexander York found himself a household name. He was a polarising figure and his actions in Topeka made him a favourite of the press. The *South Kansas Tribune* praised him as "the most widely esteemed citizen of the state." *The Kansas Chief* called him "a bad man through and through" and claimed his exposure of Pomeroy amounted to treason against the state of Kansas. Alexander quickly grew weary of the criticism. In his speech he had gone to great lengths to accept responsibility for his behaviour and failed to see why the matter continued to draw attention. On the advice of his father, Manasseh, Alexander returned to south-east Kansas and to his family in Independence, throwing himself back into the York & Humphrey law firm where he specialised in landownership cases. His children were overjoyed to once again have the presence of their father as part of their day-to-day lives. In the evenings they burst into his office and coaxed him away from his legal correspondence to the family dinner table. Always hungry for a new enterprise and eager to shake off the residue of his failed political career, Alexander also began to make frequent trips to Fort Scott, where the family agricultural business was rapidly expanding. Over long February evenings spent by the hearth with his father, he learned that his brother William felt the Pomeroy affair had brought unwanted attention to the family. The doctor had worked hard to build his practice and worried constantly about alienating his patients through political affiliation. Manasseh told Alexander that his brother avoided commenting on whether they were related, and if he was pushed said that they were not.

WHEN WILLIAM STAYED WITH ALEXANDER IN EARLY MARCH, THE two avoided discussing the matter. Alexander was too proud to raise it and William did not feel he had the time. The doctor was travelling to Fort Scott in order to visit their father and check on the older man's health. While there he intended to arrange for the transportation of plants back to his wife, Mary, and their young children. A petite, religious woman, Mary was struggling to settle into her new life seven miles south of Independence. Though she was practical and organised, she had become disillusioned by the isolation of their new home. She missed the convenience of the city and the close network of friends she had back in Illinois. William, like most men on the frontier, spent little time with the family, and she missed him intensely when he was away. Now pregnant with the couple's fourth child, she grew increasingly agitated at his long absences. Aware that his wife's anxiety was beginning to transfer to the children, William thought focusing on the garden might allow her to occupy her restless mind. The York Nursery was fast becoming one of the best in the region, and he made a list with Alexander of the trees, shrubs, vegetables, and flowers he wanted sent back. As the evening drifted on, Alexander's disappointment in his younger brother was replaced with a private relief that William was at last showing signs of recovering from the trauma of war.

WILLIAM'S EXPERIENCE OF THE CIVIL WAR HAD SHATTERED THE previously energetic and optimistic young man. After graduating from the Lind Medical University in Chicago, he was conscripted into the

Union Army; his "draft card" lists him as William H. York, Assistant Surgeon for the 15th Regiment of the U.S. Colored Infantry. Deployed immediately, William and his unit were plunged into one of the most intense regions of conflict during the war—the Union campaign to take the Confederate stronghold of Vicksburg, Mississippi. It was a brutal, desperate fight for one of the most important cities on the Mississippi River. Hampered by the Union blockade in the South, the Confederate cause relied on the stretch of the river between Vicksburg and Port Hudson for supplies. Losing the city could mean losing the war. Gunboats blasted Confederate defences and drowned men under rubble and mud. Raiders plundered supplies on both sides and myriad waterborne diseases crippled troops who were already weakened from hunger.

William, placed in charge of several field hospitals in the area, saw some of the worst violence the war had to offer. Before victory was in sight for the Union Army, he fell victim to a band of roving Confederate Bushwhackers, who raided the encampment and took him prisoner. Then began a gruelling trek to the largest Confederate prisoner-of-war camp west of the Mississippi, Camp Ford. Stripped of their uniforms, hats, and boots, William and his fellow prisoners walked the 340 miles in rags that offered them no protection and quickly became stiff with sweat and filth. They burned under the glare of the southern sun and found no comfort in the wetlands of Louisiana, where disease moved unseen beneath the waters of the bayou. Stinking and wretched, they continued west, fed only when their captors had food enough to spare. At the outbreak of the war Camp Ford had managed to keep its prisoners in relatively good conditions, largely due to the presence of a spring that provided clean water. But by the time William arrived it was overcrowded and fetid. Men huddled in holes dug into the banks or simply lay exposed to the elements.

From time to time the misery of the men's condition escalated into violence against the guards. During William's imprisonment a guard was shot while on sentry duty. When no one ventured forward with information, the prisoners present at the time of the shooting were lined up and forced to draw lots. Eighteen men, including William, drew short. A ramshackle scaffold was erected and a rope thrown over the beam for each of the prisoners. An end was tied to each man's thumbs and they were hoisted into the air. They were left suspended by their thumbs for hours, a cruel example to the man who had shot the guard and those who had sheltered him. The pain was so excruciating that many slipped into unconsciousness. Others succumbed to fever that had brewed in their limbs since their arrival in the camp. William survived, but the trauma of the event was etched as deep in his mind as the rope scars on his thumbs. Disgusted by his inability to save the men who had suffered beside him, he threw himself into his post-bellum doctoring with a fervour that often left him bedridden with exhaustion. A compassionate man with principles as firm as his elder brother's, he had found comfort in the arms of the unwaveringly devout Mary, who herself had seen first hand the trauma of war. Mary was a member of the United States Christian Commission, a group formed to provide Union troops with medical assistance and religious support. During the war she headed south with the USCC, where she worked tirelessly as a nurse in field hospitals that were overrun with wounded soldiers. In the aftermath of the war she turned her attention to teaching at freedmen's schools, institutions that provided an education to newly emancipated slaves. The details of how Mary and William met are lost to history, but they must each have sensed a kindred spirit in the other. After the birth of their second son, they followed Manasseh York to south-east Kansas to build a new life on the frontier. With his growing medical practice and growing family, William had finally begun to shed some of the guilt he had carried with him since the war.

WHEN WILLIAM SAT ACROSS FROM HIS BROTHER THE EVENING OF 3 March 1873, he did not mention the other reason for his journey to Fort Scott. In late January he received a letter from George Longcor's family in Iowa, expressing concern that the young man and his daughter had not yet arrived. William was fond of the little family, as they were some of the first friends he and his wife had made in the area. Having worried for some time that they had been waylaid on their journey, he was not surprised to receive news that they were missing. On his Traveller in the district he frequently overheard gossip about disappearances in the area, and his patients expressed concern for his safety. When the letter arrived on his doorstep, a familiar feeling of guilt rose up in William's heart and he decided to combine the visit to his parents with an initial inquiry into the whereabouts of his friend.

In the days leading up to his departure, he read in the paper that a wagon had turned up on the outskirts of Morehead, a town north-east of Independence. The description matched the wagon he had sold to Longcor. While searching the wagon for clues as to the fate of its owner, the men who discovered it came across clothing belonging to a man and a little girl. William tried in vain to keep the development from his wife, knowing the news would upset her and that she would oppose his intention to investigate the disappearance. When Mary heard the news from a neighbour that afternoon, the colour drained from her face.

In her account of the events, published in 1875, Mary recalls the morning of William's departure for Fort Scott. As she listened to him talking with their children, Mary found her "heart so oppressed with sadness, foreboding imminent danger," that she began to cry. But she also felt it was not her place to try to dissuade him from going. They said their goodbyes in the parlour. William kissed the children on the forehead and gave a firm handshake to each of the little boys. He embraced his wife and, in his arms, Mary offered up a silent prayer that he would not be overtaken by the same York impetuousness that had sunk Alexander's career. The children ran shouting and waving into the morning, following their father as far as the wooden fence that enclosed the yard. From the porch Mary watched William's progress until he was no longer distinguishable from the haze of light that drifted through the tallgrass.

ON THE MORNING OF 4 MARCH, A LOW MIST SETTLED IN THE streets of Independence. By the time William had saddled his horse and bade farewell to his brother, the sun had burned it away, leaving the land clear and sharp. Reaching the outskirts of town, he set out north towards Morehead. He was in good spirits despite his grim purpose. Brimming with adrenaline he had not felt since the war, William felt the prairie come alive around him, awash with the colours of spring. Upon arriving in Morehead, he was directed to the local stable, where the wagon had been hitched in the hope that a passer-by would be able to identify it. William took his time examining the wagon but knew at first glance that it was the one he had sold Longcor just three months earlier. He confirmed the fact with the local authorities and informed them in no uncertain terms that he was certain foul play was the reason for its appearance. Morehead was not on the route Longcor had told William he was taking to Iowa, and there had been too many disappearances in the area to write it off as a mystery. He was discouraged to hear that a group of local men had made a peripheral search of the area but were unwilling to venture far into a landscape capable of swallowing travellers up.

WILLIAM ARRIVED IN FORT SCOTT INTENSELY PREOCCUPIED WITH the fate of his friend and Mary Ann. When he sat down with his father for dinner he barely ate and dismissed the older man's concerns that something was wrong. Over the course of his four-day stay, William planned how he would begin an investigation without alerting the perpetrators. Manasseh had not seen his son gripped by such intense purpose for quite some time. When William returned to the house on the final evening of his stay riding a new horse, his father knew the purpose must be grave. William did not spend money unnecessarily and the animal was clearly expensive; a glossy even-tempered roan, far superior to the horse it had replaced. After they had eaten, William finally gave up the reason for his behaviour. He explained to his father that he intended to travel home via the route he knew Longcor and Mary Ann had taken, stopping at homesteads to question the inhabitants about their disappearance. Once he reached Independence he would organise a more substantial search and expected Manasseh's support. His father agreed that he needed to return to Mary and be at home during the investigation so as not to upset her or the children. Together they decided that William would inform the sheriff of his intent to investigate the disappearance. He did so following their discussion, then packed his saddlebags to save time in the morning. The next day he set out across the prairie when the daylight still glowed red beneath the horizon in the east.

To his frustration, in his forty-five-mile ride to Osage Mission the doctor encountered no one who had seen Longcor or his daughter. The land was full of people drawn out by the cracking of ice on the creeks, the first true sign of the spring thaw. Everyone he stopped was eager for conversation but short on answers. Logically William knew that his questions had not been fruitless; they had allowed him to narrow the area in which it was likely the two had disappeared. But the knowledge that his friend had not even reached Osage Mission filled him with a profound sense of guilt that it had taken him so long to realise they were missing. William rode into the town convinced that Mary Ann and her father were dead. He was offered a place to stay for the night by J. M. White and his family, who were excited at the prospect of having a relative of Senator Alexander York in their modest cabin. They broached the subject over dinner, questioning him about the Pomeroy affair with curious faces. William thanked them for their hospitality. But in an ongoing bid to distance himself from his brother's controversial political legacy, William denied that he knew Alexander. The next morning he was gone before they had woken up, riding south beneath the azure sky.

An Anxious Heart

———

At home in Onion Creek, Mary did her best to distract herself from her husband's absence. She rose early and walked the homestead, feeding the animals and making lists of what needed to be tended to when William returned. She took the children to visit the neighbours, all the while thinking of Mary Ann Longcor and her father. She prayed more than usual and made sure the children did, too. Though she was used to William's absence, knowing this journey had a graver purpose had taken its toll on her, and in her darker moments she worried that her unborn child would grow up without a father.

As the days crept towards 18 March, she felt the fog of anxiety begin to lift. She was certain William would return on the date he had promised, and they could start preparing for the summer. On the evening of 17 March the children laid out their father's slippers by his favourite chair and the eldest wondered out loud about what presents he might return with. At bedtime they sang together in bright spirits until, tired but content, the children drifted off to sleep. Mary woke in the night to the rumble of thunder and the glow of lightning in the skies. At the foot of the bed, her youngest son cried out in his sleep, and she scooped him out of the cot, wrapping them both beneath the sheets.

Shrieks of delight woke her in the morning. The children dressed themselves haphazardly and ran to the door at every sound of hooves on the trail outside. By noon, Mary had fed the animals twice and paced the parlour, her fingers working at the plait in her hair. In the late afternoon a heavy knock on the door startled her so badly that she cried out. On the porch stood a man from Morehead inquiring after the doctor. He was surprised to find that William was absent and explained that they had expected to see or hear from him on his return journey with regard to organising the search for the Longcors. Mary chewed at her lip. The man realised he had distressed her and apologised, making several excuses for William's failure to arrive home. He reassured her again as he left and said he would return as soon as he received any news of her husband. Mary thanked him quietly and closed the door. When the children's play-mates arrived to dinner she tried to reassure herself by telling the children that he was just delayed. Night fell slow and heavy around the family and she slept in the same room as the children to comfort them. The following morning Mary was awake before the sun, determined to prove her husband was still alive.

ALEXANDER WAS SURPRISED NOT TO SEE HIS BROTHER IN THE WEEK following William's visit on the way to Fort Scott. For some time their father's health had been in decline, and he suspected William had remained with their parents in order to monitor his condition. Not wanting to be left out of any discussions regarding the family's agricultural business, Alexander wrote to his father asking if he should join them. A large, formidable man even in ill health, Manasseh was immediately alarmed by the contents of the letter. Had he been ten years younger, he would have ridden out straight away in pursuit of his missing son. Though William was obsessive about the Longcors' disappearance, Manasseh knew he would not have alarmed his wife by arriving home late. He took the first train to Independence and arrived at Alexander's house late in the afternoon. Alexander arrived the following evening to find his father in a bluster of concern. His concerned deepened when he discovered William had become so fixated on the disappearance that he never organised for the plants to be delivered to Mary. Alexander wrote to her, promising they would be with her the following day. Manasseh set out for the sheriff's office to inform them that his son was missing. He cut an imposing, sombre figure on the busy streets of the town. Alexander sent word to the youngest of the three brothers, Edward. He told him to bring a detective and to arrive as soon as possible.

MARY CROSSED PATHS WITH THE LETTER AS SHE SAT BESIDE A FARM-hand who offered to take her to Independence. In the house she convinced herself that a letter containing an explanation for his delay waited for her at the post office. Out on the prairie the wind rang in her ears, and William felt further away than ever. Somewhere in the noise the farmhand was providing a stream of local gossip. When he chatted about the disappearances, Mary was glad of the wind no matter how much it stung her. At the post office there was nothing for her, and she stared for a long time at the clerk as though it might change his mind. Quietly, the farmhand led her outside and asked her what she wanted to do. They drove to Alexander's house, where she threw herself from the buggy and opened the front door. The house was empty.

ALEXANDER YORK'S MOTHER-IN-LAW, MRS PRESTON, HAD BEEN LIV-ing with the couple since they moved to Independence. A pragmatic woman with a kind face, she knew that the next few weeks would be a difficult time for the family and started preparations accordingly. She made her way up the garden path and reached for the back door. When it slammed open she stumbled back with a shout. In the doorway stood Mary York, her eyes big, frightened, then filled with relief that she had found someone.

Mrs Preston did her best to feign genuine surprise at the state of the young woman. "Why have you come here?" she asked, trying to usher her back inside. Mary transferred her grip on the door handle to the frame.

"I came to look for Will." Mary's eyes were frighteningly dark. Mrs Preston had always admired the younger woman's devotion to her husband, but now Mary was brittle with fear. Struggling through a suggestion that William might still be with his father in Fort Scott, Mary trailed off into silence when a look of sympathy formed on the face of the woman in front of her.

"Father York came here to look for William."

Mary took the news in silence. Mrs Preston prised her fingers gently from the door frame. When Manasseh arrived moments later he found Mary completely still. A peculiar emptiness had consumed her entire body and she found she could not cry. Manasseh tried to comfort her by being pragmatic, but she was unresponsive. When Alexander returned, he poured her tea and joined his father in cautious optimism, assuring her that the search for William would be immediate and expansive. Mary broke her silence when the stagecoach arrived to carry her to Onion Creek, a place she no longer wanted to call home. Her voice was steeped in finality.

"No—he will never return."

A Match to a Powder Mill

——

In the early months of 1873, the Benders began a slow falling-out with the community around them. Opinions about Kate in particular grew increasingly polarised. She remained popular with male travellers, and her unfriendly behaviour was never enough to deter her more dedicated suitors, who continued to call on the family. Susanna Tyack also remained devoted to her, even encouraging her husband to attend a séance at the cabin. Thomas was unconvinced but enjoyed the company of the younger Benders and the enjoyment it brought his wife. Other than with the Tyacks and the travellers, Kate had a reputation for being a nuisance. She continued to materialise on the doorsteps of sick members in the community and harass them until they accepted her services or drove her from the premises. The more superstitious citizens of Labette whispered to one another that she was a witch. In the days following William York's disappearance, a confrontation occurred that damaged her local reputation so badly that even Susanna stopped calling.

DURING THE NINETEENTH CENTURY, SPRING IN KANSAS WAS RIFE with prairie fires, a natural and necessary process through which the landscape rebirthed itself. Over winter the grasses dried out in bitter winds and froze in the sub-zero temperatures. With the spring thaw they became free of their frosted shells, turning the landscape into a tinderbox in which man or nature could provide the first spark. The fires were integral to the life cycle of the prairie, removing waste plant material and dry scrub and leaving the warm soil full of nutrients. In the wake of destruction was the perfect environment for new growth. The Native Americans who lived on the prairie knew that with the fires came lush, verdant land that encouraged an influx of animals they could hunt for food. But for white settlers the fires were frightening infernos that "crept like demons, licking up with tongues of flame the laboured toils of years." In the needless battle to eliminate the fires, vast swaths of prairieland were destroyed and countless lives were lost.

On 8 March 1872, the Dienst family lost their eldest son, John, to the fires. The men of the family had ridden out to meet the maelstrom of heat, armed with little more than buckets of water and the intention to light a smaller fire to drive the larger away from the homestead. In the crackling roar of the flames, John's lungs filled with smoke and he lolled unconscious on his horse as it fled from the blaze. He was laid out at the cabin, a mess of charred clothing and burned flesh. His mother, Henrietta, tended to the wounds as best she could, but it was clear that he would never regain consciousness. John was just twenty-six years old and left behind his wife, Delilah, and their little daughter, Cora. The Diensts were a well-liked family, and John Dienst Senior was as much a part of local life as Leroy Dick. The community mourned for the family and mourned for the man. No one was more attentive and persistent in offering comfort than Kate Bender.

After the death of her husband, Delilah found herself drawn to Kate and her reputation as a medium. The two women knew each other well and often sat together at the Harmony Grove Sunday school. Kate had always talked of her ability to contact spirits, but she pressed the matter with more urgency in the aftermath of John's death. She knew it could be a means of earning money, and clients in the throes of grief were the most susceptible to her propositions. But in the months following John's death,

Delilah's grief was so great that she could not bear the thought of hearing his voice. Though she longed to ask Kate to speak with him, she knew her mother-in-law would consider it a betrayal. Henrietta considered Kate's supposed talents to be fraudulent and warned Delilah on several occasions not to trust her. As the seasons passed, Delilah drew her comfort instead from Kate's assurance that he was still with her.

When the prairie fires once more lit up the sky, Delilah felt the anniversary of her husband's death draw near. Kate felt it too and once more began to to pressure Delilah into agreeing to contact his spirit. One afternoon as the women were leaving Harmony Grove, Kate took Delilah's hand firmly in hers and told her now was the best time to speak with her deceased husband. There was something unfriendly in the Bender woman's grip on her fingers that made Delilah think of Henrietta's warnings. She declined, unwilling to put her emotions in the hands of a woman who could be a charlatan. A flicker of contempt passed behind Kate's eyes, and she offered again in a sharper tone. Again, Delilah said no, unnerved by the sudden meanness in the other woman's voice. She removed her hand and thanked Kate for her offer, setting off to find someone else to walk her home.

A week later, the Dienst women were tending to the garden with the children when they saw Kate riding down the trail. Delilah reached immediately for Cora, scooping the little girl up against her chest. Henrietta wedged the shovel in the ground and crossed dirt-covered arms over her chest. With a steady gaze she watched Kate dismount. Kate made no pretense as to the purpose of her visit. She offered her condolences again, but Henrietta did not respond. Instead, she turned to Delilah and suggested she take the children inside to prepare for lunch. As she rounded up the children, Delilah heard Kate explaining how comforting it would be for the family to host a séance. Delilah reddened, ashamed that her mother-in-law now knew she had continued to entertain the idea. She ushered the last of the children into the cabin, relieved to be out of sight of their visitor.

Henrietta had none of the softness nor curiosity of Delilah. After a long year, the wound left by the death of her son had finally begun to

mend, and she had no desire for the family's healing process to be un-
done. Well aware that Kate's aspiration to healing and spirit talking had
been accepted by more gullible members of the local area, she feared for
Delilah, whose grief still remained exploitable. Henrietta crossed the garden to the post where Kate had hitched her horse and untied the animal.
The two women stared at each other until Kate's features lost their pretend compassion and drifted into petulance. She walked to the animal
and mounted it, but Henrietta kept hold of the reins.

In a voice clear enough for those on the homestead to hear it, Henrietta informed her that the Dienst family, living and dead, had no need of
her services and she was not to contact any of them again. Kate bristled
with indignation and snatched the reins from the older woman. She kicked
the horse and wrenched its head in the direction of the trail. Henrietta
escorted her off the property. When people stopped in at the homestead,
she made certain to tell them she no longer thought of the Benders as
neighbours. Years later she would testify in court that "Kate claimed she
could call up spirits," and had repeatedly offered to call up the spirit of
her son.

The Trace of Him Is Lost

Ladore, Kansas

APRIL 1873

When James Roach sat down in the office of his hotel in Ladore to write to the governor of Kansas, he was fed up. He was fed up with the supposed band of thieves murdering travellers, and he was even more fed up with being blamed for it. It had been two weeks since the disappearance of William York, and Ladore's reputation as a meeting point for desperadoes had put the town front and centre in the investigation. Roach was already struggling to support the ailing town whose more respectable citizens were beginning to relocate. Now he worried for the safety of his family members in the aftermath of a disastrous visit from the York brothers. Earlier that morning Roach watched with relief as they set off from his hotel—he hoped not to return. During their short stay in the town, the brothers had turned popular opinion against him and caused undue panic among the citizens. If the band of murderers had not been enough to scare more people into leaving, Ed York was well on his way to doing the job.

AT TWENTY-ONE, EDWARD YORK WAS JUST YOUNG ENOUGH TO HAVE missed the opportunity to make a name for himself during the war and was busy making up for it in other ways. Lithe and blond with his mother's dark eyes, he stood out among the family and enjoyed it. A good decade younger than his male siblings, he admired Alexander for his principles but had always been closer to William. News of the doctor's disappearance upset him, yet when Alexander sent word that he was to join them, Ed felt a rising sense of excitement. Manasseh had kept him at work in the nursery, where the hours were long and the work bored him. Ed did not really believe that William had been killed, but when he arrived at the York house in Independence with a detective in tow, he felt at last that Alexander would take him seriously. Together the York family had rallied a group of men that varied in number between sixty-five and over a hundred, depending on the weather. It was nearly a week after William's disappearance by the time the group set out on to the trail. Ed rode out front in a hat with a low crown that matched the one his father wore. The prairie bloomed and everything seemed too lush, too fertile to be harbouring death beneath the soil. Alexander kept a close eye on his little brother, and when the time came to separate into groups, he asked the detective to do the same.

They traced William to Osage Mission with relative ease. He had spoken to so many people in the area that many were surprised he had managed to go missing. When Alexander knocked on the door of J. M. White, the farmer was alarmed to discover that his guest had indeed been related to the famous senator, though he was careful not to tell Alexander that William had denied the relation. By mid-afternoon all fingers in the area pointed to Ladore as the nexus point of crime in the region, so the group circled around in a thunder of hooves and rode for the railway town.

By the time they reached the inn of James Roach, Ed, prone to putting too much stock in gossip, was spoiling for a confrontation. Alexander introduced himself and requested lodgings for his brother and the detective. Roach, wanting to get off on the right foot with the search party, had agreed. Knowing that the town would never be free of suspicion, he wanted the process dealt with as swiftly as possible. He sat drinking with the York brothers late into the night and listened carefully to their plans. Ed outdrank himself and rankled the other customers by raising the subject of the lynching from three years earlier. In the morning, Alexander paid the bill but did not apologise for his brother's behaviour. All day agitated townsfolk turned up at the inn, indignant at the way those in the search party were conducting their investigations.

In the late afternoon, Ed, rage burning high in his cheeks, materialised in the saloon and, in front of Roach's patrons, accused the man of being complicit in William's disappearance. In his sweep of the town, Ed heard numerous rumours connecting Roach to unsolved disappearances in the area during the summer of 1871. John Martin, a labourer to whom Roach owed two months' wages, vanished on his way back to the town from work on the Roach homestead. Shortly afterward, John Arbunkle, a man with heavy pockets and a dream of going West, never turned up for a planned dinner at the Roach residence. *The Tioga Herald*, along with many of the townsfolk, assumed that Roach was responsible and more than capable of organising a band of murderers to make an easy profit. It was enough to convince Ed, who informed Alexander of his findings when his older brother arrived at the saloon. Roach weathered the accusations with a sombre expression and a growing concern that the search was escalating towards unjustified violence. Alexander questioned him carefully and, to Ed's dismay, cleared him of involvement. He suspected Roach of being complicit in the disappearances of Martin and Arbunkle but knew he was not stupid enough to involve himself with the murder of a prominent citizen.

When the York brothers rode out of town the following morning, Roach was glad to see them go. The experience rattled him. Roach understood the pain of a missing relative but saw no excuse for the distress the group had caused the town during the search. The panic brewing in neighbouring counties was already in danger of boiling over into unmitigated disaster without the help of a roving group of men hungry for revenge. Roach was concerned for the safety of his family, for the safety of the town, and for the safety of those who would be implicated for little more than looking at a member of the York family the wrong way.

In his letter to the governor, Roach demanded assistance from state authorities without delay. The lack of structured law enforcement in the region posed a danger to those on both sides of the search. To support his case, Roach listed names of men who were confirmed to be missing in the area—Jones, Brown, McCrotty, York—and accused local authorities of being inept and unable to find the perpetrators. He signed off with a plea. "We are all poor and we want help from the state and we want it now and we need it so that we will spare no time until we bring the guilty parties to justice."

Assistance from the state would not arrive until it was too late.

WHILE JAMES ROACH SET ABOUT REPAIRING THE ILL FEELING AMONG the townsfolk, the search party succeeded in tracing William to a general store in Parsons. Unlike Ladore, Parsons had a good reputation and was considered one of the places to be in south-east Kansas. When Ed described William to the clerk of the general store, the man nodded, informing them that a man matching the description had purchased tobacco a week or so before. Satisfied with the morning's progress, the group splintered off to have breakfast. While the others ate, the detective walked the main street of the town and admired the newly painted shopfronts. Thomas Beers was a man of many talents, none of them quite good enough to excel in any particular career. He moved to Emporia, Kansas, with his wife where he worked as a hay-fork salesman, but decided the profession was beneath him after they took up residence in an apartment in the courthouse. The courthouse gave him delusions of legal grandeur, and when the number of disappearances on the trail began to climb, he decided to reinvent himself as a private detective. With law enforcement on the frontier still in a state of flux after the Civil War, private detectives were in high demand. Some worked for themselves, others for firms like the Pinkerton Detective Agency, which offered services from tracking down missing persons to breaking up striking workers. The job was a good fit for Beers, who was naturally inclined to pry into affairs he felt he ought to be involved in.

When he heard the York family was in need of a detective, he met Ed at the train station and offered his services. Ed was impressed with the brashness of the man and his florid manner of speaking. He agreed to take him on.

As Beers stood outside the town's printing press, he was approached by a boy no older than sixteen, who had the drawn, adult look common to all children who worked the land. He asked if Beers was a lawman, and the detective nodded. The boy said he had been stopped by a man who could have been William while ploughing a field just west of the town. He remembered the man because he had admired the horse, a red roan, the kind only rich people could afford. Beers took out the reporter's notebook he kept in the breast pocket of his coat and took down the details. The doctor had stopped to check that he was on the right road to Independence, the boy explained. When he said yes, the man thanked him and headed towards the crossing at Big Hill Creek. Elated, Beers took the boy back to Ed, to whom he repeated his story. The closer they got to piecing together an answer to William's disappearance, the harder Ed's moods were to predict. He listened to the boy with a steady expression, feeling the first seeds of grief plant themselves in his stomach. Everyone around him thought his brother was dead, and the smaller the radius of the search became the more he wished someone would look him in the eye and say it.

Alexander suggested they focus the search on the area surrounding Big Hill Creek, starting with the place where the two brothers had discovered the body of William Jones the previous fall. The waters had already begun to swell with the first of the spring rain and the boy warned them that canvassing the area would be treacherous without the help of a local guide. Alexander knew they needed someone who represented local authority as a counterweight to the increasingly aggressive search party. He asked the boy who he thought was the best man for the job. Without hesitation he volunteered Leroy Dick. Ed and Detective Beers took a few of the party and rode south with a letter of introduction and request for assistance.

The Mystery Still Unravelled

Leroy Dick was on his way back to his homestead when a small group of men on the Osage Mission Trail approached him. Dick guessed from the upright gait of their leader that they had a York at the helm. Drawing his horse alongside, the man introduced himself as William's younger brother and handed Dick a letter from Alexander requesting his assistance. Dick read it and, to his surprise, experienced a great wave of relief. When the first disappearances were reported he was certain the matter would resolve itself. Then concern about the reputation of the area hampered his willingness to openly acknowledge the issue. After William's disappearance, Dick grew deeply embarrassed by his previous lack of action. Alexander's request for help offered him the opportunity to redeem himself. Consequently, when Dick recounted events to writer Jean McEwen over fifty years later, he placed himself at the centre of the investigation, omitting his prior inactivity and describing the drama unfolding around William's disappearance in vivid detail.

ED LOOKED TO DICK FOR AN ANSWER. ED WAS EXHAUSTED BY DAYS of little sleep and fruitless searching, and his eyes had taken on an earnest desperation. Dick felt sorry for the boy and suggested they have lunch together to discuss the particulars. The group dismounted and sat about eating beans and drinking day-old coffee. Ed stared into the grass. Detective Beers introduced himself, wrote down Dick's details, and asked intelligent questions about the lay of the land. Dick had never met such a heavyset man with such a cultivated sense of refinement.

"Are there any persons or families in the neighbourhood suspected of crimes?" Ed asked suddenly. Dick hesitated. He had heard from Ladore that Ed's tactics for eliciting information were unlikely to endear him to the townsfolk.

"What about Elder King?" Beers suggested, noticing Dick's hesitation. "Folks seem to think his reputation leaves much to be desired."

Dick sighed and poured the rest of the coffee on the fire. He was disappointed that citizens were so readily offering each other up as suspects over the usual frontier grudges.

"King's just an unfortunate old humbug. He rubs people the wrong way, but there's nothing criminal about him."

Dick thought about the people in the area and wondered whether it was worth putting stock in the rumours about the Bender family. At a recent visit to the Dienst homestead, Henrietta had made her feelings about Kate very clear. Dick hadn't seen the older Benders in months; he couldn't be sure they were even still around. What did bother him was that Gebhardt's attendance at the Sunday school had waned. He had been unpleasantly defensive when Dick pressed him on the matter, and now, in the wake of everything that unfolded, he doubted his initial fondness for the man. It did not take him long to reach the conclusion that it would be no great loss to the community if the York men chased the Benders off.

"There's a family over in the mounds with unproven robbery charges. The daughter claims to be a medium." Dick immediately felt like he had done the community a service by directing the search party to a specific family. Beers flicked through several pages in his notebook, then passed it to Ed, pointing out a passage he had copied down. Ed read aloud.

"Prof. Miss Katie Bender, can heal all sorts of diseases; can cure blindness, fits, deafness and all such disease, also Deaf and Dumbness."

Dick nodded. "That's her, lives with a man called Gebhardt and her parents."

Ed shot a hopeful grin at Beers, then asked him to send a man to fetch Alexander, who had ridden on to Independence.

"We saw her advertisement in Chetopa, I thought it was hooey." Ed turned his full attention on the trustee. "Unproven robbery charges?"

Dick informed the men that the Benders were unpopular in the area, then talked the two men through the incident with Edward Ern. He recounted as much as he could remember—how Ern was one of the first people to meet the Benders when they arrived at his trading post looking for a claim; how several months later Ern's trust in the family was broken when valuables belonging to his relatives went missing during a stay at the Bender cabin. Nothing had come of the accusations, Dick explained, because Ern chose to confront the family on his own instead of reporting it to the relevant authorities. When the Benders his bluff, Ern abandoned the matter and left the state. Beers took everything down at an impressive speed, the notebook balanced in the crook of his elbow. Ed listened, completely still.

"The Dienst family won't have anything to do with them," Dick finished. "Kate wouldn't let them alone when their son died."

Several moments passed. In the tallgrass, a grasshopper sparrow looked for lunch and screeched to unseen companions every time it found an insect. Dick hated the unnaturalness of the sound. It belonged in the legs of an insect, not the throat of a bird. Ed leaped to his feet, stamping out what was left of the fire.

"We'll search the area and call on the Benders for supplies."

Among the group of men comprised largely of local homesteaders like the Tole brothers, those who had been listening closely to Leroy Dick whooped and mounted their horses. Beers good-naturedly asked them to settle down, and Dick was surprised that they complied. He had seen them drinking over lunch and a few of the men put empty glass bottles back into their saddlebags. Dick climbed into the saddle and watched the group with a wary eye. He told Ed that he would help them organise the search of the creek but that they should question the family on their own. If the Benders turned out to be no more than unpleasant neighbours, he didn't want them to know he had volunteered them as suspects.

A Disguise of Hellish Cunning

The Bender Cabin

4 APRIL 1873

Alexander was pleased with his brother's work but had no intention of including him in his initial investigation of the Bender family. Ed proved himself volatile, and Alexander did not want to risk running off anyone who knew the location of William's remains. Manasseh and his eldest son had come to the sad conclusion that William had perished before the bulk of the search party set out. Alexander bottled the sorrow and the anger, unwilling to release it and jeopardise his ability to lead before they had an answer. But Ed bristled with rage, and it had already endangered their cause in Ladore. When Alexander regrouped with his brother near Brockman's trading post, he asked Detective Beers and William's neighbour, Jim Buster, to join him in questioning the Bender family. Ed protested until Alexander promised he would send Buster to fetch him if trouble arose and put him in full control of the search of the creek. In areas where it was possible, they were to drag the water for remains.

Alexander and the two other men arrived at the cabin under cloud cover that ebbed and flowed over a land slick with rain. Pools of standing water made a fractured sky beneath their feet. In the yard a few bedraggled chickens pecked at each other and insects drawn out by the weather. As a man well informed in agricultural matters, Alexander was impressed by the state of the orchard; it was the only well-kept thing about the property and the topsoil had evidently been raked earlier in the day. On a stack of wood outside the cabin a wiry young man sat with a Bible balanced on his knee. He looked up long enough to introduce himself as John Gebhardt and then turned back to the Scripture. Alexander knocked on the wall of the cabin, then he and Buster made their way inside. Beers considered the tiny structure with a sense of unease; he harboured an intense suspicion of anyone who conducted their business outside a reasonable walking distance to the post office. Giving himself a shake, he entered after his companions. In the corner of the room, Ma Bender snored beneath a discoloured quilt. She awoke with a start when Jim Buster coughed loudly to announce their arrival. Outside, Gebhardt glanced over his shoulder at the men, closed the Bible, and listened.

Kate emerged from behind the dividing canvas with a big, confident smile. She blushed when Alexander explained that they had come to her for help after seeing her services advertised in Chetopa. Beers sat himself on the bench opposite Kate and watched, notebook in hand. Buster, who had been eyeing up the meagre goods on display with disappointment, perched on the edge of a barrel and lit a cigarette. With a grave expression, Alexander introduced himself as the brother of the missing Dr William York. He talked her through what they had discovered so far, and for a moment his resolve faltered when he spoke of the distress it was causing his family.

"I wish you would find out for me whether he is dead or alive."

York let his request settle and relied on Beers to observe the young woman while he rebottled his emotions. Later Beers informed Dick that after the question Kate's features became tense and that she smoothed the front of her skirt to disguise it, resetting her face into an expression of concern as she did so.

"That's a big mystery to solve without any preparation," she replied. A vacant silence settled on the room. Jim Buster leaned down to Beers and suggested loudly that the whole thing was a hoax.

"It's like the Dienst lady said, she can't tell us anything. Just a bunch of lingo."

At his words, Ma Bender flew into such a convulsion of cursing and coughing that the detective stood up from the bench, moved to help her, and then thought better of it. Gebhardt appeared and wrangled her back into the chair, holding her down while Kate cooed a stream of jumbled Latin and German at her in encouragement. Beers felt an encroaching sense of embarrassment about the whole scenario. Buster chewed at his cigarette and chuckled. Alexander was unperturbed. When she calmed down, Gebhardt released the old woman and left her to Kate.

"I got shot at near where they found the body of that man before Christmas," Gebhardt announced unprovoked. "I can show you, just over by Drum Creek."

Alexander already felt like they were wasting their time and Gebhardt's outburst was the last straw. With no proof that they were anything other than eccentric, unfriendly neighbours who exploited vulnerable people, Alexander agreed to let Gebhardt take him down to where he had been shot at. He put no stock in the man's claims but knew they would run across Ed and be able to regroup in the process. Alexander sent Beers out ahead to ready the horses. On his way out, Kate stopped him, touching a hand lightly to Alexander's arm.

"If you come back on an evening next week without your men, I will have an answer."

BUSTER SNORTED ON HIS WAY OUT OF THE CABIN, TOSSING THE CIGA-rette among the chickens. Kate ignored him and explained that she had to consult with the spirits before undertaking such a challenging task. Alexander removed her hand, thanked her, and declined the offer in icy tones. He gestured to Gebhardt that they should head down to the creek and followed him outside, where the other men were already in the saddle.

"These are just simple, credulous folk under the hallucination that Kate has supernatural powers," he told an unconvinced Detective Beers as the group set out towards the creek.

GEBHARDT TALKED AIMLESSLY FROM THE MOMENT HE GOT INTO THE saddle to the moment he dismounted in a small clearing near the creek. Down in the thicket he performed an awkward re-enactment of being shot at. Ed came across the party in time to witness Gebhardt describing how the ball had wedged itself in the trunk of a tree. Several of Ed's men had been drinking, and the German's claims were met with a chorus of derision. Scrambling out of the tangle of branches, Gebhardt looked to the York brothers for approval and received none. Alexander looked back at him with contempt, then gave the order to ride back to Independence where they would discuss their next steps. Beers rode up front with Alexander and left Ed and his men to harass Gebhardt. But the man was unflappable. He talked and laughed and plagued them with so many questions that they gave him up for simple and left him alone. When the group peeled west to Independence, Gebhardt turned his horse and watched. Evening light sliced through the group, sharp and red and separating each man from the next. He brushed the debris from his clothes and rode for the cabin.

THE YORK BROTHERS AND THEIR MEN REACHED INDEPENDENCE after nightfall, the land bogged down in mist that became rain and soaked through their jackets. The party dispersed and returned to their homes or to saloons. At the York residence the brothers, their father, the detective, and Leroy Dick drank and smoked and planned. Beers was sure the Benders were more than peculiar shop owners. Alexander was unconvinced. Though he did not like the family, he knew that if word got out that they were under suspicion, a lynch mob would likely take matters into their own hands. Together the men decided to use a meeting for the local elections to discuss how best to proceed with the investigation. Leroy Dick was to put forward the notion that every cabin in the area would undergo a thorough search by a group of deputised men.

With his father's encouragement Alexander and his business partner,

Lyman Humphrey, drew up a petition and sent it to the governor of Kansas. It demanded that a reward be offered for the apprehension of the "organised band of outlaws who are spreading in many localities." Lawlessness in south-east Kansas had reached the point where it "rendered life and property unsafe" and it was not good enough that state authorities had not yet intervened. No amount of economic boom and glistening prairieland could disguise the state's ugly underbelly. Sixty-three prominent local citizens signed the petition, including the sheriff and the justice of the peace. Within days of receiving the letter, Governor Osborn responded. He declared that the state would pay five hundred dollars per head for the apprehension of criminals involved in the disappearances. It was the highest reward he could legally offer.

The Night Express

The same night that Alexander York and Lyman Humphrey drafted their petition for intervention, a run-down wagon tore across the prairie, its occupants desperate to catch a train out of Kansas. The Bender family headed towards Thayer, a settlement just north of the border between Labette and Neosho. Up front, Gebhardt cracked the reins against the horses. In the back Pa was loading the family's shotgun. He spat curses whenever the motion threw him off balance, and the family dog yapped incessantly at his feet. Ma and Kate huddled together against the encroaching rain. When the distant glow of lights materialised from the mist, Gebhardt yanked the horses from the trail and plunged them into the undergrowth. Kate gripped the handle of the traveller's trunk containing the family valuables. Gebhardt pulled the horses to an abrupt stop and ordered the rest of the family out of the wagon. They emerged from the thicket, abandoned the wagon, and followed the lights from Thayer until they arrived in the town. As they neared the railway station, they began to bicker over who would speak to the ticket agent.

"Folks round here know me and John too well," Kate hissed at the older couple.

Pa relented, pulled the collar of his weather-beaten coat around his ears, and lumbered into the ticket office, accosting the ticket agent with a stream of broken English. In the distance the whistle of a train cut through the night air and sent a ripple of panic through the rest of the family. Gebhardt dragged the trunk on to the platform. The women followed him, eyes cast down and faces turned away from the agent, who was locked in an increasingly heated exchange with Pa. Eventually the man worked out the family wanted four tickets to Humboldt, a station with connecting trains to Texas and Missouri.

"That's the 9.03 from Cherryvale," he gestured to the train pulling into the station. "Last train to Humboldt before the morning."

Kate and Gebhardt were boarding the train before the agent finished his sentence. Fishing about in his pocket, Pa produced a ten-dollar bill and pushed it through the office window. The ticket agent later recalled that Pa took the tickets and the change without checking either before clambering on to the train after the rest of the family. When the dog that had followed them from the wagon tried to follow them on to the train, Pa kicked it back on to the platform, where it landed in a whining heap. As the train left the station, the ticket agent wondered why the group had been in such a hurry. The rain washed away the scent of its owners and the dog slunk back to the wagon hidden in the undergrowth.

AS THE TRAIN CARRIAGES RATTLED TOWARDS HUMBOLDT, THE Bender family made plans to separate; Ma and Pa would head into Missouri, Kate and Gebhardt would take the railway down to Texas. The next morning, they arrived at Humboldt, having stopped overnight in Chanute, where they were seen eating breakfast at the Sherman House hotel. Kate and Gebhardt left the train and purchased tickets for the Missouri-Kansas-Texas Railway. The Katy, as it was more commonly referred to, was a rapidly expanding line that joined Texas to the north in order to bolster the state's growing population. In 1896, it gained international attention when an agent for the company staged a publicity stunt in which two obsolete trains were driven into each other for the purpose of "public spectacle." Forty thousand people showed up at the temporary town erected at the site, which the railway had dubbed "Crush, Texas." When the engines collided a shower of iron, steel, and wood rained down on the terrified crowd, killing two spectators and injuring numerous others. But at the time Kate Bender and John Gebhardt boarded the carriages it stretched only as far as Denison, providing an ideal jumping-off point for those intent on disappearing westward across the plains or south into Mexico.

Conjectures of Robbery
and Murder

———

As the search continued, Mary York moved herself and her children to Alexander's family home in Independence. In the days after Mrs Preston had confirmed her fears, Mary focused on maintaining a sense of calm in order not to distress her children or complicate her pregnancy. Mrs Preston was more than happy to share her quarters with the young family, relieved that she was able to keep a watchful eye on their well-being. Mary listened as every evening men stamped the grime from their boots on the porch and crowded into the downstairs rooms. They spoke in hushed voices about the progress of the search and dissolved into silence whenever she appeared, moving awkwardly into polite conversation peppered with condolences. The house was filled with a heavy, focused sadness that the youngest children did not understand. The detective spoke with her whenever she had questions, but he talked too much and said too little. Of all the men who circled about her, she was fondest of Ed, because he did not patronise her. He updated her whenever he could and recognised when silence was better than consolation. She sensed in him the faint hope that the thing could be happily resolved, and she thought less of Alexander for letting him think so. When the days stretched into weeks, the suspense seeped out of the ordeal and the family began adjusting to life defined by a constant unknowing.

Mary did her best to avoid the newspapers, but sometimes the urge overtook her and she searched between the advertisements and the articles for anything that might hold some clue about William. On the day she read that her husband was presumed dead, she resolved to remain active to crowd out her fevered thoughts. Informing Alexander that she would take the settlement of William's accounts into her own hands, she spent the days settling debts and copying out medical notes so patients would have records to pass on to their new doctors. Between visits to patients, she made plans to move back to Illinois and spend the summer with her sister. As Mary worked through travel arrangements, she thought how much happier they could have been if they had never come to Kansas. She watched the days lengthen and the sun stay a little longer in the sky, breathing life into the earth around her. At night she prayed for the strength to hear the news when it finally came.

ON 8 APRIL, SO MANY PEOPLE TRIED TO CROWD INTO THE SCHOOL-house at Harmony Grove that Leroy Dick didn't know where to put them. Like most schoolhouses on the frontier, it was a white building made up of crisp lines, neat windows, and a high ceiling. It was the focal point of the local community and served as a town hall for the scattering of settlements around Big Hill Creek. The room was already thick with pipe smoke, and the smell of bodies fresh from farm work was undercut with expensive cologne. The gathering represented all walks of life on the frontier. Farming couples with very young children wedged between them sat beside gruff railway workers and attorneys who took up unnecessary space. People watched each other closely, looking for things that might be a sign of criminal behaviour. The Bender men were missing from the crowd, but Dick chalked it up to their antisocial tendencies. He didn't blame them. Detective Beers had told him the family behaved in such a bizarre manner when they called on them that Alexander had all but written them off as dim-witted country folk.

A bitter wind rattled in the windowpanes when Leroy Dick rose to address the meeting about the disappearances. As he outlined the situation, his audience grumbled and shook their heads. A couple of men vocalised their discontent and were shushed by their partners. Dick told them what they already knew. Over the last six months eight men and one little girl had vanished on the trail between Fort Scott and Independence. Two of those men had turned up dead. It was not an unusually dangerous route and it was apparent to all that the disappearances were localised around the eastern corner of Labette, where the county joined Neosho and Montgomery. Almost overnight the area had developed a bad reputation and it was steadily getting worse, aided by the near-daily coverage in the newspapers. Leroy Dick was interrupted first by John Dienst, and then, in more colourful language that he strongly believed had no place in a schoolhouse, by an Irishman named Jim McLain. A popular local character known for a complete lack of restraint in voicing his opinions, McLain raged that Labette County had been made to bear the brunt of the blame for the crimes. It was, he argued, no more suspicious than its neighbouring counties, which had made a great furore over the disappearances but offered no assistance. A chorus of voices went up in agreement and then broke down into smaller factions. Dick looked into the faces of the people he had lived alongside for the past three years. The hardship of life on the frontier showed in their eyes and on their bodies. Billy Tole, wiry and reliable, was in heated conversation with Henrietta Dienst; Susanna and Thomas Tyack leaned urgently over the chair in front of them and muttered in low voices to Mary Hiltz about bad spirits.

John Dienst clapped his hands and called the rowdy group to order. He read out a list of campsites where it was felt the band of outlaws could be hiding: Walnut crossing on the Walnut River, Osage Mission on the Neosho, Big Hill crossing on the claim of George Anderson, and Drum Creek crossing on the Bennett claim. Bennett, remembering the fervour of the townsfolk after the discovery of Jones's body, loudly volunteered his property as the first to be searched. Anderson offered his up next. The men exchanged a nervous look of solidarity. Dick commended the two men and, per the instructions of the York brothers, proposed a thorough search of each of the sites, including any buildings that happened to be on the land. Legal intervention was coming from the governor, Dienst assured the group. A systematic search of all properties near the trail in Labette County by those with the legal power to make arrests would be undertaken in the coming weeks. The creeks would be dragged, wells would be checked, and all suspicious persons questioned thoroughly by organised committees. A murmur of approval moved through the crowd, and those interested in joining the search arranged to meet again on 12 April to finalise a strategy with the assistance of the state authorities. With high spirits and a feeling that justice was soon to be served, the inhabitants of Labette County and the surrounding area filtered out of the schoolhouse into a grey April drizzle.

ON 9 APRIL, DETECTIVE BEERS ARRIVED AT THE YORK FAMILY HOME with news that a wagon had been discovered on the outskirts of Thayer. Named for Nathaniel Thayer, a major player in railway development, it was a busy and well-thought-of railway town in Neosho County. Since its inception, Thayer had been home to several newspapers, all of which had followed William's disappearance with great enthusiasm. Beers related the information he had collected about the wagon to the York family with grave precision. It was a well-used and badly kept wooden wagon, caked in filth from a freak snowstorm that had whipped through the area earlier in the week. When the men who spotted it in the undergrowth approached it, an angry terrier snapped at their feet, then retreated behind the wheels. The two horses had eaten as much of the brush as was in their reach and the larger of the animals was lame and grumpy about it. With considerable effort, the local stablemaster, A. H. Wheeler, and two of his workmen had stabled and fed the horses, then dragged the wagon from the ravine and printed their findings in the newspaper. Mary York listened to the detective and felt her heart sink at the thought of yet another possible murder. She did not understand how the perpetrators could still be active despite the presence of the search party and the reward issued by the governor. Alexander had offered a further hundred dollars of his own money, but it had encouraged no one to step forward.

Her heart sank even further when Beers bought her *The Head-light* on 16 April, in which more details of the wagon had been printed under the headline FOUL PLAY. The dog refused to leave the wagon and continued to be a nuisance to reporters when they tried to investigate its contents further. Wheeler complained to the newspapers that the damage done to the back wheels had made it near impossible to free it from the undergrowth. Both were dished the wrong way and two of the spokes were broken, though he couldn't tell exactly when they had snapped. Thrown in the back was a double-barrelled shotgun; one barrel was loaded with a charge of buckshot on top of the ordinary load of common shot, the other was empty. Common shot littered the floor of the wagon box. Beneath the gun was a plank on which GROCRYS had been painted in large, crude letters. One of the men pulled it out and flipped it over. On the reverse side in considerably neater handwriting was painted GROCERIES. It was nearly a month before anyone realised its significance.

A full two weeks after its occurrence, *The Head-light* also published details of the meeting that had taken place on 12 April. The attendees promised to "make every effort in our power to detect and bring to justice the murderers," but it was hard for the townsfolk to believe when it had been over a month since William York had disappeared and nearly six since Jones was discovered in Big Hill Creek. Enthusiasm for the search was drowned in the quagmire of the spring rain, which made weather conditions so appalling that even travel within the towns was difficult. Business suffered all over the state, and *The Kansas Daily Commonwealth* haughtily announced that anything it had said heretofore about the beautiful spring it was willing to take back. At night, lightning exploded onto the earth as prairie fire, extinguished by heavy morning rain in a hiss of steam and smoke. Livestock scattered, and those who had pledged themselves to the search abandoned it to hunt down the wayward animals that made up their livelihood. For the York brothers, the weather was an endless frustration—sometimes a mere inconvenience, sometimes an insurmountable obstacle. Though neither man was a stranger to bad weather, every day that they could not head out on to the prairie, every man who abandoned the search party, and every evening they returned to Mary York without answers served as a reminder that William was still beyond their reach.

THE ONSET OF MAY BROUGHT A BRIEF RESPITE FROM THE DELUGE. Billy Tole had been out in his yard hours before sunrise, wanting to make the best of a morning without rain. He raked the topsoil in the garden and breathed in the smell of the wet earth, imagining the meals he could make with the yield from the homestead's spring plot. Around mid-morning he set out to round up the cattle that had gone missing during the storm and to drive those who hadn't to a different pasture. The route along the trail took him past the Bender cabin. On his approach, a thin, desperate whine carried on the wind. He thought nothing of it until no one appeared from the cabin to tend to the animal it belonged to. From his horse he could see that something was wrong about the place. Keeping his cattle in sight, he rode to the corral and dismounted. Lying on her side in the mud was a discoloured sow, her body rising and falling with each wheezing plea for help. Billy was distressed at the state of the animal and acutely aware that he was most likely alone in the vale. He fetched his rifle from the saddlebag, checked it was loaded, and slung it over his shoulder. Walking quickly to the stable he stopped when he smelled a dead animal. Life on the frontier had treated him to all manner of dead creatures, but the stench always turned his stomach. Covering his face with his sleeve, he kicked the stable door open and was hit by a wall of flies. He gagged and moved downwind, waiting for the breeze to disperse the insects. Inside the stable everything was damp and putrid. Splayed in the centre was the body of a dead calf. Billy moved his gaze from the gangly corpse to the sack of feed and swallowed. He stepped around the animal and avoided looking too closely at what moved beneath its skin. Returning to the sow, he threw a handful of feed on the ground beside her head. She ate greedily. When he brought her water she staggered to her feet, burying her head in the bucket. Billy took a deep breath, but the air was so tainted with the smell of the calf that he gagged again. For several moments he watched the sow and wondered about the cabin. He felt its presence behind him like a void in the land. Small, squalid, and empty. The Toles were not superstitious folk, and Billy knew his brother would berate him for it, but he disliked the idea of entering the cabin alone. Drawing his rifle, he crept to the door, flattened himself against the wood, and craned his neck to see inside. In the seconds it took for his eyes to adjust, Billy thought of the dead calf and the flies. The same scent lingered in the depths of the cabin. When the darkness sharpened itself into a similar throng of flies, Billy recoiled in disgust. In a panic he dashed back to his horse, rounded up the livestock, and rode north to his ranch. In the distance, yellow-tinged clouds converged on the horizon and the sound of rain two miles out hummed in the air.

Part III

A REVOLTING
SPECTACLE OF CRIME
MADE PUBLIC

A Veil of Mystery

Labette County, Kansas

SUNDAY, 4 MAY 1873

B illy Tole was in such a state of excitement that he was nearly incomprehensible when he stopped to inform a small group travelling the opposite way on the trail of his discovery. Leading the group were Schwartz and Brooks, two local real estate agents whose business had suffered at the evidence of crime in the area. They listened with interest to Tole's description of the abandoned homestead with its malnourished animals and unkempt orchard. Billy promised them he would return to the site once he had driven his livestock back to his ranch. The group watched him in weighted silence as he went on his way. Brooks was the first to suggest they investigate, disguising his curiosity as a suggestion that the situation might provide a business opportunity.

When Billy Tole arrived back at the cabin the rain had reached the valley and the men who now littered the scene moved as grey figures among the mist. He cursed his big mouth and later made a point of repeatedly telling reporters that he was the one to make the discovery. Schwartz did his best to feed the skittish livestock with what little grain was left in the stable.

"Team is gone," he said to Billy. "Unless they're loose."

Billy chewed on his lip. "Far as I can see, wagon's gone too."

Schwartz whistled quietly. The two men looked at each other and then out across the vale. At the cabin, Brooks levered the door open and let out a cry when he was greeted by a cloud of insects surprised to have their colonisation of the space interrupted. Schwartz and Tole joined him. Billy was no stranger to the interior of the cabin, and he poked at the debris that littered the soiled dining table. A discarded newspaper twitched in the breeze that drifted through the open door and swept dirt in spirals across the floorboards. It took little more than a cursory exploration of the building for the men to come to the conclusion that if the family had fled, they had taken only the barest of essentials. On the counter an inexpensive clock had stopped its ticking at twelve minutes past nine. Cooking utensils too big to carry on horseback sat in a haphazard, unwashed stack on the stove. On the shelves an open tin of beans was the last of the meagre groceries the family had sold to travellers. Outside, the wind picked up, sending a wave of rain spattering across the floorboards and up the wagon sheet that divided the space. The smell of decay that initially drew Billy to the stable clung to the interior of the cabin. He was glad to have the real estate agents with him, but he could not shake the desire to put several miles between himself and the abandoned homestead.

"I'll go over to Harmony Grove," Billy announced suddenly and stepped out of the cabin. "Throw a little excitement into the folks at the singing school." He thought about the times he passed Kate Bender on her way back from the school and spat into the mud. From the cabin, Schwartz and Brooks watched the farmhand break into a gallop as he headed towards the schoolhouse.

By the time Billy reached Harmony Grove, he had convinced himself that his eagerness for leaving the homestead was rooted firmly in the need to alert the community. Leroy Dick later described him being as "elated at the prospect of spreading the news as a cub reporter with his first big scoop." Dick, however, was not present when Billy jumped from his horse into the small crowd of young people who were chatting outside the schoolhouse. Among the group were Maurice Sparks and the Dienst boys. The latter were particularly pleased to hear that the area was rid of the woman who had been such a plague on their family after the death of their brother. Since no major breakthroughs had yet been made into the whereabouts of Dr York's remains or the identity of his murderers, the news threw the men into a state of conjecture. Some suggested the family themselves had fallen victim to the same criminals as the missing men. The women in the group, including Leroy Dick's wife, Mary Ann, decided that whatever the reason for their disappearance, the community was better off without the Benders.

AS THE RAIN FADED INTO NIGHTFALL ACROSS THE PRAIRIE, DICK and his wife drove their buggy back to their homestead. In front the horses gleamed, their coats slick with water. Dick knew there had been some excitement after the singing school finished, but when he asked his wife for details, he was surprised then irritated to learn of its origin.

"They oughtn't have broken into the cabin without an officer present," he grumbled. After dropping his wife at their home he rode back to the schoolhouse, where the group were drinking around a fire in the yard. Billy was still enjoying the attention the story brought him.

"What is this I hear about the Benders?" At Dick's question a hush fell across the group and Billy repeated his story. He played down the actions of the real estate agents, embarrassed that he hadn't informed the authorities first. Dick took a seat among the men and they discussed how best to proceed. He suspected that Alexander York's visit to the cabin spooked the family into fleeing, whether or not they were guilty of the murder of his brother. The York brothers had made such a show of harassing suspects that it was enough to make anyone they questioned jumpy. Dick made arrangements with the Dienst boys to visit the homestead early the following morning and make an assessment of the situation. There had been so many false alarms in the hunt for William's murderers that he was apprehensive about sending word to the York family without serious evidence of foul play.

"I'll be mighty glad if the livestock can be moved on," Billy piped up as Dick made to leave. "They're so hungry they'll be wanting our sugar and bacon next."

WHEN LEROY DICK LATER RECOUNTED THE EVENTS OF MONDAY, 5 May 1873, he remembered a morning bright with sunshine that was already burning off the damp from the previous day by the time he arrived at the Bender homestead. As township trustee, the task of making an inventory of what was left of the Benders' property fell on his shoulders. In the spring of 1872, Dick had visited the homestead to collect taxes, which gave him a rough estimation of the size of the task ahead. When he dismounted and cast an eye over what was left of the scrawny livestock, Dick remembered a heated argument between Gebhardt and Ma Bender over the number of stock they should report to the authorities. Now the trustee wondered whether the animals had been stolen. Making his way towards the cabin, he was halted by the smell that had unsettled Billy Tole. Unlike the farmhand, Dick recognised it immediately. He stood motionless, hoping that it wouldn't dissolve in the breeze before he could place its origin. It was a smell familiar to many veterans of the Civil War who had lain beside fallen friends on the battlefield or crossed land soaked with blood from recent conflict. Dick knew it would not be long before he had to send word to the York family that they might finally have an answer to William's fate.

"Too fine a day for such bad business," he muttered to himself as he turned his attention to uncovering the root of the smell. A large mound of manure slouched against the side of the stable. Though Dick knew it was not the source of the stench, the soil mixed into the heap suggested the Benders had been digging unusually deep somewhere on the property. Inside the stable he found similar heaps, too fresh to have come from the excavation of the well or the cellar.

Puzzled, Dick made his way back to the cabin. When he stepped inside, the presence of the estate agents was clear in the footprints that covered the floor, but it appeared they had done little more than look around. Dick, who had never thought much of the Bender cabin, was still surprised at the squalor the family had been living in. Beneath the smell of unwashed dishes was the same waft of decay that he had smelled on the breeze. It was stronger at the back of the cabin, behind the wagon canvas. Ducking around the fabric, Dick noticed a leather strap protruding from beneath a straw mattress. He kicked the mattress aside to reveal a trapdoor. No longer blocked by the mattress, the odour reached a new potency. Dick threw the hatch open, staggered back, and covered his nose. The stench leaked out into the rest of the cabin. But when he ventured into the cellar he found no obvious source. He was both relieved and frustrated by the absence of the body he expected to find. Dirt had crumbled from the walls and packed the crevices around the stone slab that acted as a floor. Knowing he would need help to excavate the cellar, Dick resolved to organise a thorough search for the following day.

Scrambling out of the pit, Dick tried to focus on completing the inventory of the property. A cursory glance told him that apart from the table, cooking stove, and clock, little else would be worth any money. Dick knelt to inspect the condition of the stove and made an unusual discovery. Concealed haphazardly beneath the stove were three hammers of varying sizes, the first a three-inch (eight-centimetre) claw hammer, the second a little longer in the handle with an elongated head. The third was a handmade sledgehammer. In his hands, the instrument weighed about five and a half pounds (two and a half kilograms). A crude and purpose-built object that would not have unnerved him in any other context, the hammer, taken with the smell in the cellar, made him deeply suspicious. Wrapping the three tools in the discarded newspaper left on the table, Dick packed them into his saddlebags and set off to ask two local residents to take charge of the family's livestock.

IT WAS EVENING WHEN HE RETURNED TO THE SITE. DICK HAD SPENT the afternoon weaving between homesteads in the local community, informing them of his intent to conduct a full property search.

"There's a dead body buried on the premises somewhere," he'd told a startled George Mortimer after requesting the man bring his plough to the Bender cabin the following morning. When he passed Maurice Sparks and Ben Ferguson on the trail, they reminded him of the wagon that had been discovered on the outskirts of Thayer several weeks before. Dick recalled the article in *The Head-light* and the fear in the community that another crime had been committed. So far, no one had been able to identify the wagon. Sparks offered to ride to Thayer to investigate whether it could be the missing Bender wagon. Dick was busy setting up camp on the homestead when Sparks and Ferguson rode in to join him.

"It's the Bender wagon all right." Sparks reported. "Must've fled about three weeks ago."

The three men talked long into the spring night, until the only sound they shared the valley with was the heavy fall of rain. They made an ordered plan for how the following day should unfold, anticipating that the rumours would bring a crowd to the site by noon. Sparks related more details he had uncovered about the wagon, recalling the unusual structure of the wheels and the crudely painted store sign. The men dampened the fire and turned in for the night. Later, Labette officials would link the wheels to the tracks found at the scene where the boys had discovered the corpse of William Jones.

What the Benders
Have to Answer For

The Bender Cabin

TUESDAY, 6 MAY 1873

O n the morning of 6 May, Leroy Dick watched the sun rise over the Bender homestead as men rode into the valley to assist with the search of the property. They arrived in groups and talked quietly among themselves over cups of scalding coffee. When the flow of volunteers began to ebb, Dick whistled, calling the party to attention. As he divided the men into three groups, he enjoyed the feeling of purpose the task gave him despite its sombre circumstances. During the Civil War, Dick had been a sergeant and the experience instilled in him a strong sense of organisation which he carried over to his roles within the community. He instructed the first group to search Spill-Out and Drum creeks, the two waters that crossed John Gebhardt's portion of the land claim. The second group was given the task of stripping the interior of the stable and digging up the floor for signs of human remains. Dick told the third group they would excavate the cellar under his guidance. He was sure answers lay in the earth beneath the stone slab and was keen to be at the centre of events as they unfolded.

"Scatter out!" he called to the search party that set off towards the winding path of the creek. Sallow clouds drained the landscape of its colour, a far cry from the clear sunshine of the day before. When George

R. Gamble, a photographer from Parsons, arrived at the site as the men began to disperse, he bemoaned the cloud cover. Despite his charisma, Gamble set people on edge with the intensity of his demeanour. He was a tall man with an unwavering stare who, though just twenty-eight, gave the impression that he was considerably older. His photography business specialised in portraits and landscapes, but when Gamble heard whispers among reporters in the region that something nasty was unravelling at the Bender cabin, he knew there was money to be made. He watched movement begin to fill the valley, arranged his equipment, and waited.

EXCAVATING THE STABLE WAS SIMPLE ENOUGH, BUT EXCAVATION OF the cellar beneath the cabin quickly proved cumbersome. In order to check beneath the slab for human remains, the slab itself had to be dug out and broken up, something that was not achievable while the cabin remained on its foundation. Silas Tole, Billy's wiry and usually silent elder brother, suggested that they move the cabin, and the others agreed. Using a system of circular logs driven beneath the base of the cabin and ropes tied to horses, the ramshackle structure was dragged until the cellar lay exposed to the morning air. The men were relieved when the smell of decay dissipated on the breeze. The Tole brothers lowered themselves into the hole and began the process of loosening the dirt around the slab so it could be removed to get at the earth beneath it. At the stable nothing of interest had been uncovered, nor any clue to the origin of the subsoil mixed into the heaps of manure. In the displaced cabin, Dr Keables, the local doctor, picked at dark stains on the joists beneath the trapdoor and tried to make an assessment about whether their origin was animal or human.

A SHOUT FOLLOWED BY A VOLLEY OF CURSES DREW THE ATTENTION of everyone on the site. Billy Tole scrambled from the pit and staggered as far as he could before he threw up. Silas remained in the cellar, his face pushed into the crook of his elbow. His shovel had sliced deep into the muck. When it was drawn out, the scent of putrefaction leaked into the air and Silas dropped the shovel in surprise. The rancid soil spilled across the slab and the men gave the pit a wide birth. Dick reached in and lifted the elder Tole out. Silas retched and stalked away from the site to find fresh air. In a show of bravado, an older farmhand leaped into the cellar and began to dig, accusing his companions of not having the stomach for such a task. It took less than three shovelfuls of filth before he too abandoned the task to vomit.

"Human decomposition," Leroy Dick announced. After some discussion about what was the best course to take, the slab was cracked open by a sledgehammer and the shards removed by men who tied whatever fabric they could find across the lower half of their faces. Gamble joined the group with a wary eye and wondered why Leroy Dick had chosen to wear such a light-coloured suit for such a filthy day's work. As the men began to dig, flies gathered on the discarded soil. But still the shovels brought up nothing except clotted earth. When Dr Keables announced that the substance in the soil was likely human blood, Leroy Dick grew frustrated. While the presence of blood confirmed his suspicions that a murder, or several, had taken place on the property, it gave no clue as to the whereabouts of the victims' remains.

By midday the search party returned with nothing to report except that a growing number of people were on their way to the site. Entire families had begun to materialise, eager to watch the search. George Mortimer arrived with his plough and set to work on the land to the east of where the cabin had sat. Excavation of the homestead filled the afternoon with the scent of earth and sweat, but there were still no bodies, only a restless crowd. Gamble watched as a girl no older than seven explored the interior of the cabin with her parents. A group of spectators gathered around the ramshackle exterior after being berated by Leroy Dick for disturbing the interior of the building. Gamble announced his intent to take a photograph. The little girl stepped up into the doorway and placed a hand on her hip, her white dress cut out against the darkness of the cabin.

Billy Tole, still queasy from his encounter with the smell, was one of those resting by the cabin when he spotted a buggy moving at alarming speed down the trail. He called to Dick and pointed at the team.

"He's sure layin' the whip to them horses."

Dick could tell who the driver of the team was by his taught posture and the big man beside him. Some of the people on foot shouted at the buggy when it passed. It careened into the yard and Ed York leaped to the ground, crossed quickly to Dick, and handed him a letter from his elder brother explaining that Alexander was in court but was to be kept abreast of developments. Beers, who remained suspicious of the Bender family since the visit to the homestead, wished Alexander had accompanied them to the homestead. Rumours that there was a dead body somewhere on the property had reached Independence before Dick sent for them. Like the trustee, he was certain excavation of the site would yield devasting results.

ED PACED THE PROPERTY AND LOOKED WITH APPREHENSION INTO what was left of the pit. Among the jumbled earth he saw nothing but flies and the boot prints of the men. The smell still lingered, but he was too young for it to conjure the spectre of Civil War brutality it revealed to men like Leroy Dick and George Gamble. Ed could feel the crowd scrutinising his behaviour and made his way over to the cabin, ducking inside and out of sight. The disordered interior had been made worse when the building was moved to provide access to the pit. To distract himself from what lay outside, Ed started picking through the mess. He began methodically but grew agitated when his gaze fell on a bridle wedged behind the grocery counter in a lazy attempt to conceal it. Ed pulled the object free and knew immediately that it belonged to William.

Outside, Beers joined Dick in managing the digging to the east of where the building had previously stood. When Ed emerged from the cabin clutching the bridle, a murmur of disquiet moved through the spectators. Before Ed reappeared, George Gamble had started to wonder whether he had put too much stock in the homestead revealing its secrets. But now as he watched the young man stare blankly towards the orchard, he felt the day might be turning.

Ed moved suddenly towards the orchard. In the evening light he spotted irregularities in the topsoil among the saplings. As he drew closer, a thin crack in the earth caught his attention. No more than two feet (sixty centimetres) away, a second crack halted the unusual disturbance in the soil.

"Bring a ramrod." The words were so quiet that if Beers had not already been on his way to join the young man, they would have been lost. The few spectators left shuffled forward and grumbled when Leroy Dick ordered them back. Trembling, Ed took the ramrod from Beers and pushed into the ground between the cracks. Four feet (120 centimetres) below the surface the rod encountered resistance. Ed's face grew pale and Beers placed a firm hand on the young man's shoulder as he withdrew the rod. It gave way with a sucking sound and the men closest to the hole winced at the putrid odour that came with it. Beers pulled Ed to his feet and guided him back where they could better survey the orchard for more signs of disturbance.

"Bring your spades," Dick called to the men who had been standing idle. "Dig fast." They worked quickly, using the disturbance in the soil as a guide and swapping with others when the smell that poured from the hole became overwhelming. Gamble moved his equipment closer to the orchard, ignoring the complaints of the other spectators. At five feet (150 centimetres) deep, Leroy Dick's shovel found its way beneath a heavy, lifeless weight. The excited whispers that accompanied the dig fell silent as Ed returned to the side of the pit. Shaking, he watched as Dick shifted the shovel and dirt fell away to reveal the upper body of a man. Kneeling, Dick brushed away the soil that clung to the face of the corpse. All feeling on the homestead turned to Ed, who was staring down at the face in the dirt through stricken, unblinking eyes.

"My brother," he whispered.

Detective Beers confirmed the fact a little louder and a wail of distress went up among the crowd. Dr York had been a beloved member of the local community, but he had also become known to those outside of his circle in the weeks following his disappearance due to the extensive coverage in the newspapers. The discovery of his remains horrified the little group at the site and indignation began to brew at the absent

Men and women at the grave of Doctor William York. Illustration done from a photograph taken by George R. Gamble. *Harper's Weekly*, 7 June 1873.

perpetrators. In the disarray, Ed remained motionless, afraid to let his gaze move from the face of his dead brother.

The voice of Dr Keables went some way to settling the agitated crowd as he discussed how best to proceed with a full excavation of the body. Later, Leroy Dick would claim that William's head was severed from his body and presented to Ed for identification because the rest of his body was too badly decomposed to be moved. But consensus among eyewitness reports and later legal testimony agrees that after Ed and the detective made the initial identification, full exhumation of the body commenced. The *Daily Kansas Tribune* informed its readers that William "was identified by his brother instantly, as his face was very natural in its appearance, though the rest of his head was terribly smashed." The sense of horror in the crowd escalated when the dirt revealed that William had been thrown carelessly into the pit in nothing but his undershirt and a bandage fastened below his left knee. Ed confirmed that his brother had sustained an injury in the months prior to his disappearance that matched the one on the corpse.

"We must return to Independence and make arrangements," Beers told the men huddled around the pit. He was growing uneasy at the temperament of the crowd and thought it best that Ed be reunited with his family away from the spectators. As they rode away, the men remaining set about the task of removing William's body from its crudely dug grave.

After a brief argument with the district attorney over the propriety of disturbing the scene without the county coroner present, George Majors, the justice of the peace, agreed that the "red tape" could be overruled in light of the circumstances. They slipped a wagon sheet beneath the body, lifted it from the earth, and laid it gently on the ground beside the shallow grave. Dr Keables cleaned the dirt collected in the head wounds and discovered a gaping laceration across William's throat, identical to the one found on William Jones the previous autumn. As Keables examined the skull, Dick's mind went to the hammers that were stashed in his saddle-bag. When the doctor announced that the cause of the wounds was blunt force trauma from two different instruments, the trustee went to fetch them. The two men measured the tools against the holes in William's skull under a heavy silence. A few men still hovered near the corpse. Billy Tole muttered repeatedly that he ought to have been quicker to realise the family had gone.

"These are undoubtedly the instruments of murder," proclaimed the doctor. He returned the hammers to Leroy Dick, who kept them on his person for the rest of the day. Dick had already seen curious spectators taking items from the cabin and had no intention of returning the hammers to the saddlebag, where an opportunistic citizen might wait until he left them unattended. With the help of the Tole brothers, Dr Keables wrapped the sheet around William's body and lifted him into a rudimentary coffin he had brought with him to protect any remains discovered until they could be delivered to the family. Dick climbed back into the pit to check that nothing had gone unnoticed. The doctor joined him. Gamble moved his photography equipment to the side of the grave that also gave a view of the cabin. His patience over the course of the day was rewarded, and he captured the scene in the last good light of the day. At the centre of his photograph, the body of William York lies in its coffin, the cabin dilapidated and unassuming in the background as the investigation continues. Gamble's two photographs were reproduced as engravings in the 7 June 1873 edition of *Harper's Weekly*, a popular and influential magazine based in New York City that ran from 1857 to 1916. Though his name was credited beneath, the images did not bring him the financial windfall he hoped for. Nearly three decades later, still hungry for money, Gamble set fire to his photography studio and attempted to claim the insurance. The ruse failed and he soon found himself photographing criminals at the Ohio Penitentiary, where he, too, was an inmate.

THE CHILL OF NIGHT IN THE EVENING AIR PROMPTED DICK TO CALL off excavation of the site for the day. While the majority of the spectators began to disperse, several pitched tents within eyesight of the cabin, certain that the following day would bring more gruesome discoveries. Campfires cast amber halos, offering pockets of warmth in the darkness that moved in across the valley. It was nearing midnight when Ed rode back on to the homestead behind the wagon carrying Alexander and Detective Beers. Leroy Dick returned home but left orders for a vigil to be kept over William's body until his brothers arrived to claim it. The men removed their hats and nodded to the eldest of the York siblings as he climbed down. When Alexander knelt at the side of William's coffin, he thought of Mary and the couple's young children. But when he looked into the face of his dead brother, he saw only his own obstinate refusal to believe that the Bender family was clever enough to commit such an atrocious crime. Now they were gone, and William was dead. He watched as Beers and the men loaded the body into the wagon. Ed had not dismounted, his eyes fixed instead on what he knew to be the cabin hidden by the shroud of night. Alexander thanked the little group and climbed back into the wagon.

"RECKON THERE'S MORE GRAVES, SIR." THE YOUNGEST OF THE MEN pointed towards the rest of the small orchard. In the meagre light of his oil lamp, Alexander made out at least five more areas where the ground had been disturbed.

The Burying Ground

WEDNESDAY, 7 MAY 1873

Mary York was busy tidying the house in Onion Creek when she heard the sound of a horse coming down the trail. She was visiting from Independence in order to make arrangements that would allow her and the children to leave the homestead behind. Mary looked to her faith to help her make peace with the land that had taken her husband, but she could not find it in her heart to continue living on the prairie. Pausing the task at hand, Mary went to the door to greet the rider. As she watched him approach the house, the anxiety on his face began to frighten her. The man removed his hat by way of greeting but was evasive about the purpose of his visit. Mary, distressed by his behaviour, inquired as to whether he brought news from Alexander. The question hung in the air between them until he found the courage to look her in the face.

"There were some men out searchin' yesterday," he began. At his words Mary felt a surge of the same horror that swallowed her up when she first discovered William was missing. She would later describe the messenger as appearing reluctant to deliver the news in explicit terms out of concern that she would be overwhelmed.

"They found William," she replied quietly, "or else you would not be here to tell me." The man hesitated, his fingers working at the brim of his hat.

"Yes."

OVER THE WEEKS WILLIAM HAD BEEN MISSING, MARY WORKED HARD to be ready when the news finally came that he was dead. But she had forgotten the small ember of hope burning within her that William might still return to the family. Now it was gone. But the news also brought relief. No longer was she forced to exist in a purgatorial state of unknowing. "I was ready to learn all of the sad story," she wrote two years later, attributing her strength in the face of the tragedy to her faith in God. The messenger was still struggling with the gravity of his news. Mary was sorry that a member of the York family hadn't taken the task upon themselves.

"Where was he found?" Mary asked, hoping that the question would persuade him to speak freely. She also knew that if she did not hear the details from the man in front of her, she would hear them through some other avenue, where they were likely to be exaggerated for dramatic effect. Relieved that Mary had initiated the conversation, the messenger explained that her husband's body was discovered near the crossing at Big Hill Creek on the land of the Bender family. When she asked about the way he had been killed, he told her that William died instantly after being struck on the back of the head. Only later did Mary discover the details of his mutilation and the state of his body when it was unearthed. The man waited until she had no further questions, then offered to accompany her back to Independence to be with her children. Mary agreed. When they arrived in Independence, the town was already abuzz with news of the events unravelling on the Osage Mission Trail.

LEROY DICK FOUND THE HOMESTEAD IN A STATE OF UNABATED EXcitement. More spectators had joined those already on-site. Bad news spread quickly on the frontier and was frequently used as a source of entertainment. Now the mystery of the disappearances and confirmed murders along the Osage Mission Trail had an answer that exceeded even the newspapers' expectations. Everybody knew that roving bands of outlaws were a danger on the frontier. But the notion that a family would set up a place for travellers to stay with the express purpose of murdering them was a story few in the area could resist investigating for themselves. As Dick passed through the homestead, he heard the excited gossip of people in his community and hoped the site would be excavated before the news spread outside the local area and it became unworkable amid the crowds. Local officials were doing their best to set a perimeter around the cabin and potential gravesites, but curious children frequently slipped by and had to be chased off. The orchard was stripped of its saplings and what was left of the vegetable plot lay trampled underfoot. Billy Tole was busy working at the ground between another set of cracks in the topsoil. Checking it with a probe had released a stench that turned him yellow.

"Another grave," he called to the group.

Several men began to dig and uncovered another, bigger corpse. A coffin was deposited at the side of the grave and the man's body was removed in the same manner as William York's the day before. Dr Keables cleaned the face for identification.

"That's Hank!" Leroy Dick exclaimed in shock, immediately recognising the handsome features of his wife's cousin. He thought of the night Henry McKenzie spent at his homestead entertaining the children and felt an intense guilt that he put the man's lack of contact down to his unreliable character. Henry McKenzie's head was shattered in three places. He, too, was naked save for an undershirt and bore the same vicious neck laceration as William York. His arms were a patchwork of defensive wounds. Dick was unsurprised. McKenzie was a keen fighter who was not easily taken off guard. That evening, when Dick informed his wife, Mary, that her cousin was dead, she found herself equal parts upset and confused. McKenzie had nothing of value on his person except his plush chinchilla coat. When they discussed what might have drawn him to the cabin, they came to the conclusion that he must have seen Kate when he was making his way along the trail. Though McKenzie had been married to his childhood sweetheart, Nancy, for several years, he always found it hard to resist the company of pretty women. Later, Dick came to believe that several of the bullet holes perforating the walls and roof of the cabin had likely been caused by McKenzie's attempt to defend himself.

FOR THE SPECTATORS, THE DISCOVERY OF HENRY MCKENZIE WAS the opening act in a day of tragedy and horror. Next came the body of William McCrotty, identifiable only by the tattoo on his forearm that listed his name, date of birth, and the regiment he served in during the Civil War. In the days after he signed up for the war, McCrotty decided the tattoo would be a clever way of ensuring his remains were identifiable should he be killed in battle. Dan Gardner, the man from whom he had borrowed the money to pay for dinner at the Bender cabin, confirmed the identity of the remains. Rage was growing among the men excavating the bodies and the crowd alike. Like McKenzie, McCrotty was not carrying anything of great value, yet both had been murdered in a calculated, brutal manner.

COMBINING HIS ANALYSIS OF THE WOUNDS ON THE THREE EXCA-vated bodies with his investigation of the cabin, Dr Keables put together what he believed to be the family's modus operandi. Travellers would be fed and entertained by Kate, sitting with their back to the wagon canvas that divided the cabin into separate living quarters. When they were at their most relaxed, another member of the family would strike them from behind with a blow intended to stun them into submission. The hammer was then used to beat in their temples, and finally the throat of the victim was slit. They were then dumped through the trapdoor and left to bleed out in the cellar. The doctor made sure to point out to authorities, and later to reporters, that there was no way of knowing for certain which of the family members were involved in inflicting physical violence on their victims. Newspapers and local gossip plugged the gap with the most sensational scenarios they could imagine.

———

BY THE TIME THE BODIES OF MCKENZIE AND MCCROTTY HAD BEEN wrapped in sheets to protect them from the growing warmth of the day and the prying eyes of spectators, Elkanah Tresslar had arrived on-site with his assistant. Tresslar, like George Gamble the day before, was a photographer. Unlike George Gamble, he already ran a prestigious and successful photography business out of Fort Scott. He specialised in ste-reoscopic photography, a technique in which two photographs taken from slightly different angles were viewed beside each other through a handheld device called a stereoscope. The effect was to produce a three-dimensional image. It captivated people from all walks of life. At the Bender homestead, Tresslar saw an opportunity to combine a hugely popular photography technique with what was turning out to be one of the biggest stories Kansas had seen since the war. The quicker he could develop the images, the faster he could begin to turn a profit by selling them to tourists eager for macabre mementos. Tresslar started with the cabin, moving through the orchard as the cry went up that another body had been found.

The body of Benjamin Brown went unidentified until Johnson, the man he had proudly displayed his silver ring to nearly six months earlier, recognised the object. When it was removed and cleaned off, Johnson confirmed that he was certain the man had to be Brown. He set off to locate the man's widow so she could identify the body for the authori-ties. While Dr Keables came to the same conclusion over the manner of death, a man informed Leroy Dick that he was sure he had seen one of Brown's horses in Arkansas around the time of his disappearance. The team was a pair of glossy, sorrel animals much admired by many of the residents.

A wider picture started to form that suggested the Benders may have had accomplices in the area who helped the family fence their stolen goods. *The Head-light* later gave voice to this theory, telling its readers that "it is evident they must have had accomplices to so effectually dispose of horses and clothing known to have been taken from the victims." Opinion was beginning to turn against other German-speaking individuals in the area, particularly those who resided closest to the family. Rudolph Brockman, one of the two men who first welcomed the Benders to Labette County, was seen at the cabin during the excavation of William York's body but had since kept his distance. In the late afternoon, when the grave of George Longcor was uncovered, his absence was taken as a sign of guilt.

THOUGH THE DISAPPEARANCE OF GEORGE LONGCOR AND HIS EIGHTEEN-month-old daughter, Mary Ann, did not receive the same level of attention in the newspapers as William York's, their absence had been keenly felt by the local community. An already agitated crowd threatened to become unruly when news reached them that a grave containing a child had at last been found. Longcor had been cast into the earth in the same condition as the other men, his throat slit so deeply that the head fell at an unnatural angle. At his feet, her little body half hidden beneath one of his legs, was Mary Ann. The men around the grave removed their hats when the doctor lifted the body from the earth. Beneath the knitted blanket she was still wearing her dress and mittens. Dr Keables found no marks on her body and concluded that the Benders had buried her alive. Quiet descended on the valley, broken by the soft cries of a woman somewhere in the crowd. In the weeks before the discovery of the Bender crimes, Longcor's father-in-law arrived from Iowa to make extended inquiries into his disappearance. Now he came forward to identify George's corpse. He did so with a curt nod and the two bodies were placed together in a coffin ready for transportation. Robert Gilmour had never met his granddaughter.

THE ATMOSPHERE AROUND THE DIG WAS OPPRESSIVE. A BIGGER crowd was growing as people came in from surrounding settlements, following directions to the cabin printed in the day's edition of *The Head-*

light beneath a headline reading HORRIBLE DISCOVERY!!! The paper had run a full article on the discovery of William York's body and promised readers that "there are doubtless other murdered victims of this hellish crew buried there," and that authorities were preparing a full search of the property. Editions of the paper were snatched up faster than the town's small printing office could produce them. *The Head-light* was also the first to draw attention specifically to Kate. Above any description of the condition of William's body and the nature of the crime was printed the notice advertising Kate's services as a medium and a healer. Three other papers printed shorter articles, announcing the death of the doctor and assuring readers that more details would follow as soon as possible.

A sense of communal outrage combined with intense curiosity drew people to the site. People "would ride a long way to see, at first hand, a drama as exciting as the one we were unintentionally enacting," Leroy Dick recalled later. By the time rain swept across the valley, muddying the empty graves and complicating further investigation, the crowd at the Bender farm was becoming increasingly unmanageable. Dick ordered that excavation of the last clearly marked grave and the well be done as quickly as possible. Elkanah Tresslar, too, was growing impatient with the crowd who wandered aimlessly about the homestead. In his photographs from the day, figures loiter at the edge of the frame. Others stand tall beside recently emptied graves and stare directly into the camera, determined to provide physical evidence that they were witness to events soon to enrapture the entire nation.

BENJAMIN BROWN'S WIDOW ARRIVED AS THE LAST OF THE SEVEN bodies from the orchard was lifted from the earth and laid out for identification. She walked through the line of coffins without acknowledging them, confirmed the identity of her husband, and requested that he be loaded on to a wagon so that she might return to Cedarvale before nightfall. The body of McCrotty was claimed by a friend whom he had fought alongside in the war and was shortly to be taken to Parsons to await burial. Dick took charge of the remains of Henry McKenzie. When one of the bodies looked as though it would not be as easy to identify, Dr Keables reluctantly addressed the crowd and asked for their assistance. A line of curious faces looked down at the man on the sheet, but he was so badly decomposed that no one could say for sure who he was. Among the crowd was Mrs Watton, friend and neighbour of Mary Feerick, whose husband, James, had vanished in the area during the winter of 1871. Mary continued to write to her friend in Kansas since moving back to New York, desperate for news of her missing husband. When Mrs Watton heard about the events unfolding at the Bender farm, she suspected that she might finally have an answer and rode across to confirm her suspicions. She reached the corpse and stared at it for several minutes, frustrated to discover that she could not tell for certain whether it was James. Though her instincts told her that it was, Mrs Watton did not want it to be. The burden of having to write to Mary to tell her that not only was James dead, but that he had been violently murdered, seemed too much to bear. She passed over the body in silence. In the months after the discovery, Mary read of the murders herself in a New York newspaper and wrote again to Mrs Watton imploring that she find out whether her husband was among the dead. James Feerick would not be formally identified until more than a year after his body was discovered.

AS THE MEN STRUGGLED TO HAUL THE EIGHTH BODY FROM THE WELL, the afternoon grew unnaturally gloomy. Dark clouds cast the land into shadow and the rain drove the crowds into wagons and buggies. Others used the weather as an excuse to take shelter in the Bender cabin, where they picked through the debris hunting for macabre souvenirs. The body in the well had been wedged six feet (180 centimetres) down in an upright position, which made removing it an arduous and complicated task. Leroy Dick identified the man as Johnny Boyle, though later newspaper reports would also refer to him as John Geary. Little would ever be known about the man in the well, who was so badly mutilated that Dr Keables struggled to identify the cause of death. The body was loaded on to a wagon with the others bound for Parsons to keep the

The Bender cabin and stable. Illustration done from a photograph taken by George R. Gamble. In Gamble's original photograph, a little girl in a bonnet stands in the doorway of the cabin; this illustration replaces her with men on horseback. *Harper's Weekly*, 7 June 1873.

rain from causing it to disintegrate before Dr Keables could perform a post-mortem. The Tole brothers probed the rest of the orchard and vegetable garden on the instruction of the district attorney but uncovered nothing unusual. Further digging had been done in the pit that was once the cellar, but as the rain turned the soil to muck the task was abandoned. Leroy Dick was satisfied that those known to be missing were all accounted for. Eight bodies had been discovered on the Bender homestead. Along with the body of William Jones in Drum Creek, the unidentified corpse from the campsite, and the mutilated body of John Phipps, the Benders' list of known victims totalled eleven, though it is almost certain there were more who went undiscovered.

As daylight fled the prairie, a woman approached Dick and he listened with a growing sadness as she explained that she recognised the clothes Mary Ann had been buried in. Longcor and the little girl stayed with her to take shelter from a snowstorm the previous December. She warned him that the bad weather would continue, offering to house the two of them until the worst of it passed. Longcor, eager to reunite with family in Iowa before Christmas, stayed only one night at the residence and set off early the following morning despite the weather. The woman dressed Mary Ann herself, wrapping her in a knit blanket for extra warmth. Dick guessed that they had been murdered later that day, after stopping at the Bender cabin to wait out the storm. A group overheard the conversation between Dick and the woman and tensions that had been building over the course of the day finally broke. Bolstered by the assertion in *The Headlight* that the Benders must have been a part of a "regularly organised band of cut-throats and murderers," the crowd began looking within itself for possible accomplices. The bickering continued long after the bodies of the deceased were carried from the site.

IN THE NIGHT THE EMPTY GRAVES WERE IMPENETRABLY DARK. THE more superstitious members of the community returned home, spooked by the remnants of horror that clung to the landscape. Rudolph Brockman rode into the camp that had grown up in the valley with a sense of trepidation. He arrived to see if the lurid reports he heard were true and to see whether there was any money to be made selling supplies to ill-prepared voyeurs. His presence among the campfires was picked out by a small group of those who had helped to excavate the plot. Brockman was not only the Benders' closest neighbour, he was also German. Local gossip put him as a close acquaintance of the family, and it seemed impossible to the community that he would be unaware of their crimes. Drunk and enraged by what they had witnessed over the course of the day, the mob closed in around Brockman's horse. Spitting accusations, they tore him from the saddle and dragged him towards the cabin. All the way Brockman protested his innocence and kicked at the ground and the men he regarded as his friends. Inside the cabin the men wrestled a noose around his neck, cast it over a beam, and hauled the screaming man into the air. Brockman twisted like a hooked fish and clawed at the rope. Torchlight spluttered in the wind, casting monstrous shadows against the walls of the cabin. A reporter for *The Atchison Daily Champion* who witnessed the ordeal wrote, "Death was within reach of him when he was cut down. Confess! Confess! They yelled, but he said nothing." The electrified mob strung the man back up. Again, he convulsed and again they cut him loose. Still he said nothing. When they strung Brockman up for the third time, the mob saw only the eight mutilated bodies that had been drawn out of the earth. The huge man hung limply from the rope. As the group began to disperse, he was cut down and pronounced dead. Minutes later he gasped back to consciousness, revived by the cold night air drawn into his lungs. He staggered to his feet and lurched from the cabin. Drained of energy by the culmination of a day of horror, the group watched him stumble into the darkness of the valley until he disappeared.

TEN MILES TO THE WEST IN HARMONY GROVE CEMETERY, WILLIAM York was at last being laid to rest. Mary York stood at the side of her husband's grave listening to a minister lift a final prayer to heaven. The York brothers stood with their parents. Time crept closer to midnight as each member of the family bid their loved one goodbye. The notion of a daytime funeral that would encourage reporters and large crowds had horrified Alexander, and so the family had agreed to bury William after nightfall. Since the discovery of the body, Ed was listless and distracted. He comforted Mary but pulled away from Alexander. Alexander found himself consumed by guilt that the family had escaped. Despaired by his inability to recognise the Benders for the criminals they were, he had started organising a team of men to pursue them. He promised Mary the family would be found, but Mary could only find comfort in her faith. Sparing herself the image of the violence inflicted on her husband, she elected not to view his body. As his coffin disappeared beneath the earth, she wished for the day when they would be reunited. In the aftermath of his death, Mary attended memorials and strived to continue the kindness she had always shown to others. Privately, she prayed for vengeance.

Facts and Theories
of the Crimes

———

It took less than a week after the discovery of bodies at the Bender cabin for the unfolding events to become front-page news across the United States. Equal parts appalled and enraptured by the story, the general public ate up all available information on the family. Reporters from as far away as New York and California descended on Labette County to quiz its residents about the monsters who had lurked undetected in their midst. "The excitement all over the country is intense," wrote a reporter for *The New York Times* after he arrived on the site amid crowds of thousands of people. *The Courier* out of Iowa ran extensive coverage of the "farm planted with dead bodies," in which it claimed the Benders had killed several members of their own family alongside the known victims. According to the paper, Detective Beers played a starring role in the discovery of the corpses and was now exhausted by his efforts but ready and willing to embark on a hunt for the criminals. Beers, it revealed at the end of the article, had furnished the reporter with the above facts himself.

THE PUBLIC'S APPETITE FOR CRIME WAS NOTHING NEW. OVER THE course of the nineteenth century, crime and the criminal had become a staple of popular culture. In Britain, murderers, arsonists, burglars, and con men filled the pages of *The Illustrated Police News*. In America, cheap "dime" novels entertained the working classes with stories of daring outlaws and raucous frontier towns. In the cities, people could pay to visit rogues' galleries—pop-up exhibitions featuring mugshots of known criminals, some of whom were still on the loose. Crimes like the Bender family murders promised an increase in newspaper sales that could sustain a local publication until the next big story broke.

Like the frontier rumour mill, regional newspapers were a mixture of fact, hearsay, and complete fiction. Out-of-state newspapers that could not afford or be bothered to send reporters to Labette County pooled information from local articles, selected the narrative they liked best, and reprinted it as fact. In the hundreds of pages dedicated to the family across the nation, the cabin grew into a luxurious roadside inn, testimony from survivors became muddled, and the victim count ran as high as fifty. Later, local papers took umbrage with the exaggerated body count. "Every person who has 'mysteriously disappeared' in Kansas for the past ten years is now 'supposed to have been murdered by the Benders, rather a charitable way of getting rid of some of them,'" wrote a wry reporter for *The Fort Scott Daily Monitor*.

ALONGSIDE SQUABBLES OVER THE NUMBER OF MURDERED PERSONS, another debate raged over whether Kate Bender was a "young woman of repulsive appearance" or a "buxom, good-looking country girl." The more disorganised newspapers ran multiple articles contradicting one another, leaving readers wondering how she could be both well formed and an infernal hag. As the most well known of the family to the local community, Kate rapidly became the focal point of the story. Those she had tried to harass or extort eagerly relayed stories of her bad character to newspapers and the authorities alike. The Dienst family came forward with not only their own story, but the experience of Julia Hestler, Kate Bender's brief companion, who was stalked across the open prairie after fleeing the cabin in a panic. Members of the community who had enjoyed her company were quick to accuse her of being a fast-talking witch and pointed to her deception of Alexander York as evidence that she was a skilled manipulator.

In her account of the crimes entitled *The Bender Tragedy*, written two years after her husband's death, Mary York expressed a popular contemporary opinion that because the Benders had emigrated from the land bordering the Rhine in Germany, they were slow-witted and predisposed to violent crime. "Who has not heard of the awful murders and robberies committed by the bandits who infest these Mountains," she asks, before going on to assume that since Kate was raised in America, she was more intelligent than the rest of the family. When the true extent of the crimes was uncovered, the newspapers came to a unanimous decision. Ma and Pa were capable of committing the murders but were simply too stupid to have concocted such a long-running scheme on their own. Gebhardt, with his intermittent giggle, was an obvious simpleton who could, at most, feign an interest in the Bible and fence some stolen goods. Kate was the only one capable of devising such a scheme and terrorised all the other members of the family so that it could be carried out.

Kate's place at the forefront of interest in the family is unsurprising. As an attractive young woman already pushing at the boundaries of what was deemed acceptable behaviour for women during the nineteenth century, just the possibility that she was a violent criminal made her an irresistible point of discussion. By welcoming people into her home under the guise of comfort, then watching or participating in their murder, Kate had performed the ultimate corruption of the domestic environment, a place where women traditionally occupied nurturing, maternal roles. In the eyes of the public she was a perversion of womanhood, described in the papers as "a pretend sorceress and real fiend" and a "child of the devil" who used her natural charm to hide her true nature. The more sensationalist papers accused her of being the one to slit open the victim's throats.

WHILE THE PRESS WONDERED WHAT AUTHORITIES WERE GOING TO do about the missing perpetrators, south-east Kansas was doing its best to deal with the sudden flood of nationwide attention the murders had brought down on the people of the prairies. Leroy Dick deemed further excavation at the site a lost cause when he rode out the day after the majority of the bodies had been unearthed. Hundreds of people had arrived to see the site christened "Hell's Half-Acre" by *The Kansas Democrat* for themselves. They trudged across the homestead and clambered in and out of tenantless graves. Others tore up what was left of the garden and packed it into wagons and saddlebags to display in their homes as evidence that they had seen the site of the murders for themselves. The more enterprising among them heaved stones from the well where the body of Johnny Boyle had sat the previous day. Dick guessed that within a week any physical trace that the Bender family once resided in the valley would be gone.

EXCITED CHATTER ROSE FROM THE GATHERING CROWDS AS PEOPLE gossiped to one another and to waiting reporters. When Dick was asked by a man from the *Leavenworth Daily Commercial* whether he had any frightening experiences with the Bender family, Dick was evasive, afraid that revealing prior knowledge of the family's criminal activities would get him blamed for not acting on the disappearances sooner. However, he did recall being asked by Pa Bender where he lived when he stopped early one morning to buy tobacco. Other residents of the county described a similar experience, leading authorities to believe that the Bender family purposefully "sought their victims among those who came from a distance." William York, it was supposed, was killed when he asked the family too many questions about George and Mary Ann Longcor. Suddenly everyone in south-east Kansas had a story about the Benders. Others were sure that their missing relatives now lay buried somewhere beneath the golden prairies of Labette County. Newspapers were saturated with accounts of men who claimed they had taken dinner at the cabin, only to make excuses and leave when they felt a presence behind the now infamous wagon canvas dividing the space. The more brazen among them claimed to have eaten with their firearms beside them on the table. Women, too, reported narrow escapes from the family, their accounts nearly always featuring "Kate of the evil eye" as the instigator of whatever terror they experienced. One woman claimed the family had woken her in the night, demanded she join them for a séance, and then thrown knives at the wall while Kate whispered that the spirits wanted her as a sacrifice. For all the papers that gleefully reprinted the story as evidence that the crimes were diabolically inspired, there were others who took it as evidence that Kansas was a state made up of gullible citizens and criminals.

"Kansas, for some years, has been noted as the nursery of moral monstrosities of all sorts," proclaimed a newspaper out of South Carolina. "The Bender family professed to be Spiritualists, but it is evident that they were prompted to their diabolical work not by spiritualism, but by the lowest sort of materialism—a lust for the money of the unfortunate travelers, who stopped at their eating saloon, on the Independence road." If Alexander York imagined that his stand against corruption in the state would go some way to repairing its reputation, the Bender crimes did as much to undo it.

SINCE THE DISCOVERY OF WILLIAM'S BODY, THE COMPOSED DEMEANour Alexander maintained throughout the search was starting to unravel. He found himself seized by the same intense compulsion for justice that led him to forfeit his political career. But this time the feeling came from overwhelming guilt that he had let his family down. Throughout the ordeal, Mary and Ed looked to him for guidance, but when Alexander was faced with the perpetrators, he had been unable to recognise them for what they were. This fact did not escape his detractors in the press, who jumped on the opportunity as further proof of his incompetence. Desperate to rectify what he perceived to be an unforgivable mistake, Alexander began searching for a culprit.

Intense Excitement
in the Neighbourhood

On Saturday, 10 May, the Leavenworth, Lawrence & Galveston Railroad Company announced its intention to run a special train service over the course of two days to allow more people to visit the site of the "Bender slaughter-pen." The interest in the crimes was so great that the railway companies capitulated to the request of the citizens of Coffeyville and Independence, sensing an opportunity to turn a quick profit out of the tragedy.

As the sun rose on Sunday 11 May, people hurried to secure a spot on the packed railway carriages. One hundred and fifty excited citizens squashed themselves onto the train from Independence. Double that number came in from Coffeyville. Both trains stopped at a point on the railway line two miles east of the cabin. Enterprising locals who had the chance to indulge their curiosity during the previous week arrived with buggies ready to ferry disembarking passengers to the site for a small fee. The rest of the crowd walked. Over the course of the day the excursion trains brought in nearly seven hundred curious spectators. Alongside the trains came groups in wagons and carriages from Thayer, Fredonia, Neodesha, Liberty, Parsons, and Osage Mission, where people had come together to organise day trips to the site. The valley was the busiest it

A view of the Bender cabin and the surrounding landscape. The orchard containing the bodies of the family's victims is shown on the right hand side, providing a rough indication of the layout of the graves. *Harper's Weekly*, 7 June, 1873.

would ever be. While most newspapers made a great show of emphasising the deep horror, pity, and anguish felt by the crowd, *The Kansas Chief* gave a more realistic assessment. Horror was present, it asserted, but was largely overwhelmed by a communal feeling of excitement and curiosity. Spectators jostled to view the graves and fought over the remaining contents of the cabin. When there was nothing left inside, they hacked at the building itself and divided it among themselves. Some tried to sell their loot for a good price to those who arrived in the afternoon. The following day, when the last of the big crowds began to descend on the Bender homestead, they were greeted by fraudsters peddling what they claimed to be genuine possessions of the family.

Eager for his role in the saga not to go unnoticed, Leroy Dick spent Sunday and Monday at the homestead. He brought with him the three hammers assumed to be the murder weapons, exhibiting them at what he considered to be a respectable distance from the graves. The district attorney had granted him ownership of the tools on the condition that they be available to the authorities if they were needed. Dick omitted his exhibition of the murder weapons in his personal account of the events of May 1873. Like so many others in the area, he felt a conflicting sense of horror at the murders and excitement over being involved in such a major event in the history of the region. On a practical level, local businesses in the area saw a brief increase in their weekly income due to the sudden influx of people. In Parsons, George Gamble hawked postcards with his photographs of the gravesite on them. In Fort Scott, Elkanah Tresslar sold slides for stereoscopes to those who could afford them and charged less to view them in his store.

AS LABETTE COUNTY PROCESSED ITS NEW-FOUND FAME, ALEXANDER York campaigned for the district attorney to begin issuing arrest warrants. Convinced that accomplices of the Benders were everywhere, Alexander operated on the basis that it was better to arrest first and ask questions later in order to avoid a repetition of his previous mistake. His approach encouraged local officials to act in a similar fashion, prompting a flurry of arrests across the region. The first to be thrown in jail was Elder King, the travelling preacher Ed York had been sure was involved even before the Benders fell under suspicion. Among the Benders' immediate neighbours to the south, Thomas and Susanna Tyack found themselves in a similar position after one too many rumours of their involvement in the Bender family's spiritualist activities reached the ears of the sheriff. Exasperated and frightened by the prospect of a lynch mob, Susanna admitted to attending a séance at the Bender property at which the group "just sat around with our hands on the table." Her husband told reporters that the Benders had a reputation for being unfriendly, and he only interacted with Kate when she came to visit his wife. Despite their flimsy association with the Bender family, Thomas Tyack was well liked by the community for being a hard and honest worker. When the Tyacks and their eldest daughter were arrested, Susanna's youngest child bawled as her mother was taken away. The newspapers attempted to make up for their rumour-mongering by calling the arrest a "brutal outrage" and demanding that the family be released immediately. Neighbours who had pointed the finger at the Tyacks assuaged their guilt over the treatment of the family by caring for the children while the parents sat in jail.

AT HIS HOME IN LADORE, JAMES ROACH HAD KEPT ABREAST OF THE developments at the Bender farm with a growing sense of unease. Having been under suspicion himself before the discovery of the murders, there was no doubt in his mind that authorities would find a way of implicating the people of Ladore in the crimes. With the Benders presumed to have fled the state, Roach knew the York brothers would put pressure on authorities to make reactionary arrests. He was right. Within seven days of the crimes being uncovered, half the Roach family was in jail. When men arrived at the Roach property to arrest James's eldest son, Addison, there was little he felt he could do without further endangering the boy. John Harness, Roach's stepson, soon found himself in the same jailhouse as the Tyacks and Elder King. Then came the arrests of Peter Harkness, George C. Parsons, and William Buxton, whose only crime was that they were married to each of James Roach's daughters. On 11 May, Major John Mefford arrived on Roach's doorstep, fresh from Missouri and demanding to know why a warrant had been issued for his arrest when he hadn't set foot in Kansas for the last fifteen months. Mefford had once been Roach's son-in-law, but after a stint in prison, remarried and left Kansas. He announced his intention to hand himself in at Fort Scott so he could be cleared of involvement with the Bender family through the legal channels. By 14 May, he was freed after it became apparent the only reason for his arrest was his former relationship with the Roach family.

PUBLIC OPINION TURNED AGAINST THE ARRESTS AFTER THE AUTHORities quickly lost interest in those they put behind bars. The people of Ladore and the surrounding Osage township were enraged. On 30 June, the *Parsons Weekly Herald* published a letter accusing Alexander York, Detective Beers, and the district attorney of knowingly imprisoning blameless men and women as "revenge on innocent people to cover up your own ignorance." It demanded an apology from Alexander, calling him as bad as the Bender family for refusing to admit the arrests were unwarranted and condemning honest people to a legacy of association with the crimes. They felt personally betrayed by the York brothers, who had torn through the area digging up homesteads, tearing down fences, and harassing townsfolk despite the community expressing nothing but a wish to help them locate William's remains. Ladore had been unfairly vilified, the letter continued, after all, had not all the murdered men been on their way to or from Independence? Rivalry between the settlements brewed ever since Ladore lost out on the railway line. Tellingly, the letter also accused the authorities of holding innocent citizens without trial, even as detectives set out in pursuit of the family. When William Buxton was finally released, he was a hundred miles from his homestead with no money to pay his way back. Other members of the Roach family sat in jail while deputised men rooted through their houses and offered to pay people to provide damning testimony. Eventually the authorities capitulated. The Roach men returned to their wives, the Tyacks were reunited with their younger children, and Elder King continued to preach forgiveness. The letter from Ladore, published after the release of the families, never received the formal response it demanded. In a deeply personal attack, it branded Alexander a weak-souled man who would never be able to make up for allowing the family to escape undetected. He would spend the next three decades trying.

Part IV

IN PURSUIT
OF MURDERERS

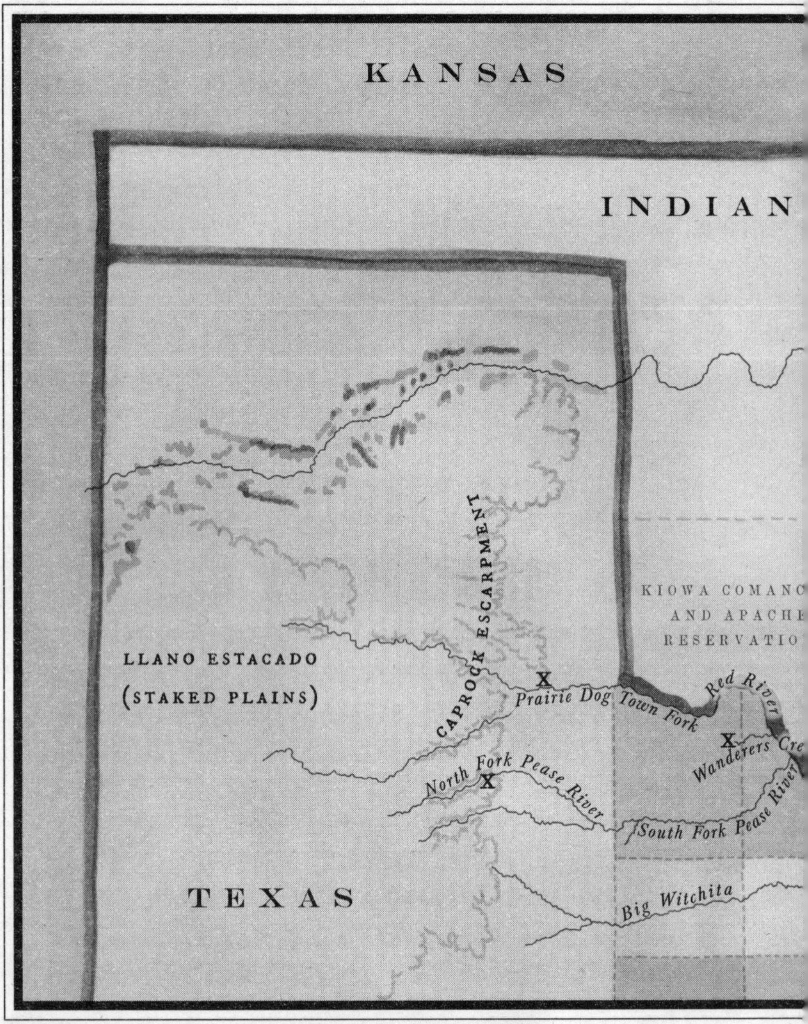

KANSAS

INDIAN

LLANO ESTACADO
(STAKED PLAINS)

CAPROCK ESCARPMENT

KIOWA COMANC
AND APACHE
RESERVATIO

Prairie Dog Town Fork

Red River

Wanderers Cre

North Fork Pease River

South Fork Pease River

TEXAS

Big Witchita

INDIAN TERRITORY
with adjoining portion of
TEXAS

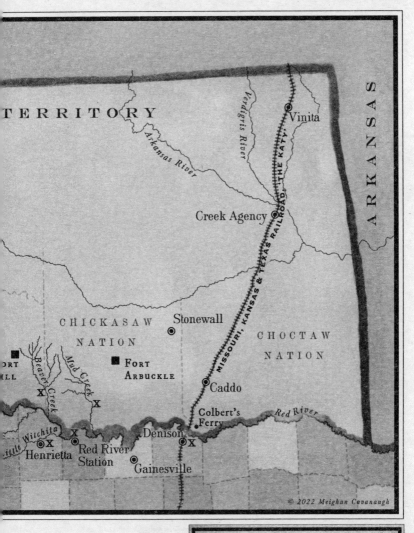

TERRITORY

Arkansas River

Verdigris River

Vinita

THE "KATY"

Creek Agency

MISSOURI, KANSAS & TEXAS RAILROAD

CHICKASAW
NATION

Stonewall

CHOCTAW
NATION

FORT
ARBUCKLE

Caddo

Beaver Creek
Mud Creek

FORT
HILL

X

X

Colbert's
Ferry

Red River

X

Denison

Little Witchita

X

Henrietta

X

Red River
Station

X

Gainesville

ARKANSAS

© 2022 Meighan Cavanaugh

✿ KEY ✿

X   OUTLAW CAMPS

╫╫╫╫╫   RAILROADS

~~~~~   RIVERS

∿∿∿∿∿   ESCARPMENT

Texas Is the Place

Denison, Texas

EARLY MAY 1873

It was little over a month since Kate Bender and John Gebhardt had boarded the train to Texas. At an undetermined point above the Arkansas River, they jumped from the train, further disguising their route from the authorities as they continued their journey through Indian Territory. With money accrued from selling goods and horses belonging to their victims, they purchased a wagon, a sturdy team of horses, and enough guns to arm the four members of the family twice over once they were reunited. Kate swapped her calico skirts for men's clothing and kept her long, distinctive hair tucked beneath her hat.

The inhabitants of Indian Territory were no strangers to white outlaws passing through on their way down south or seeking refuge in the multifaceted landscape of open prairie, dense forest, and ragged mountains. Though the United States District Court for the Western District of Arkansas was responsible for enforcing federal law in the territory, at the time the Bender family was in the area it was presided over by Judge William Story, whose corruption obstructed legal proceedings and often allowed violent criminals to walk free. Further complicating matters was the presence of tribal courts that had no jurisdiction over white criminals, making crimes that involved both Indigenous and non-Indigenous people difficult to process. With white criminals able to operate relatively free from legal repercussions, Indian Territory became a haven for those on the run.

On their journey, Kate and John slunk along a tributary of the Arkansas River, keeping close to the foliage that spilled from its banks. At the Creek Agency, they crossed the river and headed for Stonewall in the Chickasaw Nation. A town comprised of a boarding school for Chickasaw children, a trading post, and a saloon, Stonewall was a place where supplies were sold to faces that were quickly forgotten.* From Stonewall they continued south and crossed the Red River on Colbert's Ferry. Benjamin Colbert, a citizen of the Chickasaw Nation, had run the ferry since 1853 and was enjoying the profits brought in by the increasing number of cattle drivers who needed to cross the river. Horses and cattle cost ten cents a head, and though cowboys could choose not to use the boats, they still had to pay to cross the river. Kate and Gebhardt would have paid a dollar for their two-horse wagon. In the days leading up to Billy Tole's discovery that the Bender homestead had been deserted, Kate and John drifted into the outskirts of Denison. At first glance they were indistinguishable from the myriad travellers who filtered in and out of the region. Camped at the north end of the town in a wagon now more decrepit than the one the family deserted on their flight out of Kansas, the two fugitives settled in to wait for Ma and Pa.

THOSE WHO CAME THROUGH DENISON IN THE SPRING OF 1873 FOUND a lively railway town already boasting an opera house, three churches, and the first public schoolhouse in Texas. The settlement lay west of the

---

* The boarding school at Stonewall had been in operation since 1854 but closed at the onset of the Civil War. Many such institutions existed across the country, designed to strip Indigenous children of their Native culture, and the children were largely taught by missionaries seeking to replace traditional religious customs with Christianity. When the school in Stonewall reopened after the war, the Chickasaw Nation fought for more influence over the curriculum and was briefly able to keep religious and domestic training to a minimum. But in 1898, the government took full control of the schools under the Curtis Act, focusing once again on eradication of Indigenous belief systems.

Red River, situated 217 feet (66 metres) above the level of the water. The location was chosen to ensure its inhabitants could go about their lives free from the "malaria and miasmas" known to plague communities closer to the banks of the river. Surrounded by ample trees for timber and natural springs to provide water for people and livestock, the land proved an ideal home for the first railway line to penetrate south of the border. Since the first lots were sold on 23 September 1872, the sound of construction filled the air and never ceased. Every day new buildings went up on the main street. Proprietors who intended to move into buildings set up temporary structures to turn a profit as soon as possible. A tent city encircled the centre of the town, its unpaved streets lined with bars and gambling houses where men drank away the time waiting for news of work on the railway. On Christmas Eve 1872, raucous crowds gathered to cheer the first train into town and celebrate the season. "Ho! For Texas" proclaimed the premier issue of *The Denison Daily News* published three days later. B. C. Murray, the editor of the newspaper, told his readers that Denison was to be "the gate that opens to the outside world the finest agricultural region of Texas." The inhabitants of the town took the paper's praise to heart, unaware that several months later they would harbour some of the most famous criminals in the West.

IN DENISON, THE BENDER COUPLE BECAME RECKLESS ABOUT CON-cealing their identities. Kate, though she did not venture into the centre of the town, gave up the pretense of being a man. She caught the attention of Albert Owens, the owner of a boarding house opposite the land where the Benders were camped. He did not approach her but watched the couple with interest and assumed that they were man and wife. John signed up with a railway gang and ingratiated himself with the labourers. He listened closely to the chatter of the men and paid particular attention to the news coming out of Kansas.

In the tent by the wagon, Kate was sulking. On their arduous journey through Indian Territory, she kept herself distracted by envisioning her name in the papers. With her ambitions of finding wealth and fame, the prospect of being a known fugitive excited her. Instead, she and John arrived in Denison to discover that no one knew they were missing, let alone that they were murderers. When Ma and Pa arrived from Missouri without incident, the family was confident they could be long gone before detectives arrived in Texas.

The following morning, John appeared on the doorstep of Albert Owens's boarding house. In a moment of either absent-mindedness or knowing provocation, John told the man the family's name was Bender. He then explained that they were intending to head west. Owens was surprised. The citizens of Denison thought of the counties to the west as largely lawless and inhabited by the rougher people the frontier had to offer. Beyond the sparse settlements was the Llano Estacado, or the Staked Plains, a high plains region so devoid of natural features that even experienced travellers could find themselves adrift in the sun-bleached landscape.

"Better cattle range downstate," Owens replied, hoping to persuade the young man to try his hand elsewhere. John gave him a look that prompted Owens to elaborate. "Lots of desperate types out that way, no place for setting up families."

John responded with the same shrill laugh that had unnerved the people of Labette County. "My old folks reckon there's money to be made selling goods to those desperate types. Could make for a decent living."

Owens was horrified by the idea. A colony of fugitives existed in that country, he explained, and they went to great lengths to protect those in their midst from law enforcement. One expedition had seen seven of the sheriff's men ride out, none of whom came back. Disputes over where the border was between Texas and New Mexico generated ongoing confusion over whose responsibility it was to take action against the outlaw colony. As neither state took action, the band of renegades thrived.

"They keep saying they'll clean out the den," Owens concluded. "But everyone's always waiting for someone else to do it."

JOHN LISTENED TO OWENS'S SERIES OF LURID ANECDOTES WITH A growing sense of satisfaction. The Benders had pre-existing ties to the loosely organised band of fugitives, and the purpose of his conversation with Owens had merely been to gauge their reputation in the surrounding areas. He thanked the boarding house proprietor for his time with an earnest handshake and returned to the family's campsite to relay the information. Kate listened with growing excitement, then set about packing up the camp. But the family waited until sundown to leave the city, and as the shadows crept into Denison's outer streets, another man joined the family.

A COHORT OF THE BENDERS, FRANK MCPHERSON WAS A RESTLESS psychopath whose chronic eye problems gave him a mean squint to match his short fuse. Just twenty-three, his life was an escalating series of crimes that had recently boiled over into murder. In mid-April, a drunken Frank staggered into a bakery in Parsons, Kansas. Shortly afterwards he emerged covered in blood, having beaten the owner into a coma with a chair and a heavy baker's weight. Annie Eigensatz, the baker's wife, told the newspapers that Frank had "bounced" the weight at her husband after the latter discovered Frank attempting to sexually assault her. Lucas Eigensatz remained alive long enough that when Frank was apprehended he was only charged with assault. The evening of the day Frank posted bail, Lucas died. Police caught up with the outlaw in a neighbouring county and bundled him on to a train back to Parsons. Frank waited until the train drew up alongside the banks of the river, then told the man escorting him that he needed to use the toilet and the hapless officer agreed to let him go. After sidling into the adjoining saloon car, Frank launched himself from the window of the train. By the time the officer realised what had happened, Frank was making his way out of the muddy river water and into the thicket. The district attorney issued a five-hundred-dollar reward for his apprehension, but he vanished so quickly into Indian Territory that pursuit seemed largely futile.

Frank lurked in the borderlands of Texas and Indian Territory until he received word that the Bender family was ready to head out West and join the outlaw colony. With Frank as their guide, they set off toward Red

River Station. The station squatted at the southern end of one of the most famous cattle trails of post-bellum America: the Chisholm Trail. Founded by Jesse Chisholm, a half Cherokee fur trader, and Black Beaver, a Lenape scout and rancher, the trail provided a route for cowboys to drive cattle up from Texas to Abilene, Kansas. Smaller trails weaved across the Texas landscape, congregating at Red River and bringing together clusters of transient faces hardy enough to brave the rough life of the cattle drive. It was also a jumping-off point for those wishing to head further out west into the obscurity of the plains.

THE *DAILY NEWS* LATER REPORTED THAT THE BENDERS "LIT OUT from Denison" on Monday, 5 May, the same day that Leroy Dick first smelled human decomposition on the Labette County homestead. In the days following his conversation with John, Albert Owens read of the bodies discovered beneath an orchard in Kansas with a rising sense of unease.

Go Out and Lay
Hands on 'Em

Kansas

MID-MAY 1873

B ack in Kansas, Alexander York returned to the crime scene one final time after collecting William's body. Accompanying him were Detective Beers and Colonel Charles Peckham, whom Alexander had recruited to manage the search for the Bender family. Like Alexander, Peckham practised law in Independence. Though his legal practice was successful and kept him busy, Peckham missed the sense of purpose he had experienced during the Civil War. He longed to go further west, to make a name for himself in the annals of frontier history. When Alexander asked him to organise the hunt for William's murderers, Peckham accepted without a second thought. He paced about what was left of the homestead with Detective Beers, who pointed out things of interest and caught him up on the details of the case.

ALEXANDER KEPT HIS DISTANCE TO AVOID THE CROWD. NEWSPAPERS that had sided with Pomeroy in the January election jumped at the chance to blame Alexander for the Bender family's escape. *The Kansas Chief* ran an article claiming that what he had done to Senator Pomeroy was as bad as the murders committed by the Bender family. Comparing the death of eleven innocent people to the exposure of a corrupt politician was a steep comparison, even for a time when reputation was considered a man's most important possession. To protect his growing family, Alexander intended to retreat from the public eye. Asking Peckham to manage the search also allowed the York family to distance themselves from a failure to catch the Benders. They, too, had a reputation to maintain.

AFTER VISITING THE SITE, PECKHAM AND BEERS PARTED WAYS WITH Alexander and headed north to the railway station at Thayer. They found the town in a state of excitement over its role in the flight of the Benders out of Kansas. It did not take long for them to find the ticket agent who had served the family. He told the two men that a group matching the description of the Benders arrived with barely enough time to buy a ticket before catching the last train to Humboldt. From what he knew of the events, Peckham guessed that they fled the evening after Alexander's visit to the cabin. The agent confirmed his suspicions.

"I remember the day on account of the baggage," he explained. "A dog-hide trunk. I'd recognise it anywhere."

Traveller's trunks covered with hide were commonplace during the early nineteenth century, but by the late 1800s the majority were wooden with metal detailing. The Benders' trunk stood out because it was covered in hide that had clearly come from a dog. Peckham and Beers set out for Humboldt, where they learned that the younger couple had likely left the train at Chanute and headed south to Texas. Peckham immediately wired the authorities at Denison but was frustrated to learn that no one answering the couple's description had been seen arriving at the train station.

Ma and Pa were easier to track, having purchased tickets to St. Louis, Missouri, where a baggage agent recalled the trunk with a look of disgust, as it "still had the hairs on it." Overhearing the conversation, a railway porter approached Beers. He, too, recognised the description of the trunk and informed the detective that he had hauled its owners to Lafayette Park. In days spent absorbing local gossip about the family, Beers had

Governor's Proclamation.

$2,000 REWARD

State of Kansas, Executive Department.

WHEREAS, several atrocious murders have been recently committed in Labette County, Kansas, under circumstances which fasten, beyond doubt, the commissions of these crimes upon a family known as the "Bender family," consisting of

JOHN BENDER, about 60 years of age, five feet eight or nine inches in height, German, speaks but little English, dark complexion, no whiskers, and sparely built;

MRS. BENDER, about 50 years of age, rather heavy set, blue eyes, brown hair, German, speaks broken English;

JOHN BENDER, Jr., alias John Gebardt, five feet eight or nine inches in height, slightly built, gray eyes with brownish tint, brown hair, light moustache, no whiskers, about 27 years of age, speaks English with German accent;

KATE BENDER, about 24 years of age, dark hair and eyes, good looking, well formed, rather bold in appearance, fluent talker, speaks good English with very little German accent:

AND WHEREAS, said persons are at large and fugitives from justice, now therefore, I, Thomas A. Osborn, Governor of the State of Kansas, in pursuance of law, do hereby offer a REWARD OF FIVE HUNDRED DOLLARS for the apprehension and delivery to the Sheriff of Labette County, Kansas, of each of the persons above named.

In Testimony Whereof, I have hereunto subscribed my name, and caused the Great Seal of the State to be affixed.

[L. S.]   Done at Topeka, this 17th day of May, 1873.

THOMAS A. OSBORN,
Governor.

By the Governor:

W. H. SMALLWOOD,
Secretary of State.

The proclamation issued by Governor Thomas Osborn offering a reward for the apprehension of the Benders, along with physical descriptions of the family.

heard that Kate frequently spoke of an aunt in Missouri who ran a boarding house at that same address. The porter took them to the house, where they found a quiet woman who told them she was Pa's sister. He and Ma had arrived unannounced several weeks before, been ill-tempered house guests, and then disappeared without a word around the time their crimes were uncovered. The sister told the men she had not contacted the authorities because she had no idea where they had gone. Stumped, Peckham went west to Kansas City to enlist the help of Missouri authorities in searching railway depots across the state.

From the outset, the search for the family was plagued by too much information but too little where it mattered. Newspapers all over the country reported interactions with the family. The *Daily Atchison Patriot* gave its readers a helpful round up of the sightings before concluding that "a few towns in the Mississippi Valley yet remain to be heard from, but these will put in an appearance in a short time."

Alongside the deluge of information another problem was brewing. Though the entire state of Kansas was outraged at the ferocity of the Bender crimes, no one could decide whose responsibility it was to finance the search for the family. Governor Osborn took more than a week to issue a proclamation offering a reward of five hundred dollars a head for the apprehension of the family. But with the reward payable only on delivery of the family to Labette County authorities, the matter of funding the search remained an issue. Newspapers grumbled that the reward was simply not large enough to entice decent detectives into working the case. "Our Governor is so economical, our state is so poor, that it can pay only $500 a head for the capture of these beasts in human form," bemoaned *The Girard Press*. Labette County officials refused to front funds for the search, believing that the state was responsible for allowing the murders to continue unchecked. Alexander York, desperate to initiate the search for the family as soon as possible, personally paid the way for Beers and Peckham to travel to Missouri. But with no clear funding and no clear leads, the search stalled before it had the chance to get going.

A reprieve appeared in the form of Albert Owens, who arrived in Parsons in a state of agitation in the days after Governor Osborn announced his reward. Owens had barely stepped off the train before flagging down a ticket agent and demanding he be taken to someone involved in the search for the Benders. His manner was so excitable that he was escorted to the schoolhouse at Harmony Grove, where Leroy Dick had been fielding tips about the whereabouts of the family. Owens introduced himself as the proprietor of a boarding house in Denison and perplexed Dick by apologising profusely.

Dick gestured for the man to take a seat and inquired after the source of the man's apology. Owens removed his hat but did not sit down. In shaky tones he described how a young couple had been camped opposite his boarding house the previous week; how they had been joined by an older couple; how the younger man had asked him about the outlaw colony in the western counties.

Dick listened to the story with a growing sense of irritation that Owens had not arrived sooner, or they might have all been in line for the reward offered by the governor. They agreed that Owens would return to Denison by the next train so that he could offer his services to Peckham and Beers when they arrived. Dick sent the telegraph to Peckham himself. Peckham was making little progress in Kansas City, and the news that the Bender family had been sighted together in Texas filled him with relief. He wired Detective Beers and the two arranged to meet in Denison the following day. Beers took the railway through Indian Territory, where the train stopped overnight at Vinita. After supper in the town, he returned to the station, where he stopped a young ticket agent to ask whether anyone remembered handling a dog-hide trunk.

"Oh yes, sir," the boy replied. "Belonged to an old Dutch couple come through about a week ago."

Where Horse Thieves
Do Congregate

Red River Station, Texas
LATE MAY 1873

The Bender family and Frank McPherson arrived in Red River Station, where they were greeted by news that the family's murderous habits back in Kansas had finally been discovered. But Red River Station was not like Denison, and if its inhabitants were aware that a group of fugitives moved among them, they made no move to apprehend them. The cattle station was a frontier settlement with no aspirations of grandeur, its existence having grown out of the necessity for a station that banked a crossable portion of the Red River. Cowboys arrived caked in the filth of the cattle drive, wandering straight into Mollie Love's hotel for a hot meal or to lesser establishments that were often little more than crudely painted tents. The bellowing of thousands of cattle filled the skies and the minds of those passing through on their way north to Kansas. Permanent residents who were overfriendly when soliciting business became hostile when asked the wrong questions. The hiss of scalding iron in water drifted from the blacksmiths as Thurston and Yates forged branding irons that were famous throughout the West. Children picked their way through muck to the local schoolhouse, which was moved to higher ground when the number of cattle driven through the area grew so high they threatened to trample the school and its pupils. Big Red, as the cowboys called the Red River, was a volatile neighbour for the settlement and a dangerous obstacle for anyone needing to drive cattle to the other side. In the spring the river swelled to nearly twice its size, sweeping men, cattle, and horses brave enough to attempt the crossing into its churning waters and carrying them for miles.

RED RIVER STATION HAD FEW PROMINENT CITIZENS, BUT AMONG those who made a lasting impression on those passing through was the man who had agreed to harbour the Benders. William McPherson was Frank's older brother, better known across several states as Missouri Bill. Where Frank was volatile and unpredictable, Missouri Bill was calculating and patient, though he concealed a similar propensity for violence beneath his affable front. At six feet three inches (190 centimetres), he towered over nearly everyone he met, and the inhabitants of Red River often sensed his presence before they saw him. Unlike Frank, Bill did not immediately set people on edge. But, as the *Denison Daily News* would later report, he "had the reputation of being a desperado, a castle thief and a murderer." Frank led the Bender family to his brother's shack on the outskirts of the station, where Bill lived with his wife amid a stash of illegal spirits. No stranger to the Bender family, Bill agreed to help them on their way out west. He did so out of necessity, knowing that if they were caught, they would not hesitate in naming him as an accomplice to their crimes.

FRANK AND BILL HAD GROWN UP IN SEDALIA, MISSOURI, WHERE THEY proved themselves to be two indelible stains on the McPherson family's otherwise good reputation. Relying on their parents' wealth and influence to bail them out of trouble, both engaged in a series of petty crimes from a young age. In his late teens, Bill became increasingly violent. "He had an affray with some men in this city, and had to flee from justice on account of it," reported *The Sedalia Democrat*, before concluding that "he was not a man to add to the pleasures of a town." Like many others, Bill headed into Indian Territory, where he sought to take advantage of the lax administration in the region. Frank remained in Sedalia, racking up a steady stream of appearances in the local paper for attempting to use counterfeit money.

Bill first encountered John Gebhardt in the spring of 1872, when the latter was visiting family in Clay County, Texas. Bill shared a run-down log cabin with a family by the name of Slimp, who introduced John as one of "their cousins the Benders that lived in Labette Co. Kansas." Perhaps John and Bill sensed in each other similar criminal tendencies, or perhaps the former simply asked if he would be willing to help him fence stolen goods and horses. However they came to the arrangement, by the autumn of 1872, the McPherson brothers were involved with the Bender family in a criminal capacity.

Things were made easier when Frank moved to Labette County. The McPherson family had been forced to relocate after Frank attacked a saloon owner in Sedalia with a beer glass, then used shards of the broken vessel to slash at policemen who were trying to break up the fight. Frank's parents paid his twenty-five-dollar fine and moved the whole family to Parsons. But Frank preferred the company of his older brother down on the banks of the Red River, where Bill was bringing in a sporadic income as a career criminal. Along with fencing stolen goods, the brothers tried their hands at everything from selling untaxed spirits to stealing cattle. Their activity extended as far north as Colorado, encompassing parts of Kansas, Missouri, and Indian Territory, as well as Texas, where Bill had temporarily set up camp.

The months following Frank's move to Parsons were the months the Bender family escalated their own criminal activity, with seven of the family's confirmed victims murdered between October 1872 and March 1873. With the aid of the McPhersons, the Benders were able to unload stolen goods at a faster rate with lower risk of being caught. John and Pa no longer had to travel hundreds of miles to sell identifiable horses that belonged to their victims; they simply handed them over to others involved with the McPhersons' gang and returned to the cabin to wait for the next potential target. Then, when the Benders fled the state, Frank made good on his word that he would get them to their cousins in Texas without being caught.

THE BENDER FAMILY CAMPED IN THE YARD OF BILL'S SHACK AND set about making preparations to strike out further west. Kate was in good spirits, enthralled by the knowledge that her name was finally front and centre in the many newspaper accounts written about the family. After learning the governor of Kansas had offered the maximum amount for her apprehension, she settled into the idea of notoriety with a confidence that made her smug. Back in men's clothing, Kate moved freely about the cattle station, enjoying the attention brought by her unusual get-up. Missouri Bill's influence in the region extended as far as the county sheriff, and if the Benders had been reckless about their identities in Denison, they exhibited no concern about being recognised in the open country.

SEVERAL DAYS LATER, MISSOURI BILL MADE HIS WAY THROUGH THE mud-clogged streets with an urgency that alarmed those he passed. He had received word through the sheriff that not only were detectives in Texas, they knew the Bender family was at the cattle station. Though they would find little help from the Montague County authorities, detectives in the area were bad news for everyone. Bill arrived back at the shack, where he relayed the news to the Benders and Frank. John suggested they leave immediately for the western counties.

Bill shook his head. "No sense going out on the plains yet, they'll catch up to you easy. Better cross the river and head up Mud Creek," he gestured to his brother. "Frank knows the place."

The Benders agreed to lie low in Indian Territory until Bill brought word that the detectives were no longer on their trail. They packed the wagon to the bustle of the station's after-dark activity and rose as the first of the daylight glistened on the banks of the river. After riding the three quarters of a mile north to the station's ferry, the group crossed the first portion of the river on the boat, and the water beyond the sandbar on horseback. With their clothes already drying in the first real heat of the year, Frank and the Benders followed the Mud Creek tributary of the Red River north into the Chickasaw Nation. Back at the cattle station, Missouri Bill waited for the men from Kansas to arrive.

Some Blundering Detective

Texas

LATE MAY–EARLY JUNE 1873

U pon disembarking from the train at Denison, Colonel Peckham and Detective Beers were greeted by a jittery Albert Owens. Owens took the men to the site of the Benders' camp, but Beers quickly grew tired of the man's apologies that he had not reported the sighting earlier. Only when listening to Owens's assertion that the family had gone west to locate an outlaw colony near the Staked Plains did Beers begin to realise the enormity of the task he and Peckham faced. They were also out of funds. Peckham wired officials back in Kansas and paced listlessly in the street waiting for a reply. Beers passed the time by making arrangements to hire a wagon, team, and guide should they receive the money to continue.

THEN, ON 24 MAY, GOOD NEWS CAME IN THE FORM OF FIVE HUNdred dollars from the governor with a strict note on how it was to be used: "The disbursement should be limited to the smallest possible amount consistent with a successful prosecution of the search and should be allowed to cover only actual necessary expense of detectives engaged in traveling in search of the criminals." Payment for their services would come from the reward if they were successful.

Bolstered by the money, Beers and Peckham set out across the plains in the direction of the Llano Estacado, intending to question all those they encountered on the way. Acres of rolling prairie passed beneath the hooves of their horses. To the north, the great Red River cut a boundary between Texas and Indian Territory, its tributaries winding through the plains and coaxing pockets of green from the soil. The men passed through the centre of Cooke County, stopping at Gainesville to stock up on provisions and make inquiries. During their time in the town they learned that Frank McPherson had been seen in the company of the Bender family, the first indication for the authorities that the two parties were connected.

"If the Benders was with Frank," a ranch hand told the two men, "they'll be at Missouri Bill's place at the cattle station." When they asked who Missouri Bill was, the man replied that Bill and Frank were brothers. The discovery proved itself a vital lead, and it seemed locating Frank would be easier than Beers and Peckham had anticipated.

Two cowboys drive cattle across a stream in Texas. *Harper's Weekly*, 19 October 1867.

It was of great surprise to the two men that when they rode into Red River Station amid the dust and bluster of the cowboys, Missouri Bill appeared to have been expecting them. They were even more surprised to find that the physically imposing man appeared to bear them no hostility. Bill took them out to his shack and introduced them to his wife, then ensured they had comfortable lodgings at Mollie Love's hotel. When they asked him about the Bender family, he said he could find out where they were, but avoided addressing the issue of his brother's criminal behaviour.

Over several days Bill pretended to make inquiries as to the whereabouts of the Benders, eventually returning to Beers and announcing that he would take them to where the family was camped, for a fee. Though the exact terms of the deal have been lost, from correspondence written by Beers and Peckham to Labette County officials and Governor Osborn, it is clear that Bill gave every indication that he intended to deliver the Bender family to the authorities. Peckham was elated by the man's co-operation. He was so confident that an arrest was close to hand that he wrote to the governor requesting a requisition be sent as soon as possible so that the Benders could be extradited to Kansas after their arrest without interference from the Texas authorities. With Montague County law enforcement in cahoots with the McPherson gang or simply uninterested in getting involved, Beers and Peckham received no warning that Bill was not to be trusted.

MORE MONEY WAS WIRED IN FROM KANSAS, SUPPLIES WERE PACKED into saddlebags, and the three men carried enough guns to stave off the variety of dangers they were likely to encounter out on the plains. Bill was specific about everything except where the Benders could be found. Beers frequently questioned him on the matter, but Bill simply replied that they would make their way to the family's last known campsite and track them from there. His manner was so convincing and the two lawmen so excited at the prospect of finally apprehending the Benders that it took several weeks before either wanted to entertain the prospect that he was a liar. As supplies dwindled, Bill began to leave the men for several days at a time. He claimed to be riding ahead to scout for signs of the family, but when Peckham confronted him, Bill's good-natured demeanour showed signs of something nastier. Eventually he vanished altogether, leaving Beers and Peckham to navigate their own way back to civilisation.

AT THE PEAK OF SUMMER, WHEN THE SKY ABOVE THE PRAIRIES swam with heat, Peckham returned to Kansas disillusioned with the search. Both he and Beers were frustrated by the sporadic funds from the governor and the general unreliability of life out West. The debacle with Missouri Bill had been an embarrassing blow for both men. The expedition that was supposed to cement them as legends of the frontier had transpired to be little more than a wild-goose chase led by an accomplice of the family, while the Benders passed an uneventful few weeks in hiding. "The Sheriff of Montague is considered implicated with them," Beers wrote to the governor after they made it back to Denison; "It is known that he advised them to leave the station for the present." Peckham was also called back by the necessity of returning to his legal practice to finish the term of court for the year. Should the hunt continue into September, Peckham resolved to head back to the land west of Red River Station with renewed zeal.

Beers remained in Texas, but when he returned to Red River Station he avoided Missouri Bill's shack. A few quick inquiries revealed that he needn't have bothered. Bill had departed for the Bender camp as soon as word reached him that Beers and Peckham had left the area. The detective spent several days at the station making further inquiries and listening to cattle-trail gossip. He learned that a camp made up of ten white people and four Native Americans had been seen north of the Red River at Mud Creek in the Chickasaw Nation. Among them were the Bender family and the McPherson brothers.

Perturbed that the location of the fugitives appeared to be an open secret, Beers hired a guide to take him out to Mud Creek. When the two men arrived at the creek, they picked through the remnants of the camp and estimated it had been abandoned little more than a week earlier.

An Organised and
Extensive Gang

Clay County, Texas

SUMMER 1873

———

While Beers wrung his hands at the thought of narrowly missing the family, the Benders and the McPherson brothers headed southwest and crossed the Red River into Clay County, Texas. Other members of the gang remained in Indian Territory, where Beers later recalled they "scattered out" and became untraceable. Clay County was a sparsely populated territory where Native Americans had previously succeeded in driving white settlers out of the county seat of Henrietta. In the early 1870s, the Kiowa and Comanche were forced back onto the reservations, but the danger posed by raiders still deterred many from settling in the area.

One of the most famous incidents was an attack on Gottlieb Koozer, a Quaker who relocated to Clay County against warnings that he was making his family an easy target for Indian raiders. With his wife, Sarah, and six children, Koozer moved into one of the abandoned buildings in the centre of a deserted Henrietta. He told those who worried about the family that he intended to live peacefully alongside the Native Americans and hoped to build a relationship with them. On 10 July 1870, a band of Kiowa led by renowned warrior White Horse rode into the yard of the homestead. Koozer went out to meet them and White Horse shot him through the heart, killing him instantly. Koozer was scalped, his home ransacked, and his wife and children taken captive. Two days later, escalating tensions in the area led to a skirmish on the Little Wichita between a different band of Kiowa raiders and troops from the U.S. Cavalry. Fifteen Kiowa were killed, but the tribe succeeded in driving the soldiers from the area. At the same time, the Indian agent in the region, enraged by the capture of the Koozer family, sent word to the Kiowa that unless the prisoners were returned, he would withhold all government supplies issued to the tribe. On 18 August, the Kiowa brought the girls to the agency and demanded a ransom, but the agent refused to budge on the matter until all members of the family were produced unharmed. Upon delivery of Mrs Koozer and the rest of the children, the Kiowa were paid one hundred dollars a head for the family and issued their government supplies. The tribe returned to the reservation and the Koozers returned to their life in Montague County.

BY THE TIME THE BENDERS ARRIVED IN 1873, THE DEMOGRAPHIC OF the land was changing once again. First came the routes of the great postwar cattle trails, trod into the earth beneath the hooves of thousands of livestock. Then trading posts and ranches sprang up across the plains to support the cattle drive, some little more than ramshackle cabins offering hot meals to cowboys and buffalo hunters. Yet the vastness of the landscape and the gruelling, transient nature of the cattle drive ensured that Clay County remained popular with fugitives.

ALONG THE BANKS OF THE LITTLE WICHITA RIVER, THE GANG WAS making its way towards the double log cabin several miles south of Henrietta, where their cousins lived. The cabin was an ungainly but sturdy building that, unlike its previous inhabitants, withstood a series of raids carried out by Kiowa and Comanche in 1868. When the Benders arrived, they were greeted by Floyd Slimp. A skinny, frontier-hardened twenty-three-year-old, Floyd was pleased to see his cousins and the

McPhersons. Since a run-in with the district court in western Arkansas the year before when he was accused of stealing mules, Floyd kept busy growing maize and left the more dubious activities to his father and elder brother, Clint. He chatted aimlessly as the group began setting up a camp adjacent to the cabin, passing around a bottle of the spirits Bill still kept on the property. Floyd was surprised to see Kate in men's clothing, as he had always known her to be particular about her appearance. Ma Bender was also in men's clothing, but she did not suit it quite as well as her daughter. When they sat down to eat, Kate told Floyd she had to go by a false name.

"On account that I'm in all the papers," she explained. "So you should call me Jennie Gardener." They drank and ate as the dark closed in, their rowdy chatter rising with the smoke from the fire to be dispersed on the wind. If Floyd Slimp knew the appalling details of the murders committed by his cousins, he avoided bringing it up in conversation. The McPherson brothers were gone before sunrise.

THE BENDER FAMILY PASSED THREE DAYS AT THE CABIN OUTSIDE Henrietta amid the prairie grasses and distant cattle calls. After weeks of squatting in the undergrowth near Mud Creek, where the red silt of the riverbed stained their clothes and hands, it was a relief to be camped on open, dry land. When Floyd's brother and father arrived back at the cabin, discussion began on where the Bender family should head next. John felt the family shouldn't bother heading further west, but Pa was not so sure. Nor did the Slimps like the idea of being caught with fugitives in their yard if the military presence in the region was persuaded to get involved with the search. Several of the men set out the following morning in search of a secluded place on the banks of the Little Wichita where the Benders could pitch their next camp. Floyd and John stayed behind and played cards with the women. In the middle of the afternoon, Ma left the cabin to start up a stew for dinner. To her surprise, she was greeted by the sight of a man she did not recognise picking his way through the disarray of the campsite towards the house. He looked up and saw her.

Ma gave him such a look that he hollered for Floyd. In the cabin, Kate reached for a rifle propped against the table.

"It's Merrick" came the voice from outside again. Floyd jumped up and waved for Kate to put the gun down. He went out to greet his friend. John followed but ordered Kate to stay in the cabin. She tucked her hair back under a hat and listened.

"This here's Sam Merrick used to live with us," Floyd said by way of introduction, gesturing to the man in the camp. Ma made no effort to acknowledge Merrick even after he touched his hat to her. John gave him a curt nod and a disconcerting laugh.

"Mrs Bender and her folks arrived from Denison 'bout three days ago," continued Floyd. "They been living in Kansas."

Kate was impatient to see their visitor. Ignoring John's warning that she should stay hidden, she stepped out of the cabin, where she introduced herself as Jennie Gardener.

"Pa's out lookin' for somewhere safe to camp. Reckons Little Wichita." She folded her arms across her chest. "That sound right?"

Merrick told her the Little Wichita was as good as any place south of the Red River. He was visiting the cabin to collect a bridle from Floyd but, intrigued by the family, hung around the camp hoping that the men would return from scouting on the river. When they failed to materialise, he set out to retrieve some cattle he owned from a nearby ranch. In descriptions of his first meeting with the Benders, Merrick recalled that Kate "was pretty good looking [with] red cheeks" and that "they all wore men's clothes."

SAMUEL MERRICK HAD LIVED WITH MISSOURI BILL AND THE SLIMPS during the spring of 1872. But unlike Bill, he did not meet the Bender family until 1873. After spending an extended period in the Rocky Mountains, Merrick returned to warmer climates, intending to find work in the cattle drive. In Texas he had a reputation as a good cowboy. In Indian Territory he had a reputation as a thief. His nickname, Limber Jim, stuck to him both sides of the river. Having grown up in the noise and grime of New York, Merrick tried his hand at anything that kept him beneath the western sky with enough money to satisfy his baser urges whenever he rode into town. Though he enjoyed stealing horses, he disliked violence and steered clear of ingratiating himself too closely with the McPherson brothers' criminal activity.

The next time Merrick saw the Benders was three days later, when he returned to spend the night. German mingled with the voices as Merrick sat down to join the group. Pa Bender had returned with the rest of the Slimps and the mood in the camp was cautiously optimistic. Satisfied that Merrick could be trusted, the Benders, particularly Kate, grew to enjoy his company. Over the course of the evening Merrick learned a great deal about the family, except what had happened to make them flee Kansas. Though the Benders never expressed remorse for their crimes, they must have been aware that the specific details of the murders had the potential to make them unpopular with other fugitives. The systematic murder of those looking for shelter, including that of eighteen-month-old Mary Ann Longcor, was a long way from stealing horses or robbing a stagecoach. Despite being vague about the nature of her crimes, Kate was not shy about bragging that every member of the family was armed.

"Winchester rifles and the new Smith and Wesson pistols, two apiece," she told Merrick with confidence. As the night wore on, John expressed an interest in Merrick's knowledge of the surrounding area, telling him the family wanted to stay near the Wichita River, where they had easy access to supplies.

"Ain't you afraid you'll be found out this close to Henrietta?" Merrick asked. John let out a shrill laugh.

"No," he replied. "Law don't like it past Red River Station and folks out here mind their business."

THE NEXT MORNING MERRICK SET OUT TO MOVE SOME STOLEN HORSES. Ten days later he returned to the Slimp cabin looking for a place to convalesce, having been shot through the shoulder by a disgruntled accomplice. To his dismay, instead of Kate he found Frank McPherson. Frank informed him that the family had changed its mind about staying near Henrietta, instead heading north across the Red River and up Beaver Creek into the Chickasaw Nation. With no one but Frank around to converse with, Merrick headed on to the open plains. Summer scorched the greenery from the landscape and the clothes of cowboys turned ochre with dust kicked up by their livestock. The Bender family moved further west to Wanderers Creek, where a large grove gave them protection from the weather. Outlaws from all walks of life came and went from the camp. Samuel Merrick did not see the family again until the winter of 1874.

Be Sure Your Sins
Will Find You Out

By the end of August 1873, Detective Beers was at his wits' end with Texas. After discovering the abandoned campsite at Mud Creek, his guide suggested they head into Clay County and question the residents of Henrietta. Beers agreed, though his experience with Missouri Bill left him deeply suspicious of everyone they came across. The residents of the county were tight-lipped until Beers promised them a portion of the two-thousand-dollar reward money, should they be able to assist in the capture of the Benders. A farmer who had settled near the banks of the Little Wichita proved particularly useful.

"Bill came through here couple weeks back," he told the detective, "said there was some German people come to this country with Frank. Asked me for money on account of they was in trouble."

Along with the farmer's testimony were a collection of eyewitness accounts. Some said the Benders had been seen on the Little Wichita at the beginning of August, others reported seeing Frank McPherson with the family on the Big Wichita not that long before Beers arrived in the town. Beers, aware of the impossibility of tracking and apprehending the Benders with just two people, returned to Denison to request help. "It is the prevailing opinion that the family is with Frank," he wrote to Colonel Peckham. "I want to go back on Wichita as soon as I can. Will you come down or write me immediately." The Benders once again seemed tantalisingly within reach of the authorities if only the detectives could gather the funds and the manpower. Peckham, desperate to start what he termed a "vigorous pursuit now in this direction [to] secure the parties," wrote to the governor in what would be his final appeal for help. All involved in the search clung to the hope that Governor Osborn would agree that the seven thousand dollars Pomeroy had used to bribe Alexander York should "be devoted to ferreting out the Benders." But Osborn was up for reelection and felt that devoting funds to a search that had yielded little result was harming his chances of a second term in office. In the late autumn of 1873, he demanded that Beers and Peckham submit their expenses and abandon the search.

Beers would later blame the governor's lack of co-operation for his inability to catch the Benders. The *Texas Democrat* made a less flattering assessment of the situation. Colonel Jacob Biffle, a Confederate war hero turned cattle rancher, informed the *Democrat* that he had spoken to the Bender family at Buffalo Springs in Clay County in July. The family then moved to a camp on the east fork of the Wichita River before heading north into Indian Territory. Launching a scathing attack on Beers, the paper accused him of "playing detective a good deal like the Bender woman kept tavern." He would go as far as Red River Station, get scared and come back to Denison, declared the article. Everybody in Montague County knew that the Benders were north of the Red River in Indian Territory, so why had the family not yet been "caught and burned at the stake"?

Back in Labette County, Leroy Dick received word that the official pursuit of the Benders had been called off and entertained the idea of setting out into Texas himself to locate the family. But when Beers returned to Labette and relayed his experiences in the region, Dick changed his mind. "I wrote to the Texas Rangers' headquarters in Austin soliciting their aid in bringing the notorious Benders from hiding," he recalled later. The Rangers suggested he write to Fort Sill, a government outpost in Indian Territory. The response from the fort directed him back to the Rangers. Dick was forced to conclude that for the time being "the search was definitely blocked."

NEWS OF THE BENDERS RARELY LEFT THE PAPERS. SO FERVENT WAS interest in the family that one blacksmith ran an advertisement for his services in the *South Kansas Tribune* under a large misleading headline reading BENDERS FOUND. A shop in Topeka went for a similar angle: "It is hard to find the Benders" read their advert, "but you can find all kinds of fruit jars at Angle's drug store." Three years later, the man who organised the advertisement was briefly arrested after being mistaken for Pa Bender. An exasperated Detective Beers arrived on the scene and confirmed that he was not. The family appeared in advertising as far east as Pennsylvania, where a newspaper informed its readers that any man who used perfume on his facial hair was "a vile compound of Judas Iscariot and the Bender family." Alongside the adverts ran intermittent reports that members of the family had been found or murdered. They varied from the reasonable to the outlandish. One article gave a detailed description of Kate emerging from the Wasatch Mountains with the spring thaw, naked and begging for food. But as more reports rolled in of innocent citizens being hounded by "some of the numbskulls that have been playing detective," public opinion turned against those in pursuit of the family. When one detective arrested a member of the Kansas Legislature after tracking him for nearly a year, it seemed authorities involved in the hunt were capable of arresting everybody except the true culprits.

Even the Pinkerton Detective Agency, one of the most infamous organisations of the late nineteenth century, had sent a man to look over the gravesite at Labette County. Agent Nathan J. Pierce took multiple stereoscopic images of the area, assured locals that when he encountered

Kate he would capture her with ease, and disappeared into the Wichita Mountains, where he was never heard from again.

THE SPRING OF 1874 WAS WET AND FERTILE, BRINGING THE PROM-ise of a golden harvest to settlers across the prairies. Rivers ran full and fast, spilling over into creeks where children caught fish, and those on their way out West watered horses and set up camp. In the early morn-ings, prairie iris unfurled like stars amid the grasses, each bloom to last only until sunset. Railway expansion continued unabated and the news-papers were crammed with advertisements for fresh produce and ice cream.

In Las Animas, a town on the Arkansas River in Colorado, a man was writing a letter to Governor Osborn. Fascinated by the Bender crimes from the outset, James Sullivan had spent weeks poring over the details of the case in the newspapers. Little is available about Sul-livan's history before he involved himself with the Bender search, but he was persuasive enough in his ability to locate the family that Osborn agreed to finance his attempt. Sullivan also befriended Alexander York, becoming privy to the detail that the McPherson brothers were involved with the Benders, something that was not public knowledge at the time. Knowing the McPhersons often dispersed stolen horses in Colorado, Sullivan travelled to the region to gather intelligence on the movements of the gang. Initially unwilling to risk his own life, Sullivan sent out a scout. The man returned less than three weeks later with a report that the Benders were two hundred miles from Las Animas in the Rocky Mountains. Sullivan took the news to nearby Fort Lyon but found that "all the soldiers were out on a scout and I cannot get any help here." Without assistance from the soldiers, Sullivan knew an at-tempt to apprehend the family would be futile. "I can make this cap-ture now," he wrote to Osborn, imploring that the governor send him one hundred dollars. Osborn sent the money but received no further updates.

———

ALEXANDER YORK HAD ALL BUT FORGOTTEN ABOUT JAMES SULLI-
van until the man turned up on his doorstep later in the year. Alexander
let him in after he announced that once again the Bender family was
within reach. Frustrated by his lack of success in Colorado, Sullivan had
taken a different approach to the case. He had written directly to Missouri Bill.

Make This Sacrifice
and All Will Be Right

The Benders had little trouble evading capture by sticking with their outlaw gang throughout 1874, but the number of settlers in the area was on the rise. Henrietta's post office reopened for business in July 1874, and the town later found itself the headquarters of law enforcement in the Texas Panhandle. Buffalo hunters flocked to the area and Sam Satterfield opened a storage yard for buffalo hide that was half a mile long. The Satterfield dry goods store proved an attraction for cowboys and hunters alike. Next to Red River Station, Henrietta was the best place for business west of Denison.

The outlaw gang kept their distance from the growing town and headed for the region of the Panhandle where the land rises into mesas covered with tough, verdant foliage. Settling at a bend of the Red River called Prairie Dog Corner, the size of the gang was constantly in flux. Kate quickly grew sullen and disenchanted with her outlaw lifestyle. Missouri Bill and the Slimps ensured the camp had a steady stream of supplies, but she had not expected to end up permanently on the run.

Setting up camp in the Panhandle during the summer of 1874 was a dangerous business, but it came with an advantage for the Bender family. Around them the Red River War raged between the U.S. Army and the

Kiowa, Comanche, Arapaho, and Southern Cheyenne. The conflict was the result of the federal government's refusal to enforce its end of the Medicine Lodge Treaty. Comprised of three treaties signed in 1867, the documents promised the Southern Plains Indians protection against white intruders in exchange for the relocation of the tribes to reservations. But the U.S. government failed to uphold its promise to provide the tribes with adequate food, and when buffalo hunters crossed into Indian Territory and began slaughtering the herds on which the tribes subsisted, the government did nothing to stop them. As conditions on the reservations became worse, the tribes headed out on to the Texas Panhandle and into the magnificent riddle of deeply etched canyons and searing rock formations known as the Caprock Escarpment. The escarpment forms the eastern border of the Llano Estacado and, with its vast system of winding chasms, provided an ideal refuge for the tribes, whose warriors were vastly outnumbered by the three thousand army troops sent out after them. With the military forces in the region focused on driving the tribes back on to the reservations, the Benders were the last thing on the minds of the authorities. Merrick later reported that the outlaws were constantly trading with tribes in the area, particularly the Comanche, who were always after more ammunition, just as the outlaws were after more horses.

AT RED RIVER STATION, BILL MOVED NORTH OF THE RIVER INTO THE Chickasaw Nation in an effort to avoid the authorities. The previous winter, he had served jail time for selling untaxed spirits, an experience that taught him his influence over local law enforcement was growing precarious. Already paranoid that a more permanent sentence was around the corner, Bill's fears were confirmed when he received James Sullivan's letter. In it Sullivan said that he knew Bill was connected with the family and that Frank "had been in company with them since their escape." Giving voice to Bill's own concerns, Sullivan warned him that he and Frank would never know peace unless they gave the Benders over to the authorities. He concluded by offering the outlaw a deal: lead authorities to where the Benders were camped and Sullivan would secure a pardon for Frank for the murder of Lucas Eigensatz.

A combination of paranoia and loyalty to fellow fugitives prompted Bill's decision to respond. He did not trust that Sullivan would allow his brother to go free, nor did he believe the authorities would leave them alone once the Benders were apprehended. But the possibility that the man could secure a pardon for Frank intrigued him and he sensed an opportunity to make money. Bill replied to Sullivan immediately, and confessed that he knew where the Benders were and that he would be co-operative for a pardon "and for a deed of money." He also stated that he did not expect to receive anything until after the Benders were caught, a magnanimous statement that ought to have made Sullivan suspicious. The two men arranged to meet on 10 December at Caddo, a sleepy railway station in Indian Territory. Bill did not send word to the Benders that someone new was on to them.

Sullivan wrote to Governor Osborn to confirm that his meeting with the outlaw was going ahead. Alexander York and Colonel Peckham had both expressed support for the plan, though they cautioned Sullivan against placing his full trust in Bill after his behaviour the previous year. Sullivan disregarded the warning, confident that the promise of a pardon for Frank would be enough to ensure that Bill kept his word. Frank's murder of Lucas Eigensatz had since passed out of the minds of Kansans, but news of the Benders still appeared on front pages nearly every week. Issuing a pardon for Frank seemed a small sacrifice to make. Osborn agreed and Sullivan set out with the pardon in the folds of his jacket.

ON 10 DECEMBER, BILL STOOD ON THE PLATFORM AT CADDO STA-tion. Snow fell heavy and unforgiving, obscuring all but the sound of the engine as it made its way down the track. Smoke rose from the train, casting a flume of grey among the white as it pulled into the station. A lithe man dressed not at all correctly for the weather stepped off the train and looked about in a state of nervous excitement. Bill approached the man and his assumption that it was James Sullivan was proved correct.

They remained in Caddo long enough for Bill to cast his eye over the pardon for his brother before suggesting they immediately head south to Texas to make further arrangements.

On the journey he informed Sullivan that the place where the Benders set up camp for the winter was four hundred miles west of Sherman, a town just south of Denison, whose turbulent history had done little to unsettle its place at the centre of trade in the region. Bill assured Sullivan that the Benders trusted him enough that there "will be no trouble in making the capture." He also promised that they would identify themselves as soon as they had been brought in by the authorities. Sullivan took his plan to the county sheriff who, swayed by the former's enthusiasm, agreed to send men to assist in the capture of the Benders once Bill had located the family. The following morning, Sullivan wrote to Osborn in high spirits. He was so certain that glory was on the horizon that he concluded with a very specific request.

"I do not think I would be asking too much of the authorities of Kansas to let me have charge of one of the members of the family to make a short trip through some of the largest cities of the Union, and I would be willing to let half the proceeds if there should be any to the people of western Kansas."

Parading one of the murderers throughout the states seemed a perfectly reasonable request to Sullivan, who felt he had sacrificed a great deal more than the governor gave him credit for. Despite Missouri Bill informing him the trip would take at least thirty days, Sullivan told Osborn it would be only "a few days" until the Benders would be captured alive. Buoyed by visions of crowds eagerly producing money to see one of the "Bender Ghouls," Sullivan took the letter to the post office and made final arrangements for the trip.

Satterfield's

Missouri Bill led James Sullivan towards Henrietta, unaware that John Gebhardt and several other members of the gang were in the area. At the Slimp cabin, the outlaws collected supplies to take with them when they returned to the plains. John was after more ammunition to trade with Native Americans in exchange for better horses. Samuel Merrick rode in after dark to join the group, intent on travelling back with them to the outlaw camp at Prairie Dog Corner. The men bundled into the cabin when the temperature dropped and lit a meagre fire as a poor defence against the cold.

"Bill says there's a man in town knows you're here," said Frank McPherson absent-mindedly. "Sullivan his name is. A detective." The mood in the cabin soured. "He's gonna fix it so he don't find us. Like he did with them others," Frank added, trying to rectify his mistake.

"How does Bill know?" Gebhardt asked, the words drawn out and slow like he thought the younger man was too stupid to understand. Frank shrugged and focused on warming his hands. An uncomfortable atmosphere stifled any promise of an entertaining evening, and the group turned in. Merrick awoke before the daylight to a sharp kick in the leg.

"We're goin' to Henrietta." Rage pricked at the edge of Gebhardt's voice. "Get a look at Frank's detective." Merrick didn't fancy riding back the way he came, nor did he like the idea of showing his face when a detective was about. Gebhardt and Floyd Slimp left for Henrietta without the others. Merrick packed as much as he could on to two horses and drank coffee until Frank woke up. The two men wrapped themselves up against the dry cold of the plains and set out for the camp at Prairie Dog Corner.

In town, James Sullivan had also risen early and told Bill he wanted them to start out for the Big Wichita as soon as possible. Sullivan was beginning to feel exposed, and Frank's pardon weighed heavy in the folds of his coat. He remembered Alexander York's warning that Missouri Bill was not to be trusted and tried to keep the man in front of him when they were riding. To comfort himself, Sullivan decided to stock up on ammunition before they left town. He finished breakfast and set out to Satterfield's dry goods shop.

BILL WAS NOT EXPECTING TO BE ACCOSTED BY JOHN GEBHARDT WHEN he sat down for breakfast at a saloon trying to pass itself off as a decent establishment. The younger man was tense and something feverish lurked in his eyes. Bill realised that Frank had let slip about Sullivan. As he recounted the correspondence and the possibility of earning money, Bill watched the man opposite him visibly relax.

"Where is he?" asked John.

Bill shrugged in the same manner as his younger brother. "Satterfield's, I guess. Wanted more supplies. Dressed *real* nice." Bill nodded in the direction of the shop. Though somewhat reassured by the man's explanation, John was still keen to set eyes on the man to judge whether or not he was a threat. Thanking Bill, he left the saloon and walked briskly down the street. Mist drifted in from nearby Little Wichita, softening the coming daylight and settling in the alleys between buildings. John slowed when he reached the shop. The front was slick with a recent coat of paint, the owner's name printed in stocky letters on a wooden sign that hung from the balcony. Through the glass John could see a man in animated conversation with the shop clerk, his clothes more suited to a town like Independence than the elemental backdrop of western Texas. Confident that he was unlikely to be unidentified without the rest of the Benders, John went inside. Sullivan was counting out dollar bills on the counter, all the while asking questions about the land west of the Wichita rivers. John hung back under the pretense that he was waiting to speak to the clerk. When Sullivan finally turned to leave, John gave him a polite nod as he passed. Sullivan reciprocated, his mind too focused on the task ahead to pay the man any real attention. John watched him until he turned down the street and out of sight.

"THAT GENTLEMAN DETECTIVE DON'T BOTHER ME," JOHN TOLD AN uncertain-looking Floyd as they climbed into the saddle later that afternoon. Samuel Merrick later recalled the exchange: "He told Floyd Slimp he was not afraid of that man, he was too stylish." Back at the camp, Floyd told Merrick he didn't think people would ever stop searching for the Benders.

OBLIVIOUS TO HIS CLOSE ENCOUNTER WITH A MEMBER OF THE BENDER family, Sullivan readied himself to continue the pursuit. Armed with knowledge and ammunition, he felt good about his chances when he and Missouri Bill set out once again. But when Bill returned to Red River Station in the new year, he was alone.

Information Wanted

The heavy snowfall of December 1874 settled on the boots of Mary Feerick when she returned to Kansas three years after her husband James went missing. Mrs Watton, the woman who was once her neighbour in Montgomery County, had finally told Mary the truth about the unidentified body in the Bender orchard. After a year of worrying that the information would be too upsetting for the young woman, Mrs Watton informed her that she was certain the body belonged to James. Mary boarded a train to Independence, already dressed in black mourning attire. The years since James's disappearance had been marred with grief, and she wore black for her husband and for their son. The boy had died while she was in New York. Alone and just twenty-three, she mourned the child and the dreams she and James had shared of raising a family out on the prairie.

When Mary arrived in Independence, she visited the office of the *South Kansas Tribune* and placed an advertisement in its pages requesting assistance from those who had helped to "disinter the unknown body." The notice received several responses, each confirming that the description printed of James's defining features matched those on the corpse. But, like Mary York, she wanted a definitive answer as to the fate of her husband. Travelling to the cemetery near Cherryvale, Mary Feerick requested that the county coroner give permission for the remains to be exhumed. He agreed, suggesting that Leroy Dick oversee the task. The bitter cold of many winter nights made the disinterment hard work. Persevering, the men broke through the soil and hauled the coffin to the surface. Mary was given the space to make the examination unobserved. Though the years had eroded the face she had fallen in love with, she knew that the features belonged to her husband. James Feerick had been a man with a distinctive appearance: red hair, broad cheekbones, and a canine that grew sidewise instead of straight. Mary informed Leroy Dick that the body was indeed her missing husband, and though the matter was a sad one, she was relieved to finally know what had become of him. Even though she had experienced tragedy in Montgomery County, she now had closure, and realised she still longed for a life on the frontier. Mary decided to stay in Kansas, and within the year she was married to a popular local carpenter by the name of Alfred Campbell. Together the couple raised two children in Coffeyville, a town just south of Independence.

IN THE YEARS FOLLOWING THE DEATH OF WILLIAM YORK, HIS FAMILY was busier than ever. Alexander, exhausted by ongoing court proceedings related to the Pomeroy case and the trauma of William's murder, wrote to the district attorney in charge of prosecuting Pomeroy and requested that the charges be dismissed. The newspapers agreed with the motion. "The truth is York and Pomeroy are in the same boat. Both are politically dead," declared the *Manhattan Beacon*. It took until May 1875 for the matter to finally be resolved, but peace was short-lived for Alexander. Less than a month later, his wife, Juliette, died unexpectedly and plunged the household into a state of mourning once again. To bring joy back into the family and to his children, Alexander opened up the York home to the people of Independence, hosting "moonlight socials," where lemonade and ice cream were readily available and the profits donated to charitable causes. The sense of community went some way to alleviating the grief he felt over his wife's death, but he still could not shake the escape of the Bender family from his conscience.

To distract himself from the horror of being the one to identify his brother's corpse, Ed also threw himself into the local community and his work at the family nursery, dividing his time between Independence and Fort Scott. In the autumn of 1875, he married seventeen-year-old Elizabeth Carter; *The Workingman's Courier* announced the news, wishing the couple a pleasant future. Ed was already a favourite of the regional newspapers, which reported him doing everything from playing in a baseball game against nearby Longton to taking part in a debate about whether science had done more for the advancement of civilisation than the Bible. Ed argued in favour of science, while arguing in favour of the Bible was William's widow, Mary.

WHILE IT BECAME CLEAR TO MARY THAT AUTHORITIES WERE LOS-ing faith that the Benders would be apprehended, she held strong to her belief that God would deliver vengeance upon the family. At first Alexander sought to keep her informed of developments in the search, but she found it hard to trust him, believing that his pride had allowed him to be easily deceived by the Benders. Reluctantly, she agreed that the couple's sons be sent to live in the care of their grandfather at Fort Scott. Long before his disappearance, William had made the request that the boys be raised by Manasseh if something happened to him, but Mary was still devastated by the separation. "The little girl I have kept with me," she wrote in 1875, "she with her baby sister were all I had left." Lulu, the child she was pregnant with during the ordeal, was born the October after William's body was discovered. For a brief period, Mary's heart was full again. Though she still grieved for her husband, the laughter of the two sisters began to mend the rift in her heart. But in November 1874 Lulu fell ill. When she died, Mary told herself that God had taken the little girl so that William would have company in the heavens. The thought brought her some comfort, but she now considered "the cords of affection sundered" between her and the rest of the York family.

With her eldest daughter, Bertha, in tow, Mary began to travel. She made her way across the Midwest, where she repeated her story to friends and new acquaintances. Recounting the events made her feel closer to William and assuaged her fear that he would be forgotten. Though everyone she encountered listened attentively when she spoke of her husband, they also pressed her for more details about the Benders. Mary loathed the ongoing fascination with the family. She had always intended to record the events for her children, but in 1875, angered by rumours and misreporting of the story, she published her account so that it was available to the public. Several newspapers noted its release and expressed interest in its publication. But when it was released, those eager for the more lurid details of the crimes and the family were disappointed. They found instead a deeply personal narrative filled with love and reverence for a murdered husband.

Soon after its publication, Mary left Kansas for good, returning to Illinois to live near her sister. The two girls had been orphaned as children, and Mary's sister was the only person who still felt like family to the bereaved widow. Bertha yearned for the bustling streets of frontier Kansas and longed to grow up alongside her brothers. As soon as she was old enough, she left her mother and returned to Fort Scott and the rest of the York family. Heartbroken and in need of security, Mary remarried. Though she never abandoned her faith, she resigned herself to an empty existence. Writing in 1875, she had come to a sombre conclusion: "I do not ever expect to understand, in this sad life, why God has permitted all these sorrows to come upon me."

The Bold Front of the Plains

Texas

1875

In the aftermath of the Red River War, the Bender family pushed further west, away from the buffalo hunters and cowboys that flooded into the region. They followed the Pease River until it deposited them near a point on the Caprock Escarpment described by Merrick as "very broken and bad to go through." Kate complained on a daily basis about life amid the rugged canyonlands and arroyos. The men's clothes she wore were soiled and ratty. Hair that was once the envy of her Labette County neighbours clung to her head in dust-matted curls. When Merrick arrived at the camp in the winter of 1875, he thought the authorities would be hard pressed to recognise her even if they did come across the colony.

"John and Pa's huntin' buffalo. Ma's asleep," she replied when he asked her where the rest of the family was. White outlaws milled around the camp, some of whom Merrick knew, others he could make an educated guess at. As the day drew to a close, a group of Mescalero Apache rode into camp. When the buffalo hunting party returned, the true size of the colony was revealed. Frank and John were pleased to see Merrick. Over a dinner of buffalo meat, Frank said he needed Missouri Bill to send provisions. Merrick was surprised. He had heard through cattle trail gossip that Bill was sick with pneumonia and the U.S. marshals had jumped on the opportunity to arrest him while he was unable to put up a fight or flee. Taken to the military prison at Fort Sill, Bill was transferred to the site's hospital when he showed no signs of getting better. When Merrick informed Frank that his brother was sick, the younger McPherson shrugged it off and continued outlining his request.

"He's gotta buy all the old pistols and guns he can get at Sherman-Denison." He punctuated his sentences by tearing at the buffalo meat. "From them plain shops that do 'em cheap." Frank wanted the goods to trade with the Indians. John explained that the deal had already been made; they just needed the arms and ammunition to fulfil their end of it. The goal of the white outlaws was to acquire better horses in larger numbers. In addition to the Apaches there were "a few Kickapoos and some Comanches from their camp at the Rich Lake on the Staked Plains," Merrick recalled later. They all wanted arms and ammunition. Merrick said he would take the message to Bill, though he wanted no real part in ac-

Buffalo hunters camp out on the plains and smoke the meat from animals shot earlier in the day. In the mid to late 1870s when the Benders and the outlaw colony were in Texas, they would have set up camp in a similar manner. *Harper's Weekly*, 10 March 1877.

quiring the items. Too many people were familiar with his face for him to be buying a town out of its firearms.

Kate was pleased to have a new person to complain to. "I hate living like a prairie dog," she hissed to Merrick. "No bed, no dresses," she spat. "And no money to fix up even a little bit."

"No matter how poor we get, Katie, we'll always be worth a thousand dollars apiece," John teased, then laughed at his own joke. Kate curled her lip and moved away from him. "Shame we can't see none of it."

The conversation turned to where the colony intended to head once Bill sent supplies. The Apaches suggested the Guadalupe Mountains, where the tribe still fought to hold out against encroaching white settlers. The Kickapoos were headed south to Old Mexico. John didn't like the idea of Mexico, "either the Gaudaloop or somewhere on the Staked Plains," he said, trying to settle the debate. Merrick thought all the options were risky and suggested heading north. There was a good place at the head of the Colorado River of Texas, he told them.

"A place a person might pass close to and never know it."

At sunrise the next morning, Merrick made preparations to travel to Fort Sill to see Missouri Bill. Pa Bender and John were carrying on a heated discussion, in a mixture of German and the older man's broken English. Before he left, Gebhardt warned Merrick that the family was going to relocate as fast as possible. Pa was worried that the current camp was too exposed for them to remain. Buffalo hunters operating in the area might mistake it for a hunting post or get ideas about alerting the authorities to the colony's whereabouts. Merrick agreed that on the open plain they were vulnerable, no matter how well armed and willing to fight they were. When he said goodbye to Kate, he found her bad temper from the night before had not improved.

Fort Sill had bad news for Merrick. Missouri Bill was dead. To keep his promise to the Benders, Merrick rode to Red River Station and located Bill's young wife, passing on Frank's request for guns and ammunition. She agreed to organise it, but told him it was the last thing she would do for Frank. *The Sedalia Democrat* announced the news of Bill's death with an observation that "it is probable that the influences of the wild country and of the men among whom he wandered at the time of his death did not serve to improve his character." The *Denison Daily News* told its reader that on his deathbed Bill said he "never committed an act he was ashamed of."

Restless Spirits

As the seasons turned into years, Governor Osborn continued to receive correspondence requesting descriptions of the Bender family from all corners of the United States. In a letter from Minnesota, a man named B. W. Simmons informed the governor that he knew a "desperate character" who had helped Kate Bender escape from Kansas. According to the desperate character, Kate was now in the company of the Osage, while the rest of the family bided their time before returning to Kansas. The man then boasted to Simmons that he was well acquainted with Jesse James and the rest of the James-Younger Gang, one of the most infamous groups operating on the American frontier. Simmons described his criminal acquaintance as of German descent, five feet eight inches (173 centimetres) in height with pale blue eyes. Osborn lost interest when the age was listed as between twenty and twenty-five. At the time of the murders, Gebhardt had been in his late twenties, and since the discovery of the murders, many criminals claimed to be associates or members of the family. By the end of his term as governor, Osborn resigned himself to the possibility that the Benders would never answer for their crimes.

————

LEROY DICK HAD COME TO A SIMILAR CONCLUSION, THOUGH HE STILL kept abreast of sightings of the Benders when they appeared in the papers. Some even warranted him sending word to inhabitants of Labette County to ask for help confirming whether suspects in custody were indeed the guilty parties. People were becoming increasingly inventive in methods of tracking the family, and the case was popular with spiritualists who channelled supposedly unidentified victims, claiming to know the location of Kate in particular. Dick read of one such incident in the papers in April 1876. A medium in Lawrence, Kansas, had entered into a trance and made the following pronouncement:

"I am Nathaniel Green, born in Decatur Illinois, murdered by the notorious wretch, Kate Bender, and buried under a manure heap. I come because I want to tell the people that Kate Bender has joined an Indian tribe near Utah."

The *Western Home Journal* gave the man the benefit of the doubt and deemed the information of interest if it were true, but the medium's claims were quickly forgotten. Over a decade later, spiritualism would find itself once again front and centre in the Bender murders when it was used as the basis for a trial that promised the Bender women would see justice after all.

Hell on the Border

Indian Territory
1877

D own in Chickasaw Nation, the sun rose over Wild Horse Creek, the water bright as mirrored glass. The creek lay on the trail between Fort Arbuckle and Fort Sill. Though Fort Arbuckle became obsolete as a military base after construction of the larger Fort Sill, it remained a popular site for settlers of all races who were looking to build a life in an area where they would largely be left alone. People formerly enslaved by the Indian Nations came together to form self-governing, all-Black communities, where profitable agricultural practices allowed for the development of other Black-led enterprises. They were joined by those who fled Southern states, where the practice of sharecropping left many unable to provide food for themselves or their families. Though not all towns were successful, life in the region was initially relatively free from the racial violence Black communities experienced on other parts of the frontier. More than fifty settlements existed in Indian Territory during the latter half of the nineteenth century before the introduction of Jim Crow laws began to drive Black communities from the area.

———

ON THE BANKS OF THE CREEK, SAMUEL MERRICK WAS PREPARING to spend the day driving stolen horses across into Texas. He was in between visits to the Bender camp, having spent a brief stint as a guide for the Texas Rangers before deciding he preferred the freedom of choosing where he went. With him near the creek was Babe Mahandy, a twitchy cattle thief who had narrowly escaped the jailhouse two years earlier. Merrick kicked dirt over the remnants of the campfire and climbed into his saddle. The two men bickered over whether to keep to the trail. Mahandy was certain that soldiers from Fort Sill would already be out to track them down and was desperate to use a route that took them through land with better cover. He was also worried that the Native Americans from whom ten of the horses had been stolen would come after them themselves. Merrick was unconcerned.

"Won't be nobody out this early," he chided the younger man. "We see anyone, we'll just roll off." When he guided the animals towards the trail, Mahandy grumbled and fell in beside him.

They had been riding less than an hour before a figure appeared, cut out against the greenery of the spring prairie. In a panic, Mahandy jerked his horse off the trail towards a thicket that indicated the presence of a creek. Startled by the sudden movement, the remaining animals spread in a way that made them conspicuous. Merrick groaned and set about driving them down towards the creek bed where Mahandy had taken refuge. The two men circled back towards Arbuckle. When dusk descended on the plains, they made separate camps. Neither lit a fire.

THE SAME EVENING, A GROUP OF COMANCHE ARRIVED AT FORT SILL to report that ten horses had recently been stolen from the tribe. They spoke to Lieutenant James Parker, describing in great detail the markings on each individual horse. When news came in that a group of horses matching the description had been spotted on the plains earlier in the day, Parker set out to track down the thieves. He rode to Fort Arbuckle to enlist the help of a man more familiar with the area and the habits of its outlaws.

Upon arriving at the fort, Parker called on Robert Pettus for assistance. Pettus was a former buffalo soldier, the nickname given to Black regiments of the U.S. Army by the Native Americans who encountered them during the Indian Wars. The primary duty of the buffalo soldiers was to control the Indigenous people of the Great Plains, but they also escorted stagecoaches, built forts, and policed areas where white outlaws like the McPherson brothers and Samuel Merrick profited off illegal trade with the tribes. Pettus had been in the area since 1872, when he was part of the regiment that constructed Fort Sill. There was no one better equipped to pursue the outlaws.

"I am no longer in the employ of the government," Pettus reminded Lieutenant Parker when the man approached him with the task. After leaving the army, Pettus dabbled in cattle rustling himself and wanted to avoid ending up in a court of law, even if it was for the prosecution. But the horse thieves were proving themselves to be a persistent nuisance to everyone in the area, so he agreed to go after them. Pettus set out before daybreak the following morning. With him rode two fellow Black settlers, John Boyd and Thomas Jefferson, and two Native Americans, Jim Nelson and a man referred to only as Thomas. Pettus was armed with a Winchester 1873 carbine, a rifle designed to fire the same ammunition as the revolver he also carried with him. The streamlining of ammunition combined with the lever-action repeating nature of the firearm earned it the title "The Gun That Won the West." Pettus later testified that the other men carried "a pistol apiece." None of the men were officers, and though Parker set out with them, he split from the group in order to cover more ground.

BY LATE AFTERNOON, RAIN MISTED THE AIR. PETTUS AND HIS MEN tracked the horses for thirteen miles. At last they came across the animals, spots of colour against the grey sky. A sorrel mare with white stockings was tied to a large, dark bay. Occasionally the animals tugged at the rope and shook their heads. Pettus rode through the group, his gaze fixed on the surrounding landscape. A quarter of a mile away, something dipped below the horizon. Pettus gestured to the men to advance, indicating the movement near a line of trees; he was reluctant to move quickly on what he suspected to be the horse thief, lest he vanish into their depths. Drawing closer, his suspicions were confirmed when the movement revealed itself to be Merrick.

The outlaw watched the group and knew they had come to take him to Fort Sill. Still far enough from the forest to consider himself exposed, Merrick turned his horse and began a gentle trot towards cover. Pettus cursed and picked up the pace of his own animal. The men beside him drew their pistols. At the sound of increased movement behind him Merrick bolted for the trees.

"Stop!" roared Pettus, breaking into a gallop as Merrick vanished into the trees. The group raced after him. Ahead, Merrick ducked and weaved, appearing at intervals between the columns of trees. Branches tore at faces and clothes. Men cursed and horses pulled at their reins, frustrated by the pocketed undergrowth of the forest floor.

"Run him on to the prairie," Pettus called over the commotion. The group separated, peeling away from each other to better surround the outlaw. Boyd and Jefferson closed in on Merrick as tightly as the trees would allow, sending him careening towards the open prairie. When they exploded from the tree line, Pettus opened fire. A great whooping and shouting rose from the others. Gunfire filled the spring afternoon, scattering birds and animals. Unable to return fire and with no obstacles to put between himself and the riders, Merrick knew there was no hope of outrunning them. To the west he spotted a cabin, close and solid enough for cover. The stink of horse breath and sweat replaced the smell of gunpowder. Flanking him on both sides and too close to fire, Pettus and his men pressed the outlaw between them. Reaching for the reins, Pettus again ordered the man to stop. Merrick wrenched the animal violently to the right, rolled from the saddle, and crashed to the earth amid pounding hooves and furious shouts from the riders. Crawling from the chaos to his feet, he sprinted towards the cabin. Dirt thrown up by bullets clattered on the door as he slammed it shut. He moved quickly through the rooms in search of guns and ammunition. He found both. Two children watched him silently from beneath a large oak table. When women's voices cried out from beyond the cabin, the youngest began to sob.

OUTSIDE, PETTUS SPAT AND HANDED THE REINS OF MERRICK'S SKIT-tish horse to Jefferson with orders that he begin to round up the other animals. The rest he instructed to surround the house. He, too, had heard the cries and intercepted the women as they tried to make their way to the front entrance of the cabin. With some coaxing he persuaded them to keep their distance. Pettus dismounted. Boyd and Thomas reholstered their guns, unwilling to risk firing and hitting one of the children.

"I have orders from Lieutenant Parker to escort you to Fort Sill," Pettus called to the man in the house. "If you give yourself up peacefully, you won't be harmed." In the silence that followed, he advanced slowly on the cabin. Merrick appeared suddenly in the door and Pettus felt the searing pain in his arm before his mind registered the gunshot. A tree was the unlucky recipient of the rest of Merrick's fire. The agitated outlaw retreated back inside.

"Got provisions in here to last a month," he crowed, knowing that realistically he would be unable to hold out for more than a day. Pettus saw to his arm and listened as one of the women tried to persuade Merrick to let her inside to fetch the children. He declined, and an uneasy silence settled over the homestead. As the rain came down harder, Pettus repeated the promise that Merrick would not be hurt if he gave himself up with no further trouble.

"You be kind enough to give me my horse and the two of them others that's roped together," came the response. "You and your boys can take the rest of them animals back to the good lieutenant."

Merrick had no desire to put the children in harm's way. His reluctance to give them up stemmed solely from the knowledge that they were the only thing preventing him from being shot at. Pettus declined his proposition. Merrick shouted back that he was willing to die in the cabin. The men were gridlocked by concern for the safety of the children, and their adrenaline fizzled out into frustration. Pettus elected to leave Boyd and Thomas on-site while he rode out to inform Lieutenant Parker of the situation. By the following morning, Merrick had given himself up. He threw his guns from the cabin door, announced his intent to exit the building, and emerged chewing on a strip of newly fried bacon.

THE NEXT TIME ROBERT PETTUS SET EYES ON THE MAN WHO SHOT him, Samuel Merrick was clapped in irons at Fort Sill ready to be transported to the more formidable Fort Smith to stand trial. A gloomy Merrick asked to see the wound inflicted by his bullet and seemed genuinely sorry he had caused such an injury. The jailhouse at Fort Smith was just seven feet high (213 centimetres), comprising two rooms below ground level in the foundations of the courthouse. With no separate cells for inmates, petty thieves and detained witnesses shared the same flagstone floor as violent murderers and rapists. Grated windows tucked under the veranda porches of the building above offered little light and even less ventilation. Straw mattresses rotted in the damp conditions and the stench of waste was so bad in the summer months that it plagued those who sat on the courthouse benches.

When Samuel Merrick arrived in Fort Smith for his trial, he would have found himself one of up to eighty men crushed into the unsanitary space. Along with the miserable conditions of the jail, those detained at the fort took little comfort in the knowledge that they were to be tried by Judge Isaac Parker. Now known in popular culture as the "Hanging Judge" for his liberal use of the death penalty, Parker had recently become the district judge of the United States District Court for the Western District of Arkansas, a court that also had jurisdiction over Indian Territory. It was a monumental task. In his first year alone, Parker sentenced eight men to death and established his reputation as a man unafraid of coming down hard on criminals. But he also oversaw the recruitment of Bass Reeves, the first Black U.S. marshal to serve west of the Mississippi River. Reeves was a former enslaved man who escaped during the Civil

War and fled to Indian Territory. With his knowledge of the terrain and ability to speak several Indigenous languages, Reeves proved a glittering asset to law enforcement in the region.

IT WAS THE END OF AUGUST WHEN MERRICK FINALLY APPEARED BE-fore the court. In an atmosphere thick with heat and the smell of the jail, he listened patiently as the charges were read out against him. He was to be charged with two counts of larceny and one count of assault with a deadly weapon. The first of the larceny charges involved one horse to the value of one hundred dollars, the property of James Williams, a white settler. The second encompassed ten horses to the value of fifty dollars each, stolen from a Native American by the name of Hoan-a-to-sah. Merrick took the stand to explain that the horses were acquired through a legitimate trade and it wasn't his fault that he had bought stolen horses. The explanation did not satisfy the jury, who sentenced him to a year for each case. Last came the assault charge. Robert Pettus took the stand and gave a detailed, unemotional account of the day he had been shot, repeatedly referring to the safety of the children as the reason he had initially been unable to apprehend the suspect. In his defence, Merrick informed the court that Pettus failed to inform him he was under arrest until he had barricaded himself in the house out of fear for his life.

"I was riding leisurely along a trail near the timbers when those men saw me. One of them set up a whoop and started galloping and shooting at me without giving no reason," he stated for the record. Merrick's easy-going demeanour and unwillingness to admit wrongdoing did him no favours in court. The jury found him guilty and he was sentenced to two years of hard labour for the assault.

TWO YEARS LATER HE WAS TRANSFERRED FROM FORT SMITH TO the Detroit House of Correction. The prison was nine hundred miles north-east of the court and received a steady stream of criminals sentenced in Indian Territory. Though Judge Parker could have sent inmates to closer institutions, he favoured the conditions at Detroit, believing that the prison operated with the intent to reform those within its walls. "The whole system of punishment is based on the idea of reform, or it is worse than nothing," he wrote in a letter to the attorney general in 1885. But when Samuel Merrick arrived, the only thing on his mind was how to get out of there, no matter the cost.

Part V

BENDER OR BUST

OFFICE OF THE SUPERINTENDENT
DETROIT HOUSE OF CORRECTION
SEPTEMBER 20TH, 1879.

Dear Sir,

I have a man confined here who claims to know where the "Bender" family are, who I think could be induced to disclose their whereabouts for a much less consideration than was offering. Should you think it best to pursue the inquiry further I will give you every assistance in my powers. I feel satisfied this man knows much about that gang that might be turned to give account should you deem it worth your time. I would like your reply. If any action is proposed find an honest person as whispering machines permeate the whole county.

Very Respectfully Yours,
Jos. Nicholson, Supt.

The Way I Became Acquainted with the Bender Family Is This

AUTUMN 1879

In the Detroit House of Correction, Samuel Merrick was talking freely about his time spent with the Bender family. With his laid-back demeanour and penchant for storytelling, Merrick quickly found himself a favourite with prison officers. His tales of life as an outlaw in the Panhandle eventually brought him to the attention of the prison's superintendent. At first Joseph Nicholson wrote Merrick off as a bored prisoner looking for attention. But Merrick spoke with such casual familiarity about the Benders that Nicholson became convinced he was telling the truth. Deciding to take the matter further, he wrote to the new governor of Kansas, John St. John. Nicholson also wrote to the Pinkerton Detective Agency but was perturbed to discover they believed the family to be dead. Their reply ordered Nicholson to keep the information secret but did not divulge any details of how or where the family had been killed. Nicholson thought the response was suspicious and he expressed this sentiment to the governor, hoping to get out in front of any correspondence between the two parties that might dissuade further investigation into Merrick's story.

WHEN GOVERNOR ST. JOHN OPENED THE LETTER WITH THE RE-
turn address of the Detroit House of Correction, it had been six years
since the discovery of the bodies at the Bender family homestead. In the
boxes of Governor's Correspondence sat hundreds of letters with supposed information concerning the whereabouts of the family. Some offered absurd theories, while the more optimistic simply offered their
services. St. John, a charismatic man with a sharp mustache and stead-
fast dedication to his moral compass, took the ebb and flow of Bender-
related news in his stride. Satisfied that the letter was sensible, he wrote
back suggesting that the man conduct an extended interview. Unlike his
predecessors, Governor St. John could not be convinced into action without quantifiable evidence.

OVER THE NEXT MONTH, MERRICK WAS INTERVIEWED SEVERAL TIMES
by Nicholson to ascertain just how much he knew of the Bender family
and their whereabouts. The two men developed a healthy respect for
each other, though the latter would write to the governor that he was
certain Merrick "was at one time more intimately connected with the
gang than he cares to tell." Privately Nicholson suspected Merrick of
having designs on Kate, the only member of the group he bothered to
describe in any physical detail. From the outset, Merrick showed no hesitation in detailing the movements of the fugitives throughout the mid-
1870s. He gave first names and surnames, directions to the mile, and
aliases used by the family when they went into populated areas. But he
also advised Nicholson that going after the Benders was a dangerous
endeavour in an unforgiving landscape. When Nicholson suggested the
soldiers stationed at forts in and around the Panhandle could be used to
apprehend the family, Merrick shook his head.

"The soldiers won't fight," he told the superintendent. "I've been
scouting with 'em more than once and they won't do it."

Nicholson was disturbed by the revelation, but it explained why the family had been at large for so long. Without the soldiers, any group setting out after the Benders was at an immediate disadvantage. When Nicholson asked Merrick to write a statement for the governor, the outlaw reiterated the sentiment. "A man's life wouldn't be worth more than a cartridge for he would be killed," he warned, before concluding that any man venturing into the region "must be well armed and of the gun at least Cal. 45 to 50 [with] plenty cartridges."

AS THE SNOW FELL HEAVY AND SILENT ON THE GROUNDS OF THE prison, Samuel Merrick wrote a second, longer statement for Governor St. John. Despite it being a comprehensive account of his time spent with the Benders, Merrick was careful to paint himself as an observer, not an accomplice. He described living with Missouri Bill, and how Floyd Slimp introduced the Benders as his cousins. He wrote of Kate's disdain for life on the plains and Frank McPherson's incessant bragging about the murder of Lucas Eigensatz.

"They have either gone further south on the Staked Plains or in the Gaudaloop Mountains," Merrick stated in his concluding paragraph, adding that it was also possible they followed the Kickapoo to Saltillo, a town south of the Mexican border. If the Benders remained on the plains, he explained, then they would get their supplies from Fort Concho or Fort Stanton. If they had returned to the red shadows of the Caprock Escarpment, their supplies would come in from Henrietta, likely through a network of characters that ensured the family did not have to show their faces in the town. Though the Slimp family had long since left to pursue farming elsewhere, Merrick guessed that at least one of the boys still knew the location of the Benders. He considered it likely that the family themselves were disguised as buffalo hunters. When he last saw them, all four carried "the big 50," a Sharps .50-calibre rifle designed specifically for killing buffalo. At the time the Benders were on the run, buffalo hunting was beginning to reach its peak. A decade later, the last of the great herds would be gone.

SAMUEL MERRICK'S WRITTEN ACCOUNT WAS DETAILED ENOUGH TO be used as both a tool to track down the family and to corroborate existing knowledge of their crimes and accomplices. Perhaps Merrick believed it was simply too difficult to catch the Benders and so had no qualms about giving over information in exchange for early release. But it is also possible that during his time in prison Merrick learned the appalling truth about the nature of their crimes and decided they did deserve to hang. In the first of his statements he advised that "whoever goes will have to be a good frontier man and understand the Indian ways and will have to rough it." In the second statement, he scribbled a postscript in which he offered to catch them himself:

"THE ONLY WAY TO TAKE THEM WITHOUT A BIG FIGHT WILL BE TO get in with them and get everything fired then drug them. It can be easily done in their coffee. I could do it."

Strife and Agitation

Kansas

DECEMBER 1879

Governor St. John prided himself on being a man who didn't suffer fools when it came to the Bender case, and Merrick's second statement convinced him the prisoner was telling the truth. The sheer volume of information contained within its pages alone would have been sufficient, yet one small detail convinced him above all others. The presence of Frank McPherson. Several weeks before his correspondence with Superintendent Nicholson began, another envelope landed on the desk of Governor St. John. Inside was a letter saying that Frank McPherson, "a fugitive [who] committed cold blooded murder in the city of Parsons," had been spotted in Texas. St. John wrote immediately to Alexander York, certain that a serious breakthrough in the case had at last been made.

ALEXANDER YORK READ SAMUEL MERRICK'S STATEMENT SEVERAL times over several days. He was alarmed to discover that the account corresponded exactly with reports written by Detective Beers and Colonel Peckham cataloguing their time in Texas. Again Alexander regretted that the search had been unable to continue unhindered in the months directly following the discovery of his brother William's body. The window of opportunity for enacting justice on the Benders seemed to always be shrinking, and Alexander still felt he was responsible for allowing them to escape. He suspected that in the years between Merrick's imprisonment and his decision to give up what he knew about the Benders, the family had either moved on or been killed. Alexander's own experience corresponding with Texas law enforcement also gave him little confidence that the family would ever be apprehended. Regardless, he returned the statement to the governor with a letter confirming the accuracy of the report. In it, he listed the information contained in Detective Beers's report that corroborated Merrick's account.

In his initial investigation, Beers had traced the family through Indian Territory to Denison and then across to Red River Station, "at which place Beers had an interview with McPherson," noted Alexander. From Missouri Bill, Beers learned that the Benders had gone west on to the frontier of Texas. Alexander omitted the disastrous chase through the country that Bill led the detectives on before they realised they had been duped. For Alexander, the key to accepting the credibility of Merrick's statement was the appearance of James Sullivan in the winter of 1874. "Sullivan mentioned in Merrick's statement visited me at Independence and went from there to Texas in search of them. I have never heard from him since," he told the governor. Though Sullivan had made a brief appearance in the newspapers as a false identity used by Governor Osborn to skim state funds, his involvement in the pursuit of the family was not public knowledge. It infuriated Alexander to think that the man was within reach of John Gebhardt but had not known it. Even more disheartening was that Sullivan had fallen into the same trap Missouri Bill laid for the detectives that came before him.

"I have never had any doubt that the Benders fled South and West," he concluded, then advised that the governor send the documents to the Pinkerton Detective Agency. For Alexander it seemed like the only reasonable avenue to pursue. But Governor St. John remembered Nicholson's letter informing him that the Pinkertons claimed the family was dead and wanted nothing more to do with the case. Instead he wrote to authorities in Texas, where he encountered the same disinterest Leroy Dick experienced in 1873. It was clear that Texas authorities considered the fugitives to be the responsibility of Kansas and Kansas alone. Tracking the family in such a treacherous region of the state would take weeks, and there was always the possibility of discovering that they were already dead, rendering all funds and lives risked in the search a waste. Disheartened, St. John kept Samuel Merrick's statements in the hope that they might one day be used to locate the Benders.

THE SUMMER AFTER MERRICK GAVE HIS STATEMENT FOR THE GOVernor, a frenzy of reporting erupted around an elderly couple in jail in Nebraska who had confessed to being Ma and Pa Bender. But when the hapless pair were transported to Labette County and the prospect of being hanged suddenly seemed to be a reality, they admitted the confessions had been a hoax informed by newspaper reports of the murders. In the aftermath of the so-called Bender Boom, Charles Morris, the man who had once worked as Governor Osborn's secretary, spoke to a journalist from *The Emporia Ledger* to repudiate the claim that the search for the Benders had long since been called off. Morris told the reporter that over the years the executive office of Kansas had accumulated reliable information as to the whereabouts of the Benders. Documents including reports and ongoing correspondence sat "in the pigeon holes of the Governor's office, all tending to show where the Benders have been at different times, and the impossibility of arresting them." The *Ledger* assured its readers that Osborn and St. John had evidence as to the family's whereabouts over the years, but that both were forced to reach the same conclusion: apprehending the Benders was impossible without assistance from the military.

AS 1880 DREW TO CLOSE, SAMUEL MERRICK'S TERM OF IMPRISONment in Michigan was coming to an end. Both he and Superintendent Nicholson had grown frustrated when the correspondence with the governor dried up. With the man due to be released, Nicholson wrote to

St. John one final time, offering to send Merrick to Topeka. "He is quite confident of not only being able to identify them, but also to find their hiding place, and put the authorities in position to affect their capture," he promised the governor. But St. John simply echoed the sentiment published in the *Ledger* several months earlier. The venture was too risky and hard to co-ordinate. Even with a man like Merrick, who knew the frontier and the family, success was not guaranteed.

In December, a North Carolina newspaper printed a fanciful account in which Kate Bender was alleged to have donned men's clothing and joined a vengeful party that bayed for her execution. In Michigan, Samuel Merrick walked out of the prison and into obscurity. But nearly a decade after Merrick's release, it appeared as though the Bender women had returned from the high plains of Texas of their own volition.

Dreams and Detective Work

——

1889

It was late summer and the people of Kansas gathered at county fairs to mark the passing of the season. Attendees bartered over pumpkins, marble cakes, maize, peppers, tobacco, ginger biscuits, and pickled pears, while judges awarded prizes in a number of food categories. In the afternoons, people congregated along the edge of racetracks for the day's entertainment, their pockets full of sugared treats. At more than one fair across the state, crowds cheered a horse named Kate Bender over the finish line.

Over in Labette County, local officials were in heated discussion over what to do about another Kate Bender. Since the early summer, letters had been arriving from Niles, Michigan, informing them that the Bender women had been located. Their author demanded that the women be arrested and charged with the crimes. Frances McCann had dedicated nearly four years of her life to her pursuit of the Bender women, and she was determined that they not be allowed to escape justice again.

BORN AROUND 1851, FRANCES MCCANN WAS ORPHANED AT AN AGE too young to remember her parents. She spent her childhood in an orphanage in Iowa, where she grew into a compassionate but stubborn young woman driven by what *The Oswego Courant* would later describe as "the desire to find out something about her parents and what became of them." When she was old enough to leave the orphanage, she married and settled with her future husband in McPherson, Kansas. At just four feet ten inches (147 centimetres), with penetrative grey eyes and prominent bone structure, Frances made a strong impression on all who crossed her path. The *San Francisco Examiner* introduced her to its readers as a "slight, agile little woman and a veritable composition of nerve and animation."

A lively member of the community, Frances had a reputation as an eccentric; she held firm to a belief that she possessed psychic abilities. A self-styled clairvoyant healer, she claimed to be able to treat her patients by putting her subjects into a trance, often with the use of a magnet. Her supposed abilities were not dissimilar to the talents Kate Bender advertised to the citizens of Labette County, though when questioned on the issue, Frances went to great pains to make sure reporters knew that she was not a spiritualist. But like spiritualists, those professing to have clairvoyant abilities found it easy to take advantage of vulnerable, impressionable people. Genuine belief in psychic powers could also be equally damaging to individuals who believed they possessed them.

WHILE RESIDING IN KANSAS, FRANCES CAME ACROSS A WOMAN BY the name of Sarah Eliza Davis. Touched by Sarah's plight as a single mother of three children, Frances endeavoured to help her by hiring her as a washerwoman. A slight woman whose former beauty was still evident when she laughed, Sarah quickly proved herself a difficult person to get along with. During her employment with Frances, she was obstinate and evasive when answering questions about her past and muttered to herself as she went about her tasks. Frances found the behaviour suspicious and became fixated on the woman. Speaking to the newspapers in 1889, she explained that the origin of her investigations into Sarah's criminal past came to her in the form of a dream in which

Frances witnessed the murder of a man by two women, whom she took to be mother and daughter. Distressed, she shared the dream with Sarah. *The Oswego Courant* imagined Sarah's supposed response in particularly vivid terms:

"Mrs Davis jumped to her feet, held both hands high above her head and exclaimed: 'Don't tell any more of that story; it is no dream but a reality and I know all about it. The man murdered was John Sanford your father, and he was killed by my half-sister. I was present and so were you. You was only about three years old.'"

It was a staggering revelation for Frances, but Sarah would not elaborate on the matter and frustrated Frances by pretending the exchange had not occurred. When Sarah fell ill with a fever, Frances took the opportunity to make daily visits to her under the guise of administering treatment. Sarah, later described by her defence attorney as an "ignorant, superstitious woman," allowed Frances to attempt to treat her using a magnet. The same lawyer claimed that Frances had then hypnotised Sarah using the magnet in a bid to get her to divulge more information about the murder of John Sanford. Sarah recovered from her illness and, horrified by her behaviour, refused to answer any further questions on the subject. The situation escalated when Frances, "guided by influences," became convinced that Sarah Davis was Kate Bender.

In his personal account of the events that transpired in 1889, Leroy Dick omits the dream as the inciting incident. He states instead that Sarah accidentally let slip that her mother was Ma Bender when complaining about the conditions she lived in. Sarah refused to elaborate until she fell ill, and then, with "a fever-heated brain," she confessed to knowing the truth about Frances's parents and the Bender family.

SHORTLY AFTER HER ILLNESS, SARAH FLED TO MICHIGAN TO ESCAPE Frances's continued harassment of her and her children. Frances was certain the woman was fleeing because she was guilty. Undeterred, Frances followed Sarah, leaving her own family for months at a time in order to keep Sarah under surveillance, sometimes concealing herself in out-buildings for hours. Sarah was living with her mother, Almira Monroe.* Almira was a stooped, short-tempered woman, and it was an easy jump for Frances to come to the conclusion that she was Ma Bender. Her belief was bolstered by the local gossip that painted both women as dishonest and criminally inclined.

WHEN FRANCES FIRST WROTE TO LABETTE COUNTY AUTHORITIES proclaiming that she had found the Bender women, County Attorney Morrison dismissed her as a "crank" and told the papers she was "la-bouring under a delusion." But when a letter landed on his desk from the sheriff of Niles in support of Frances, Morrison capitulated and wrote to the governor of Kansas: "I expect it will turn out another hoax, but there is sufficient in it that I think action should be taken." The man in the governor's office in 1889 was Lyman Humphrey, the long-time friend of Alexander York and the man who had organised the petition demanding help in the search for William back in 1873. He, too, was unconvinced by Frances's investigation, having developed a deep aver-sion to all things supernatural in the aftermath of the Bender murders. But the matter was already in the papers and Frances was an engaging enough storyteller that it continued to gain traction.

Beset by the idea that Sarah and Almira would escape while Labette County authorities decided what to do, Frances concocted a scheme to have at least one of the women arrested. Then events unexpectedly played into her hands. Sarah approached an officer and informed him in no uncertain terms that Almira was Ma Bender. It did not take much to persuade the incensed Almira to file a phony larceny charge against her daughter. Almira accused Sarah of stealing a frying pan, several pewter plates, and a pair of baby's stockings. But after realising what she had done, both she and her daughter attempted to flee. They were caught on

---

* Almira is alternatively referred to as Almira Monroe and Almira Griffith throughout 1889 and 1890.

the outskirts of the town and thrown into the jailhouse at Niles to await Sarah's larceny trial.

LEROY DICK WAS AWARE OF FRANCES MCCANN'S STORY WHEN HE was summoned to the Labette County sheriff's office in the autumn of 1889. Since the spring of 1873, when he had been present at the unearthing of the bodies in the Bender orchard, Dick had occupied a variety of administrative positions in Labette County. He retained his good humour, but sixteen years of life on the Kansas frontier had worn the cheery, open face of his youth into one lined with experience and responsibility. County Attorney Morrison had already been to see the women, dismissing them as "a family of the criminal class" who did not match the description of the Bender women enough for the matter to be taken further. But Morrison had never met the Benders and it was decided that someone who knew the family should be sent. The sheriff informed Dick he was to travel to Michigan to view the prisoners, but Dick thought the entire narrative was nonsense. "I was mad as a bumblebee," he recalled later, "told him in straight language [that] the Benders were in Texas." Instead of arguing with Dick, the sheriff tried a different tactic. He asked the man in front of him if he would be kind enough to look at some pictures. Producing an envelope from his drawer containing tintype portraits, he laid them one by one on the desk. Shocked, Dick pointed to the one that showed Almira Monroe.

"That's old Mrs Bender!" he exclaimed, picking it up and squinting at the likeness. The next morning, Dick was on the first train to Michigan.

A Siege of Examination

Niles, Michigan
OCTOBER 1889

A town with a rich and varied history, Niles in the late 1880s was booming. Situated on the banks of the St. Joseph River, it had once been a stop on the Underground Railroad, a network of trails, safe houses, and individuals who helped thousands of Black people escape the bonds of slavery. In the aftermath of the Civil War, the town grew as an agricultural centre and its streets hummed with activity. Upon his arrival in Niles, Leroy Dick was greeted by Sheriff Wrenn, and the two men went to Wrenn's house for supper. Dick had not yet met Frances McCann but, certain the woman in the tintype was Ma Bender, was eager to hear more about the circumstances of the Bender woman's arrest.

"What I don't understand is why the old woman brought that charge against her daughter," he told the sheriff, unable to see what purpose the charge served for a woman whose best interests were in keeping herself as far from the law as possible.

"I reckon Mrs McCann and her detecting got her frightened. Figured she'd beat the law by stating in court that Sarah is the real Kate Bender. Dump all those murders in Kansas on her girl." Wrenn took a long drag on his cigar. In the minds of the public, though all four members of the family were involved in the murders, it was Kate who had been the ringleader and thus the one responsible for the crimes. Accusing Sarah of being Kate came with higher stakes than the accusation that her mother was the older Bender woman. Almira knew that if she could put enough distance between her and her daughter, she just might escape the noose herself.

As the time drew closer to midnight, Wrenn invited Dick to accompany him on his nightly rounds of the jailhouse. He suggested that Dick wait on the stairs, where he could see the women but they would be unaware of his presence. Jumping at the opportunity to make a positive identification in person, Dick followed the sheriff out the door and into the cold air of the Michigan night. At the jail, he walked as quietly as he could behind the sheriff, then waited as he heard the key to the cell turn in the lock. Unable to make out the face of the younger woman, Dick moved on the stairs. The noise prompted Almira to turn in his direction, and Dick found himself staring into the face of a woman he was utterly convinced was Mrs Bender.

"That heavy old figure, that peculiar squint as she peered out were too characteristic to allow me any further doubt," he told an excited Wrenn over breakfast.

THAT EVENING, DICK RETURNED TO THE JAILHOUSE, INTENT ON tricking Sarah and Almira into disclosing their true identities. Both women treated him with suspicion. Sarah, who was nursing a young infant, did her best to make light of the scenario using provocative humour, but her attempts fell flat. It did not take long for both women to ask to speak to Dick alone. Almira pressed a newspaper clipping about the discovery of William York's body into his hand, telling him she knew that Sarah was the very Kate Bender responsible for his death. In turn, Sarah accused Almira of being Ma Bender, professed her own innocence, and begged Dick to protect her and her child. Each woman, desperate to secure her own freedom, saw no way of doing so except by hurling the other into the line of prosecution. Sheriff Wrenn, happy to do anything that would stop the bitter quarrelling between the pair, agreed to hold them in separate cells.

In the weeks leading up to the larceny trial, Leroy Dick developed his own theory concerning how the Bender women had come to be in Michigan. Patching together eyewitness testimony from their acquaintances, he concluded that the women had returned from the outlaw colony separately. Ma and Pa, now older and unsuited for life on the run, made plans to return to Michigan. Pa then abandoned his wife at a train station, and she never saw him again. Disheartened, the older woman returned to Niles and to life as Almira Monroe. Kate left the colony after falling for an artist who came across the group by accident. The two settled in McPherson, Kansas, but the man abandoned her when she fell pregnant. It was during this time that she was employed by Frances McCann and revealed her true identity as Kate Bender. Exposed for the murderer she was, Kate fled to Niles, where she reunited with her mother. It was a neat theory that, on the surface, supported the claims of Frances McCann.

ON 22 OCTOBER, A SOUR-FACED SARAH DAVIS STOOD IN FRONT OF a court in Niles. The rumours that Sarah and Almira were the Bender women had drawn curious spectators from the local area, and the courtroom was busier than usual. Watching the proceedings carefully were Leroy Dick and Frances McCann. McCann had written to the governor of Kansas several days earlier, imploring him to agree with the results of her investigation. She finished her letter with a request that the women be "made to confess fully as to a knowledge of the murder of [my father] John William Sanford." Frances thought the Kansas authorities owed her at least that much.

FROM THE OUTSET, THE TRIAL WAS AN UNMITIGATED DISASTER FOR Sarah and Almira. Their willingness to accuse each other of appalling crimes made them unsympathetic but highly entertaining on the stand. *The Evening News* out of Emporia, Kansas, informed its readers that Sarah poured forth "blood-curdling and horrible revelations" that made it impossible for Almira to be anyone other than Mrs Bender. The revelations had started as soon as the trial began. When asked what she had to say in response to the charge of larceny brought against her, Sarah snapped back that it was a false accusation.

"Ma gave me those things when I was married. She don't want me here for that. She wants me mixed up in this Bender business."

Almira did not lose her composure and several newspapers later remarked that she remained "cool and calm" for the majority of the trial. Almira told the judge that her daughter was Kate Bender and she herself knew nothing of the crimes but what had been printed in the papers. The judge replied that the crimes in Kansas were not the matter at hand, then turned his attention back to Sarah. With the Bender crimes off the table, Sarah changed her tactic. Clutching her child in her arms, she tearfully told the court that she was so frightened of her mother that stealing from her would be unthinkable.

"She's threatened my life ever since I was a girl," she declared. When the judge asked her to elaborate, Sarah recounted an episode in her childhood when Almira had beaten a neighbourhood child to death. Unable to dispose of the body by herself, she took the then ten-year-old Sarah with her and forced the girl to watch as she dumped the other child's remains in a nearby swamp.

"Said I'd better not tell no one otherwise she'd do the same to me."

The story was so upsetting that the court descended into chaos. Above chatter that prickled with outrage, Sarah and Almira spat insults at each other. By the time the judge called the room to order, Sarah was in tears. Seated beside Leroy Dick, an open notebook on her lap, Frances McCann felt in her heart that the years spent dedicated to following the two women had at last been vindicated.

AS THE NEXT TWO DAYS UNFOLDED, IT BECAME APPARENT THAT Almira's plan to escape justice by throwing her daughter into the line of fire was collapsing. She was not as sympathetic as her daughter, and the snowballing of accusations levelled at her by Sarah and the judge caused her to become increasingly belligerent. Any pretense that the larceny charge was the purpose of the trial had long since been abandoned, and *The Parsons Daily Journal* referred to the matter as a "case arranged by detective for the purpose of drawing out the history of the past lives of the two women." Informed by the detective work of Frances McCann and Leroy Dick, the judge subjected Almira to intense questioning about her previous husbands. Dick had discovered through interviews with Almira's other daughters that she was once married to a man named John Flickinger. Flickinger bore a close enough physical resemblance to Pa Bender that Dick saw no issue in telling the judge they were one and the same. Conveniently for Dick, Flickinger was dead and unable to defend himself.

On the stand, Almira gave a comprehensive account of the many times she had been married, guessing the number to be around seven. Some Almira left, others left her. More often than not a mutual dislike drove them apart. When asked about her first husband, Almira told the court that one day the man simply collapsed and died. To the consternation of Leroy Dick, she denied ever being married to a German. In the closing hours of the last day of the trial, the judge asked her again. Again she denied it. Frustrated by her obstinance, the judge confronted her with the new information.

"Mrs Monroe, at what time were you married to a German by the name of John Flickinger?" The judge's question plunged the room into silence. Almira tensed up, an expression of fear appearing on her drawn features.

"I've been married so many times it's no good tryin' to remember them all," she finally retorted. Though she refused to say any more on the matter, the damage was done. By hiding her marriage to Flickinger, Almira made herself appear guiltier than ever. It was enough to convince everyone in the courtroom that she should be taken to Kansas and subjected to further questioning. The women were released, permitted to briefly visit their families, then rearrested at gunpoint by Leroy Dick, a deputy sheriff, and Frances McCann. Sarah's four children were not yet old enough to fend for themselves so were taken from their mother and dropped at a local poorhouse. Only the youngest went with Sarah. She was given permission to keep the child with her because she was still nursing.

By the time the women arrived in Kansas, Almira had been accused of all manner of heinous crimes. According to the newspapers, not only was she responsible for the murder of John Sanford, Almira had also killed an old beggar woman, burned a child to death, bludgeoned a husband with the handle of an axe, poisoned her son, and attacked a pregnant daughter-in-law in a jealous rage. The *Chicago Tribune* confidently declared that "Mrs Monroe has had seven husbands and a number of them have mysteriously disappeared." None of the papers bothered to explain how she had avoided being charged with any of the crimes. The rumours were bolstered by Dick's accounts of his detective work in Michigan, stories he was more than happy to relay to reporters. Though there was unanimous consensus that Almira was a "ghoul in human form," public opinion, particularly in Kansas, was growing increasingly divided over whether she was Ma Bender. "The story as told by Sheriff Dick is a very sensational and probably over-drawn one," wrote a wry reporter at *The Wichita Star*, before concluding that exciting times lay ahead for those in the newspaper business.

Evidence Against Them

Oswego, Kansas
NOVEMBER 1889

Leroy Dick knew that the problem with convincing the people of Kansas that Sarah and Almira were the Bender women was that many of the state's inhabitants believed that the entire Bender family was already dead. Since the family first disappeared in the spring of 1873, reports that they never made it out of Kansas continued to surface in the newspapers. Some whispered that the Benders were hunted down and executed by a vigilance committee. Others were certain that Ed and Alexander York returned to the cabin after the initial interview with the family, slaughtered them, and dumped their bodies in the Verdigris River. The York brothers had even threatened legal action against a man who claimed to have been with them while the act was carried out. Alarmed that they had been accused of such behaviour, the family issued a swift rebuttal through the press in which they promised to call upon the man behind the rumours and "request proof of his statements." They also offered two thousand dollars to anyone with evidence that the Benders were dead, a testament to Alexander's belief that the family was still at large. *The Leavenworth Times* told its readers that if a vigilance committee had disposed of the family, its members would not have spoken of the act. "The ordinary vigilante never gives anything away," in order that he may retain his place as a model member of society, read a column dedicated to the fate of the family. Death, it ascertained, was the only possible answer to the fate of the Benders. They were simply too stupid to have evaded the authorities for so long.

The Oswego Independent was not so sure. The paper agreed to publish a local attorney's offer of five hundred dollars "to any person or persons who can and will give satisfactory proof to the legal authorities of Labette County that the Bender family [. . .] was ever captured by any party of men and put to death." It was an opportunity, promised the article, for those men who wished to make the papers believe they knew more than the average man about the Benders to come forward and make a "snug little sum." All those in the know had to do was show the authorities where the family was buried. No one came forward to claim the reward.

ON THE TRAIN JOURNEY FROM MICHIGAN TO LABETTE COUNTY, Sarah Davis tried repeatedly to convince Leroy Dick that she was not Kate Bender. Later, Dick would use her ever-changing stories as evidence that she was trying to cover up her role in the murders. Frances McCann was ignored by Sarah and Almira, who addressed her only when they felt like issuing a threat. Labette County authorities had been eager to keep the identity of the prisoners a secret to avoid crowds causing disruption on the journey. But it did not take long for Dick to confide in the other passengers that they were on board a train carrying the women thought to be Kate and Ma Bender. Soon the entire train was abuzz with the news. When it pulled into St. Louis, reporters pushed their way on to the cars, wrestling with one another for a sighting of the women or a chance to speak to Frances. She revelled in the attention, talking "glibly of her impressions and dreams and her detective work." Her direct manner impressed reporters, who were surprised that such a small woman contained so large a personality. To avoid giving Sarah and Almira the chance to speak to reporters, Dick had the women escorted to a waiting room. A writer for *The Fort Scott Daily Monitor* caught a glimpse of them as they were ushered back on to a train to Kansas City. "The two women were dressed in plain, dark clothes, both wore veils which were pulled down over their faces the entire time they remained in the depot." At the stations where Almira did have the opportunity to engage with reporters, they found her in good spirits. After a brief exchange with her, one correspondent from *The Pittsburg Dispatch* sent a telegram informing the paper that Almira "treated the whole matter as a huge joke." Sarah's little child gurgled and laughed, endearing herself to reporters and other passengers alike.

THE PRISONERS AND THEIR ESCORTS STEPPED OFF THE TRAIN AT Oswego to a sea of curious spectators. If Leroy Dick and Frances McCann expected a hero's reception for their supposed apprehension of the Bender women, they were disappointed. As soon as reports came down the telegraph wires that an arrest had taken place in Michigan, the Kansas newspapers resurrected the debate over whether the family had been killed. Though they did not necessarily agree on where their bones lay or who was responsible, many were so convinced that vengeance had already been enacted that they worried for the fate of the prisoners. For those who were yet to make up their mind as to whether Sarah and Almira were Ma and Kate, catching sight of the two on their way to the Oswego jailhouse was their first opportunity to see the women in person. To their dismay, many returned home less certain than before. Summoned by the sheriff, older citizens who had shared the prairies with the Benders drifted in and out of the jailhouse, having been given the chance to speak to the women before any legal matters began.

AS THE CLOCK CREPT TOWARDS MIDNIGHT, THE EDITORS OF *THE Oswego Courant* worked quickly to set the type for the following day's edition. Having been permitted an interview with Sarah and Almira, they had come to the conclusion that the prisoners were not who Frances McCann and Leroy Dick wanted them to be. Between them, the two would-be detectives had indulged in an absurd fabrication that endangered the lives of two innocent women. Those who read the front-page article the next morning were told that Sarah, distressed and exhausted, showed only the characteristics of someone who had "seen much trouble, hard work and exposure." She bore no resemblance to the "gay and festive Kate Bender who was so popular with frontiersmen" during the time she lived in the area. Almira was "a typical Yankee woman" who could not be Ma Bender because the latter was obviously German both in manner and in speech. Several of the witnesses brought in to speak to the women had returned home via the newspaper office to give their opinion that the women were not the Benders. The paper reprinted the knowledge with confidence, assuring its readers that if there was even a possibility of truth to the accusations, they would be more than willing to see the women put on trial. It was not so kind to Frances McCann. The *Courant* accused her of hounding Sarah Davis, manipulating her through false acts of kindness, and being proud that she had abandoned her own children in favour of her bid to prosecute the two women. After a description of Frances's dream, it attacked the newspapers for encouraging her delusions. Those who read the *Courant* were left with two solid conclusions: Sarah and Almira were victims, "poverty stricken women being dragged over the country to produce a sensation." Frances McCann was a fraud.

A NERVOUS ATMOSPHERE SETTLED OVER OSWEGO IN THE LEAD-UP to the preliminary hearing. County Attorney Morrison set the date for 1 November. Privately he hoped that the matter would be dismissed before it was even brought to trial. Morrison sent for Silas Tole, the elder of the two brothers who lived closest to the Bender family. Silas had also been among the men who dug the victims out of the earth. The attorney placed great weight on the man's personal knowledge of the Benders. When Silas arrived at the jailhouse, Morrison told a correspondent from *The Oswego Independent* that "if Tole does not identity Mrs Davis as Kate Bender, then I shall believe we have the wrong parties." After half an hour of conversing with the two women, Tole emerged and shook his head.

"Those aren't the Bender women. Apart from the height there's nothin' similar about Kate and Mrs Davis." When asked about Almira he simply replied, "That old woman don't resemble Mrs Bender at all."

Though the statement was enough to convince Morrison, Frances McCann was disinclined to entertain the possibility that she had made a mistake. When the newspapers printed stories that she had offered Sarah and Almira fifty dollars each to testify against each other, she remained undeterred. The *Independent* remarked that Frances had "more determination concealed about her small body than is usually vouchsafed a community of women." It agreed with the *Courant* that the prisoners were working-class women who had devoted most of their lives to raising children. The week before the hearing it ran the headline MRS MCCANN GETS REVELATIONS FROM THE WRONG SPIRITS. But in spite of the efforts of the papers to discredit Frances McCann, Leroy Dick was able to produce witnesses who supported her claims. The possibility that Sarah and Almira were not the Bender women was not an option for Dick. Still harbouring guilt that the murders continued for so long in a community he was charged with protecting, he had at last been presented with an opportunity for closure that he was not willing to give up. The sixteen years that had elapsed since the citizens of Labette County stood in the orchard planted with bodies looked increasingly as though it would work in favour of the prosecution.

ON MONDAY, 18 NOVEMBER DEFENCE ATTORNEY JOHN TOWNER JAMES made the last of his preparations before setting out for the Labette County Courthouse in Oswego. James was in Arkansas when he heard that two women accused of being the Benders were in need of representation. Knowing that the case was high profile, he travelled to Oswego to interview the women, where he became convinced that they were innocent. Neither Sarah nor Almira had the expenses to pay for legal counsel, so James agreed to represent them without payment. Writing of the hearing in 1913, he gave his reason for accepting the case pro bono as "trusting in the reward of the future which will always come to the worthy lawyer." But both he and his fellow attorney, Judge H. G. Webb, knew that they were in for a difficult fight.

The time drew closer to ten o'clock and the courthouse crackled with anticipation. Amid the crowd of faces new and old were those who remembered being present at Harmony Grove schoolhouse sixteen years ago, in the spring of 1873, when the county did not yet know that the Benders were responsible for bloodshed. The hearing drove a wedge between those who identified the women as the Benders, those who were certain they were not, and those who struggled to come down on either side of the argument. Delilah Keck and her mother-in-law, Henrietta Dienst, sat side by side and avoided discussing Kate Bender's harassment of their family. Silas Tole entered and sat awkwardly among his peers. Also present were John Handley, the freight hauler whose large dog spooked the family into asking him to leave, and Doctor G. W. Gabriel, who frequently had to deter his patients from believing Kate had spiritual powers. In its report of the hearing, the *Labette County Democrat* drew attention to the "fair portion of ladies" in the audience. The gender imbalance was enough that James also recalled the number of women in his memoirs written twenty years later.

AT TEN O'CLOCK, SARAH DAVIS, HER LITTLE GIRL, AND ALMIRA Monroe were escorted into the courtroom by the sheriff. Almira showed no interest in the whispers that moved around the room behind her. The little girl tugged at her mother's hair and chuckled when Sarah tried to shush her. Both women knew the trial in Michigan had been a sham. But after being presented to the staring faces in the Labette County courtroom, Sarah was suddenly overcome with fright. As the judge opened the hearing, she grew pale and clutched her daughter tight against her chest. Those who believed she was Kate Bender took it as a performance to garner sympathy.

Before the hearing, it had been decided that the women, if they were

An illustration of Sarah Davis and her daughter in the courthouse at Oswego, Kansas. Taken from *The Benders in Kansas*, an account of the Bender murders and the trial of 1889, written by Sarah and Almira's defence attorney, John T. James.

the Benders, would be charged with the murder of William York, the most high-profile victim of the Benders. At the hearing, Judge Webb, the second defence attorney, admitted that William's body had been discovered at the Bender homestead. The statement waived the need for the court to be subjected to an extended description of William's life and the circumstances of his death, something both defence attorneys knew would swing the mood of the room against the women. All that was left for the court to decide was whether Almira Monroe and Sarah Davis were Ma and Kate Bender.

After nearly ten hours of testimony, the identity of the women was more in dispute than it had been at the start of the day. In a turn of events neither side had expected, far more witnesses claimed to recognise Sarah as Kate than were able to place Almira as Ma Bender.

Charles Booth, the first witness for the state, squinted hard at Sarah before announcing that she bore an "awful striking" resemblance to Kate Bender. He was qualified to say so, he explained, because he was a cook at the hotel where Kate worked a brief stint as a waitress. In 1872, he and Kate had attended a dance at Big Hill, where he constantly reminded his friends that she was his date. When asked about Almira, Booth shrugged. He had never encountered Ma Bender.

Next came John Handley. "That is Kate," he announced. When he pointed at Sarah her expression dropped. "And that," Handley turned his attention to Almira, "is old lady Bender." Handley's self-confidence earned his identification of the women affirmative mutterings from the crowd. When Delilah Keck took the stand, she struggled to look both women in the face. After giving a brief history of her acquaintance with the family, Delilah told the court that Sarah shared the same high cheek-bones and mannerisms as Kate. She apologised to the judge that she was unable to identify Almira.

"I knew the old man, John and Kate, but Kate was the one I knew best," she concluded after cross-examination. Later in the evening, her mother-in-law, Mrs Dienst, gave a more detailed description of Kate Bender.

"I saw the girl Kate twice. She had very nice auburn hair done up in a roll once and plaited the next time." Mrs Dienst said that while Sarah did somewhat resemble Kate, she was not willing to state unequivocally that they were the same person. Throughout the day, the colour of Kate Bender's hair had established itself as a major point of contention. Several witnesses, including Delilah, claimed that Sarah's dark brown hair made her a perfect match for Kate Bender. Others stated that her hair was the very reason she couldn't possibly be Kate. Eventually the matter became so heated that one unfortunate witness was accused of being colour-blind.

AT MIDNIGHT, EXHAUSTED SPECTATORS FILTERED FROM THE BUILD-ing and steeled themselves against the winter air. But exhaustion was no impediment to gossip. Two testimonies in particular had gripped the imagination of those in the courtroom. The first was the statement of Rudolph Brockman, the stocky German who had first welcomed the Benders to the area, and then three years later found himself at the end of a noose. Brockman told the court that the women were not the Benders. Along with Silas Tole, Brockman was one of the few in the region who were genuinely acquainted with the family. On the stand he was initially composed, offering detailed descriptions in answer to questions regarding the family's appearance.

"Kate had a full face, high cheekbones, a big mouth. Not like this lady." He gestured towards Sarah. Brockman also recalled a scar below her left eye that he suspected might have been a burn. Though he was fairly certain that Sarah was not Kate Bender, he was absolutely sure that Almira was not the old woman.

"Old Mrs Bender was much bigger than this lady," he told the prosecuting attorney. "They weren't no Americans neither. That old lady didn't speak a word of English."

Leroy Dick was visibly agitated by Brockman's testimony, and he shook his head when the matter of language was raised. At the evening recess those who disagreed with Brockman reminded others in hushed tones that he was once suspected of being an accomplice to the crimes. In the days following the trial, papers like the *Labette County Democrat*, which sided with the prosecution, omitted the parts of Brockman's testimony that suggested the women were innocent.

The good that Brockman's statement had done for the defendants unravelled with the last witness testimony of the day. Maurice Sparks was a farmer who had lived in the region since 1870. During the trial, he was considered to be a key witness, having interacted with the family on several occasions, though it later transpired he had never spoken to Kate or Ma. On the stand he confirmed that Kate had a scar below her left eye. Asked to inspect Sarah's face for a similar mark, he stepped down to look at the defendant. After a moment of consideration, he announced to the court that yes, Sarah Davis also bore a mark in the same place. The observation threw the courtroom into stunned silence. On the stand Sarah clenched her jaw, but the tears she had struggled to keep under control all day finally spilled over.

Bound Over

Oswego, Kansas
1889

Darkness still lingered in the thickets of the prairie when the court-house opened its doors for the second day of the hearing. A great many more people tried to squash themselves between the benches, having heard from neighbours that the case against Sarah and Almira was heating up. Several spectators pointed at the two women, speculating loudly as to whether they were the murderers. Under the strain of the previous day's session, Almira's composure was beginning to weaken. Her mouth twisted at the accusations being levelled at her from the crowd. Sarah started fighting back tears as soon as she entered the courtroom. She sat on the bench with her child clutched against her chest and avoided looking anywhere but the floor. Frances McCann returned to her perch beside the prosecution and readied herself for the testimony of Leroy Dick. Dick, who spent the previous weeks making his opinions on the women known to all who would listen, took the stand with an air of ostentation. After a long description of his various roles within the community of Labette County, he offered a list of notable occasions on which he had interacted with the Benders.

"I have sufficient remembrance of the Bender family as to distinctly remember how each one looked," he concluded in a clear, solemn tone.

"And have now, in my mind, how the women looked at that time I knew them."

Almira glowered at him. Sarah did her best not to look up. Both the women and the defence attorneys knew that Dick's testimony could act as the deciding factor in the hearing. The newspapers picked up on it, too, reporting that "the testimony of Dick was of the most importance and damaging to the defence." Dick remained one of the most well-respected citizens of Labette County. In the minds of the people, he was in a unique position to comment, as the three hammers with which the Benders had murdered their victims were still in his possession. At the urging of the prosecution, Dick described the scene of the crimes. An uneasy hush settled over the room as he relived the day the bodies had been drawn out of the earth. He let the sadness linger long enough to penetrate the minds of those present. Then he informed the court that though she denied it, Almira Monroe spoke perfect German.

"When I first talked with the old lady before me in Michigan, the exchange was in German."

Almira shot to her feet at the accusation. As Dick continued, she thought better of interjecting and sat down with an unintelligible mumble. He told of how when questioned in Michigan about their whereabouts during the early 1870s, neither woman was able to offer a satisfactory account. When asked if he thought Sarah and Almira were the Bender women, he turned to the defendants, then to the prosecuting attorney.

"They are Mrs and Kate Bender. I have no doubts as to it."

DEFENCE ATTORNEY JOHN JAMES ROSE TO CONDUCT THE CROSS-examination, opening with a request that Leroy Dick give a detailed description of Kate Bender. Dick obliged, detailing a woman barely out of her teens, with auburn hair, hazel eyes, a large mouth, and a sprightly demeanour. It was obvious that the description could not be applied to Sarah Davis, even when the sixteen years passed since the crimes were taken into account. James knew that Dick's own feelings of guilt, the enthusiasm of Frances McCann, and the chance to finally play a starring role in the downfall of the Bender family had all contributed to the man's belief that they were guilty. But James also knew that Sarah and Almira had done themselves no favours. On multiple occasions, often in front of other witnesses, both women had tried to convince Dick that the other was guilty.

UPON FIRST MEETING THE WOMEN, JAMES CURTLY INFORMED THEM that if they continued to tell stories they would end up on the gallows. James was openly critical of Dick's behaviour throughout the trial, later remarking that his testimony "did not bear analysis by the trained legal mind." He placed equal blame at the feet of the district court for failing to subject the man's motives to an appropriate level of scrutiny.

By the end of Dick's time on the stand, his statements amounted to little more than a smear campaign against both women. He pointed to Almira's multiple marriages as evidence that she was bad-tempered and irresponsible, hinting strongly that more than one had ended in a mysterious death. When questioned about Sarah's guilt, he repeated that her attempts to blame her mother were evidence enough. The *Labette County Democrat* praised his efforts under the headline PRETTY STRONG TESTIMONY.

Yet as witness after witness was called for the defence, the mood in the courtroom began to change. Silas Tole told the court with absolute conviction that the defendants were not the Benders. Dr Wright, a doctor who occasionally supplied Kate with medicine, testified that Kate Bender was much taller than Sarah Davis. After Almira was ordered to converse openly so that her voice might be heard, three more witnesses stated that her English was too good and too natural for her to be Mrs Bender.

"My name is Almira Monroe an' I was born Almira Hill in Cattaraugus, New York," she began. As she relayed the history of her life, those in the courtroom were surprised to find her an engaging speaker whose prominent sense of humour undercut her testimony. But she struggled under cross-examination, where her answers became lost in a jumble of dates, names, and places. When asked about Leroy Dick, Almira did not hide her anger.

"I don't speak German and I never have," she replied. "Don't have a clue about whatever language that man says he heard me speak and don't you dare say that I ever lived in Kansas or was the wife of some John Bender." Almira was even angrier when the prosecution revealed that they were aware she had served a prison sentence at the Detroit House of Correction.

"That's not yours nor the court's business," she huffed. Abrasive towards any further questions, she was dismissed. Almira returned to her seat flustered and defensive.

Sarah took the stand after her mother. Reporters noted that her daughter "played around as if nothing was being done, not knowing that if her mother is identified as Kate Bender it means life imprisonment or death on the gallows." Despite exhibiting more emotion throughout the trial than Almira, Sarah's testimony was recorded in the papers as being "very direct and straight, differing from Mrs Monroe, who several times made conflicting statements." She recounted the events of her life in chronological order, including her time spent in Wild Fowl Bay, Michigan, which accounted for her whereabouts during the period the Bender murders were committed. Sarah married several times and was widowed twice, and her life was a patchwork of misfortune and poverty. She had married again in the summer of 1889, but the man now refused to support her on account of the charges, and her three children were currently in the Poor Farm at Berrien County.

"I never said my mother was Mrs Bender," Sarah said, "though I did say that if she were the type of person to have her own daughter arrested, she weren't no better than old Mrs Bender." She was dismissed without cross-examination and the closing statements from both sides were read.

In the two hours the counsel took to deliberate, those in the courtroom drifted outside, where they debated the matter among themselves. Like the witnesses, opinion was almost perfectly divided. In total, seven of the sixteen witnesses had positively identified the women as the Benders, seven had declared they were not, and the remaining two were unable to come to any conclusion. When news came that the counsel had reached a decision, the eager populace crushed themselves back into the courtroom.

TO THE DISMAY OF THE DEFENCE, THE JUDGE DECLARED THAT THERE was enough evidence to hold the women until the next term of court began in February, when they would then be charged with the murder of William York. James was furious but unsurprised. In his memoirs, he acknowledged that "with so many reputable and respectable citizens testifying that they were the Bender women," the result was a foregone conclusion. It did not seem to matter that three of the witnesses for the prosecution had been members of the Dick family, one of whom had never even met the Bender women. James also knew that with a similar pool of witnesses likely to be called for the trial, the possibility of a death sentence for the two women was very real, and he did his best to console Sarah and Almira. As the town prepared for Christmas, he returned to Fort Smith and began gathering evidence, desperate to prove it was logistically impossible for either woman to have been involved in the Bender murders.

Hope Gone

Winter settled cold and bright on Labettē County, and the citizens of Oswego developed a fondness for the two incarcerated women who were starting to relish their status as unusual local celebrities. While the nearby towns of Parsons and Cherryvale leaned more towards believing Sarah and Almira to be the Bender women, the majority of Oswego deemed the whole situation to be a farce. Encouraged by the newspapers *The Oswego Independent* and *The Oswego Courant*, law enforcement relocated the women from the jailhouse to the house of a local resident, where they were treated kindly by the family. At Christmas, when Sarah's child fell ill with pneumonia, the local doctor arrived to check in on the girl and brought with him "a small doll and a sack of sweets." Sarah cheerfully informed reporters who called on the women that she received regular letters from their defence attorney updating her on the evidence being accumulated to secure their release before trial.

Despite the promising news, Sarah and Almira continued to withhold information from their attorneys, often out of embarrassment surrounding certain events that had unfolded in their lives. Out of James's direct influence, they restarted their habit of accusing each other of criminal behaviour. An exasperated James later referred to Sarah as "the most colossal liar of my experience in criminal practice." Her lying extended beyond the case. In January, Sarah informed the sheriff that she was pregnant and in need of new clothes. The sheriff, sympathetic to her plight, afforded her an allowance with which to purchase what she needed. When the doctor appeared several days later to check her condition, it became apparent that Sarah was not pregnant. *The Parsons Weekly Sun* called her a "gay deceiver," the *Parsons Daily Eclipse* advised readers that should they wish "to mention the matter to Sheriff Wilson, do so at long range."

JAMES ARRIVED BACK IN OSWEGO WITH THE LAST OF THE WINTER and a "pocket full of affidavits." His own investigations into Sarah's and Almira's history had yielded plenty of people willing to testify to their whereabouts during the early 1870s. Most important among the documents he carried were those relating to Almira's term in the Detroit House of Correction. Almira was admitted on 18 May 1872 and discharged on 24 March 1873, and her sentence covered the period in which the majority of the Bender crimes were committed. She had been convicted under the name Almira Shearer, having married Chauncey Shearer in Michigan in December 1869. Almira purposefully omitted her marriage to Shearer in court out of fear the conviction would be discovered. She had been charged with manslaughter, but reluctantly confided in James that the circumstances of the case involved an abortion. Ashamed of the charge and knowing it would affect the way she was viewed in court, Almira had done her best to conceal the evidence that eventually became her alibi. Alongside the documents from the House of Correction was an affidavit from Daniel Perry, the man from whom Almira had rented a house during 1870 and 1871, in Jackson, Michigan.

As early as November, correspondence between the sheriff of Labette County and the sheriff of Huron County, Michigan, had all but confirmed that Sarah Davis was also innocent of the charge of being Kate

Bender. Sarah had given information that she lived at Wild Fowl Bay with her husband, Hiram Johnson, between the years of 1871 and 1873. The sheriff of Huron County set out to investigate and found multiple people able to corroborate her story. Among them were former neighbours and the doctor who had delivered and then helped bury her infant daughter, Belle, in November 1873. After considering the evidence, James came to the sad conclusion that a life defined by poverty had taught Sarah to look out only for herself and her children, but it had also left her vulnerable to manipulation.

Before visiting County Attorney Morrison, James spoke to a correspondent from *The Sedalia Weekly Bazoo*. "It would be difficult to imagine a stronger case of alibi than these affidavits make, all of them from good and reputable citizens. I am satisfied that when I present this proof to the prosecuting attorney, he will agree with me as to the impossibility of these women being in any way connected with the Benders." James was right to be full of high spirits. When he presented his evidence to Morrison, the attorney was relieved to finally have tangible material evidence with which to dismiss the case.

On 10 April, James filled habeas corpus proceedings so that Sarah and Almira might finally be released. In court, the affidavits confirming the identity of the two and their whereabouts during the period of the Bender murders were read aloud. Almira apologised for not revealing her marriage to Chauncey Shearer at an earlier date. Sarah, under orders from James, stayed quiet until the charge was dismissed. With clear evidence that the court no longer had jurisdiction to hold the women, Sarah Davis and Almira Monroe were freed. *The Lawrence Weekly Journal* and *The Lawrence Tribune* took a dim view of those involved in the prosecution, suggesting that "if these unoffending women had 'inflooence' there would be suits for false imprisonment." Leroy Dick was incensed by the sudden turn of events. When he recounted the events in 1934, he claimed that all the documents related to their release were fraudulent. No doubt he was inspired by Frances McCann, who reached a similar conclusion when others came forward later in an attempt to claim the reward for themselves.

IN THE DAYS AFTER SARAH AND ALMIRA WERE PUT ON A TRAIN
back to Michigan, Frances arrived in Oswego and demanded she be
shown the evidence that resulted in their release. The local officials were
surprised to see her, as a recent dispatch from Sarah in Michigan claimed
that Frances was sitting in jail, having been arrested for her role in the
affair. Frances laughed at the dispatch, but she was saddened by the
thought that her investigation had led to nothing. Disappointed but
not deterred, she made her way back to her home in McPherson, where
she kept abreast of any news related to the Bender family. She would appear again a little over ten years later when a supposed sighting of the
Benders came in from Colorado. Frances wrote to the *Parsons Palladium*
and informed them that the Benders couldn't possibly be in Colorado
because they had been found in Michigan in 1889. "The disappearance
of the Benders has been made plain and is no longer a mystery," she
wrote, before attacking the claimant in Colorado and arguing that she
was the only person entitled to the two thousand dollars reward money.
A newspaper in McPherson told its readers that those who knew Frances
personally thought she was insane, but noted that "as has often been
demonstrated, sanity is not a necessity in the acquiring of notoriety in
Kansas." Frances eventually left Kansas, spending the rest of her life in
Joplin, Missouri, where she was active and well liked in the community.
She died in autumn of 1946 and is buried in Fairview Cemetery beneath
a headstone that reads "Frances E. McCann, 'The Little Detective.'"

SARAH DAVIS AND ALMIRA MONROE WERE ALMOST CERTAINLY NOT
the Bender women, and their experience in Labette County was shaped
largely by attitudes towards working-class women during the latter part
of the nineteenth century. Even those who worked to prove that they were
innocent of the Labette County murders concluded that "their lives are
not much better than the history of the Benders." Multiple marriages,
rumours that both women engaged in sex work, and the willingness of

both to testify against the other set public opinion against them, though in reality the charges were based on little or no evidence.

UPON RELEASE FROM THE JAILHOUSE AT OSWEGO, ALMIRA MONROE returned to Michigan and the poverty in which she had lived her whole life. In 1896, at the age of seventy-six, she married Charles Eaton, and the two remained together until his death five years later. Almira lived out the rest of her days in an almshouse in Muskegon. She died in 1913 at the age of ninety-three, having outlived six of her thirteen children, including Sarah.

IN THE AFTERMATH OF THE HEARING, SARAH DAVIS RAGED THAT she and her mother had been forced to endure such an ordeal. In a matter of weeks, she was back in Oswego with her children in tow and announced to anyone who would listen that she intended to "make it hot" for Leroy Dick. Dick recalled meeting her on a street corner, where she haughtily informed him that she intended to sue him for ten thousand dollars. When nothing came of the lawsuit and her anger burned out, Sarah returned to Michigan, where she worked intermittently as a housekeeper. Marrying at least three more times, she was granted a divorce from her final husband on the grounds of "extreme cruelty." Sarah died in the summer of 1908, at age fifty-eight. Her death certificate lists the cause of death as "extensive gasoline burns of body and shock," but the circumstances surrounding the burns were not recorded. Neither Sarah nor her mother ever received an apology from the officials who had facilitated their arrest.

THE CITIZENS OF LABETTE COUNTY CAME TO VIEW THE CASE BROUGHT against Sarah and Almira as an embarrassment, not because it had endangered the lives of two innocent women, but because it had cost the county $1,300, and the question of the Benders still remained unanswered.

The Oswego Independent blasted the entire fiasco as "a foolish or extrava-
gant expenditure of the county funds." It told readers that the matter of
the women in the Bender family would now remain unsolved, as none of
the witnesses who provided a positive identification would ever have the
nerve to take the stand again.

As to the Benders

O ne name was noticeably absent from the events of 1889 and early 1890. No one in the York family had taken the stand, nor were they seen in the courthouse. Initially, the family's silence on the matter was interpreted as evidence that they had killed the Benders themselves, particularly as Ed York, still a much-beloved citizen of Fort Scott, had not even spoken to the papers about the arrest of Sarah and Almira. In the years after his wife's death, Alexander remarried and moved to Denver, Colorado, where he was busy establishing a real estate business at the time news reached him of the situation unfolding in Labette County. Though Alexander had interacted with the Benders, he thought himself ill-equipped to recognise them over a decade later, when his impression of the family had been coloured by what he knew them to be capable of. A reporter for the *Chicago Tribune* visited Alexander in Denver, and he took the opportunity to dispel rumours of his involvement in the deaths of the Benders. He also confided in the reporter that if Sarah and Almira could be proved without a doubt to be the guilty parties, he would "feel that a great burden has been lifted from my shoulders and my duty discharged as far as possible in this world towards the memory of my brother."

ALEXANDER YORK MAY WELL HAVE TOLD THE NEWSPAPERS THAT he hoped Sarah and Almira were the Bender women, but privately he had his reasons for believing they were not. Since the summer of 1873, when Detective Beers was forced to leave the Texas Panhandle empty-handed, Alexander held fast to the theory that the Benders were out West. This was only encouraged by the statement of Samuel Merrick, who suggested a number of places where the family and the outlaw colony might be camped, all of which littered the borderlands of Texas and New Mexico Territory. Alexander paid special heed to sightings of the Benders that matched Merrick's account of their life on the plains. In 1883, news of one such sighting came in from Gila County, Arizona.

The man behind the sighting was Thomas Gates, the owner of a lucrative silver mine in the region. Certain the Benders were "living like hermits" in the area, Gates wrote to the then governor of Kansas, George Glick, to request information on the amount of money offered for their capture. When Alexander was informed, he was elated, convinced that a breakthrough had at last been made. "I attach more importance to the claim of Mr Gates that he has seen them than I have to any particular report for years," he wrote in a letter to the governor, adding, "I expect to see them hang yet." When Thomas Gates wrote back that the reward was so small and the conditions of a capture so dangerous that he was not willing to risk it, Alexander was devastated. Several months later, when reports drifted in that the Benders were ranching at an undisclosed location in Colorado, he reiterated his belief that they had "made their way out to the Rio Grande and concealed themselves in that South West Country."

WHAT ALEXANDER FAILED TO TAKE INTO CONSIDERATION WAS, IN his own words, that the outlaw colony was in the habit of "gathering mules and horses for the Colorado trade." Authorities in Kansas had known since the summer of 1873 that the McPherson brothers' reach extended as far as southern Colorado. Given the Benders' position as fugitives, they would have been almost constantly on the move. Alexander's preoccupation with the land west of the Rio Grande blinded him to the very real possibility that the Benders had been in New Mexico Territory and Colorado, especially as one of their accomplices had made quite a name for himself in both of those places.

SINCE SAMUEL MERRICK REPORTED LAST SEEING FRANK AND THE Benders in 1875, the younger McPherson sibling had developed a reputation for violence that followed him across the West. In 1881, while working as a railway tie inspector for Watson and Levy in Pecos, New Mexico, Frank shot and killed two Mexican men in cold blood. Romero, one of the victims, was a well-respected railway contractor who had pushed back against exploitation of Mexican labourers in the region. Frank, it was assumed in the papers, shot him in a dispute over the price of railway ties. *The Gunnison Daily News-Democrat* reported that Frank was on the run and "one of the worst characters in the Western county." By 1883, Frank was a resident of Gunnison, Colorado, a growing settlement nestled at the base of the Rocky Mountains about to experience a cattle boom. He lived in the region for the next three years and made frequent visits to see his younger brother, John, a well-respected businessman in Missouri, until a disastrous incident in a saloon sent him back to Colorado for good.

IN 1887, A MAN NAMED EDWARD LANGSTON STAGGERED INTO A SAloon in Kansas City, cried out that he needed a doctor, and collapsed at a table. He had been stabbed so deeply in the back that the blade tore through a lung and pierced his heart. Two doors down in another saloon, Frank McPherson was wiping the blood off a pearl-handled knife using the hat belonging to the man he had stabbed. An abrasion on his nose made by brass knuckles dripped blood into his mustache. He left the building, followed by his brother, and headed for a pharmacy. When officers arrived to arrest him, they found Frank in the back room washing Edward Langston's blood from his hands and shirt cuffs.

Officers brought Frank to Langston and the man identified the prisoner as his attacker. Langston also told officers that this was not the first assault of this kind Frank had committed, and a picture quickly emerged of the events leading up to the attack. Langston was a deputy marshal from Kansas and recognised Frank as being wanted for murders committed across several states. Wanting to make sure, Langston began asking the barman what he knew about the man. Frank overheard the conversation, threatened the barman, then turned on Langston. "The men had a tussle together . . . when within a dozen paces of the door McPherson drew his knife," the barman later told *The Kansas City Times*. In court, Frank claimed self-defence, blaming an afternoon of drinking and Langston's inability to hold his alcohol as the source of the fracas. Langston surprised everyone by surviving the attack, but never appeared in court. Without the key witness, and assisted by the expensive lawyers hired by his brother, Frank walked free.

AFTER THE ASSAULT ON LANGSTON, FRANK'S BROTHER WARNED HIM against staying in Missouri, and he headed west to Colorado once again. Throughout the rest of his life he occupied a series of positions that allowed him to commit violence on behalf of the law so he was unlikely to be punished for it. He worked first as a guard at the Cañon City Penitentiary, where he enjoyed mistreating inmates until one of them stabbed him in the side, nearly killing him. He recovered, and by 1903 was working as strike-breaker in the Colorado labour wars, a series of labour strikes in which tension between union members and government forces and their private contractors escalated into some of the worst violence seen in the history of American labour. Frank shot at least one man, an Italian named Mancini, but there is no doubt that he beat many others. Frank eventually settled in Las Animas, where the city directory from 1907 lists him as owning a saloon in a mining settlement by the name of Tercio.

IF FRANK MCPHERSON'S TRAVELS PROVIDE A CLUE TO THE MOVEments of the Bender family, his presence in New Mexico Territory suggests that the outlaw colony followed Merrick's advice to head to the top of the Colorado River in Texas, where it was a short ride over the border into New Mexico. Or perhaps they went with the suggestion of the Mescalero Apache and followed the Native Americans to the Guadalupe Mountains. Should it have been the latter, the Benders would have found themselves run out of the area in 1881 when the Texas Rangers ambushed the remaining Apache, forcing them north on to the reservation. If the Benders were still alive when Frank went to Colorado, it is likely they went with him. Snow-scattered mountains and vast expanses of verdant wilderness would have been an appealing prospect to anyone who had spent many years in the dry heat of the high plains. John Gebhardt was familiar with the region, having spent the best part of a decade driving stolen horses into Las Animas County with Frank. The rowdy mining towns comprised of transient workers would have allowed the family to move about with relative freedom, especially if the older and younger couple separated.

WHETHER THE BENDERS PERISHED AT THE HANDS OF THE TEXAS Rangers, tried their hand at prospecting in Arizona, or moved between settlements in Colorado, the two men with the most knowledge of their whereabouts never gave up their secrets. Samuel Merrick, the outlaw who had once offered to track down the family himself, disappeared from the records after his release in 1880. Whether he regrouped with the Benders is impossible to know. Frank McPherson returned to Missouri to die in 1917. His obituary made no mention of the four people he was known to have murdered. *The Kansas City Star*, which once printed details of his brutal attack on Edward Langston thirty years before, reported his death under the headline WESTERN PIONEER DIES HERE. Over the course of his life, Frank undoubtedly killed more than four people and—I would speculate—was an active participant in the Bender murders. But his ability to slip through the legal system ensured he never paid for his crimes. Whatever he knew of the Benders and their fate he took with him to the grave.

From the Old Century
into the New

———

As the world pushed forward into the twentieth century, life accelerated on the frontier. Between 1880 and 1890, the population of Cherryvale increased from 690 to 2,104. By 1910, it would reach 4,304 and include a little girl named Mary Louise Brooks, who went on to become a glittering icon of the Jazz Age. Independence entered its boom period, bolstered by the discovery of natural gas near the city in 1892, which was quickly followed by the appearance of oil fields in both Montgomery County and neighbouring Neosho County. Outlaws who had once roamed freely through the Cross Timbers, a region of dense forest and open prairie in Indian Territory, headed further west, away from the settlers who flooded into the region. On 22 April 1889, the newly formed Oklahoma Territory was opened for settlers, and fifty thousand people arrived to lay claims on the first day alone. Black settlers, some of them formerly enslaved people of the Indian Nations, arrived in their thousands to join existing Black communities that had sprung up after the Civil War, hoping that together they could be a force to stop segregation from gaining a foothold in the region. But in 1907, when Indian and Oklahoma territories entered the Union as Oklahoma, the newly established legislature immediately enacted segregation laws. While some Black communities thrived in spite of Jim Crow laws, oppression in the state continued to escalate.

IN THE MONTHS FOLLOWING SARAH AND ALMIRA'S RELEASE IN 1890, Ed York left Kansas and moved to Denver with his ageing parents to join Alexander's real estate business. In the summer, Irwin York, William's eldest son, whose fair hair and blue eyes gave him a striking resemblance to his late father, struck out west to California. William's widow, Mary, was also on the move, heading south into Texas with her husband, James Jackson. Upon her death in March 1898, *The Fort Scott Daily Monitor* extended its sympathies to Mary's "many friends in Bourbon County who will be pained to hear of her death" and remembered her as a "cultured and refined lady [who] had many harrowing experiences" in her life.

THOMAS BEERS, THE PRIVATE DETECTIVE WHO TRACKED THE BENDERS as far as the plains beyond Henrietta, Texas, remained in Kansas, entertaining those around him with increasingly far-fetched stories of his youth. In the newspapers of July 1901, Beers came across the same reports from Colorado that had upset Frances McCann. Not to be left out of the excitement, he gave an interview to the *Emporia Weekly Gazette* in which he claimed "the Benders are not in Colorado . . . I'm watching them and they are watching me as closely as I am watching them." Where and how he was watching the Benders never became apparent. He died three years later and was greatly missed by the people of Emporia, who regarded him as an authority on the early history of the region.

COLONEL CHARLES PECKHAM, BEERS'S ASSOCIATE IN THE HUNT FOR the Benders, entered the twentieth century in a quagmire of legal trouble. After agreeing to take the role of defence attorney in a murder case, Peckham pocketed the money paid him by the defendant and then deserted the man. He left Kansas for Oklahoma Territory, where he resumed work as a legal adviser for railway companies in the region. In the winter of 1901, he dropped dead of a heart condition five miles outside Lawton.

AS THE WORLD CREPT TOWARDS WAR AND AUTOMOBILES APPEARED alongside horses on the frontier, interest in the Benders continued to ebb and flow in the public imagination. In 1910, great excitement at a death-bed confession from a woman in California claiming to be Kate Bender proved that interest in the family showed no signs of subsiding. Katha Peters had run a "resort of ill repute" in Sacramento, where she informed a friend that she was the only member of the Bender family who escaped being shot as they fled Kansas. The people of south-east Kansas responded to the claim with their usual scepticism. *The Chanute Weekly Tribune* printed an interview with a local justice of the peace who said he believed that the Benders did escape initially but were killed somewhere on the frontier. "They ought to be dead," he concluded. "They have been reported dead often enough."

LEROY DICK NEVER FALTERED IN HIS CONVICTION THAT SARAH DAVIS and Almira Monroe were Kate and Ma Bender. The strength of his belief is reflected in the numerous articles that refer to Ma Bender as Almira, though there is no evidence the actual Mrs Bender was known by that name. Dick kept the hammers he had discovered in the Bender cabin for his whole life and enjoyed recounting the story of the murders to those who were interested in the early history of Labette County. Upon his death in April 1939, Parsons mourned "a remarkable character, who seemed so much a part of his community," and many residents recalled with fondness the stories he told of life in the early days of Labette County. The murder weapons passed to his son, who in turn donated them to the

Cherryvale Historical Museum in 1967, where they remain on display to this day. Others for whom the crimes were still in living memory grew old and passed their recollections down to younger family members and reporters, who were always willing to use the story to pad out newspaper columns.

ON AN OCTOBER EVENING AT A DETROIT BOOK FAIR IN 1937, ONE of south-east Kansas's more famous one-time residents also claimed a connection to the Bender family. Laura Ingalls Wilder, author of *The Little House on the Prairie*, stood in front of an audience and told them that some of her experiences in Kansas as a child were not appropriate material for a children's book. One such experience was her interaction with the Benders, whose cabin lay between her family home and Independence.

"We stopped there, on our way in to the Little House, while Pa watered the horses and brought us all a drink from the well near the door of the house," she told her listeners. "I saw Kate Bender standing in the doorway. We did not go in because we could not afford to stop at a tavern." Wilder went on to describe how the search for the Benders went on for many years, but her father was never interested in reports that they had been apprehended. Instead he told his daughter that the family would never be found.

At first glance Wilder's description of her family's fleeting interactions with the Benders provides a tantalisingly dark backdrop to her work. It is easy to imagine her as a child, glancing towards the cabin to see Kate in the doorway, a sight shared by those who had already fallen victim to the family. But recent scholarship on Wilder's supposed connection with the Benders has proven her claims to be untrue. The source of the stories lies not with Wilder's father, but with her daughter and fellow writer Rose Wilder Lane. Keen to capitalise on her family's proximity to such a famous crime, Lane concocted the tale of her grandfather's role in the demise of the Benders, then attempted to coax her mother into including it in her writing. Wilder pushed back and the Benders never made an appearance on the pages of her published works. But, as her lecture at the book fair shows, she wasn't quite able to resist the lure of being associated with such a famous case.

BY THE TIME WILDER PROFESSED TO KNOW THE FATE OF THE BENDER family, Alexander York had been dead for nearly a decade. If he had been alive to hear her claims, he would not have believed her. As he grew older, Alexander became weary of talking to the newspapers about the Benders. In January 1911, he granted a rare interview to *The Wichita Eagle*, in which he again denied that he and Ed had killed the Benders themselves. "There would have been no reasons not to disclose it had we done so," he said, "because it would have been considered a laudable act at that time." Alexander then explained that the family had been tracked as far as the Texas Panhandle, where he suspected they were slaughtered by the very outlaw gang they were part of. Alexander had never vocalised this opinion before, nor would he do so again. But it is a theory that allowed him a measure of closure in the absence of real justice. Imagining that the Benders met a gruesome death at the hands of other criminals relieved him of some of the responsibility that they had escaped. Like Mary York, Alexander also tried to find comfort in the knowledge that William's murder had led to the discovery of the crimes and given answers to those desperate for news of their missing relatives.

When Alexander died in February 1928, his passing prompted a series of newspaper articles declaring that his death had forever sealed the secret of what happened to the Benders. *The Centreville Press*, out of Alabama, told readers "it is generally believed Col. York and his men hung the entire Bender crew." Many papers also took the opportunity to reprint Alexander's exposure of Samuel Pomeroy. *The Parsons Daily Sun* praised him for securing the election of John Ingalls, one of the most important governors in the history of the state and a distant relative of Laura Ingalls Wilder. Alexander would have mixed feelings about his legacy, but would no doubt take comfort in the knowledge that his impact on the state's politics is still being talked about today.

_____

OUT WEST, ED YORK EVENTUALLY SETTLED IN OREGON, FAR FROM the land where the memory of William's murder lingered on the prairies. He arrived in Cottage Grove in 1926, the same year silent film actor and director Buster Keaton descended on the town to film _The General_. With Keaton came eighteen freight carriages packed with reproduction Civil War–era props and set dressing. Over the course of the summer, the film crew constructed an entire frontier town with the help of over 1,500 local residents. _The General_ was by no means the first film to put the Civil War on-screen, and the mythologising of the West had begun long before the emergence of silent cinema. But it must have been strange for Ed, then in his seventies, to watch as the world he had grown up in was rebuilt around him, a Hollywood facsimile of an age born of blood and division.

Epilogue

Independence, Kansas

28 OCTOBER 2019

Mount Hope Cemetery does not look vast from the entrance, or even from the road, but once inside, the path dips, opening into a sprawl of headstones that easily numbers in the thousands. My partner and I have come to find the grave of William York. I have a rough guide as to where his headstone is located, but when we start to walk among the graves, we struggle to understand how to apply it on the ground. Half an hour into our search, the rain that has been threatening all day finally starts to fall. It is cold and sharp and almost snow. Then, drifting in from a location we can't pinpoint, comes "The Star-Spangled Banner." A moment of disbelief later, we realise an American football game is being played somewhere nearby, and the encouraging shouts of the spectators accompany us as we continue looking. My partner is the one who finally finds the slab of smooth marble bearing William's name and Civil War regiment. It is nearly 150 years since William's family stood in this same place under the cover of a spring night in 1873. I think of Mary York, pregnant and newly widowed, working hard to imagine William, in her own words, "as a resident of that Heavenly Land where all is bright and beautiful." I think, too, of Ed, and the burden of being the one to identify a dead loved one. But most of all I think of Alexander, who stood at his brother's grave with the knowledge that he was one of the last people in Kansas to look into the eyes of William's murderers.

I HAD INITIALLY PLANNED TO CALL THE FINAL CHAPTER OF THIS book "Exit the Benders," but that would have been a misnomer, as the legacy of the Benders is still very much alive. When I mention the Benders in conversation with staff at an axe-throwing bar in Lawrence, Kansas, I am met with knowing nods. Several days later, during a game of pool with the hosts of our Airbnb in Independence, Robert tells me the Benders are at the bottom of the Verdigris River. His is the prevailing opinion among the residents of south-east Kansas today, where the lines between fact and folklore relating to the family are often blurred.

CHERRYVALE, THE TOWN CLOSEST TO THE BENDER CABIN, HAS A complicated relationship with the murders. In 1961, a reconstructed replica of the cabin was put up as part of the Kansas State Centennial Celebrations and received over two thousand visitors in the first three days after its opening. Despite continued success, the cabin had always been a source of controversy, and it closed its doors in 1978 after being moved to several different locations. During our visit to the Cherryvale Historical Museum I am handed directions to the land where the Bender cabin once stood, tucked inside an envelope from 1992. On the front is a large ink stamp commemorating "Bender Day." It shows the cabin, three hammers, the grave of William York, and Kate, who lurks behind the canvas waiting to strike a hapless victim. The stamp was the winning design in a competition for local schoolchildren, organised by a beloved local schoolteacher. Fern Morrow Wood's love of local history led her to write the first real account of the Benders and she worked tirelessly to assign them their proper place in the history of the region.

SEVERAL MONTHS AFTER OUR VISIT TO THE STATES, I NOTICE THE land on which the Benders committed their crimes is up for sale. "Ever want to own a gruesome piece of American history? Well, you're in luck" reads the opening sentence of an article written for the American TV news channel CNN about the auction. A number of outlets picked up the story, including the British *Daily Mail*, which announced the news under the cumbersome headline LAND OWNED BY AMERICA'S FIRST FAMILY OF SERIAL KILLERS GOES ON SALE WHERE "THE BLOODY BENDERS" BASHED THE HEADS OF 11 VICTIMS WITH A HAMMER, SLIT THEIR THROATS AND DROPPED THEM THROUGH A TRAPDOOR. *Mental Floss*, *Smithsonian* magazine, and *People* all ran pieces on the crimes, taking the details from an article written by Amy Renee Leiker for *The Wichita Eagle*.

As I read them I am reminded of the flurry of news articles released about the Benders in the wake of Sarah and Almira's arrest in 1889. At the time, a reporter for the *Burns Mirror* noted that "the arrest has given a large number of newspapers an opportunity to publish once more the life and adventures of the Benders," and it seems not much has changed about the stories that capture the public imagination. The Benders live on because the story of their crimes does not have an ending, and unsolved mysteries have the greatest afterlife. The family themselves are ghosts in their own narrative, patched together through the voices of those who knew them, those who lost loved ones to their crimes, and those who continue to tell stories passed down through generations. These are the voices, both new and old, to whom this story truly belongs.

Acknowledgements

I am hugely indebted to the staff at the Kansas Historical Society State Archives who went above and beyond in helping me navigate the wealth of material available about the Bender family, as well as making my partner and me a list of the best places to eat in Topeka. I would also like to thank Mike Wood at the Cherryvale Historical Museum for taking the time to show us around and answer all my questions. Thanks to Jenny and Robert Soper at the Magnolia Blossom Inn for being such wonderful hosts during our time in Independence and to everyone in Kansas who made us feel welcome and helped us on our travels.

I am endlessly grateful to my editor, Terezia Cicel, at Viking for her enthusiasm and patience, but most of all for her suggestions that helped shape the second half of this book into what it is now. Thank you to Chris White at Scribner for sharing my excitement about the story and to my agent, Georgina Capel, who knew my interest in the case was worth pursuing as a book before I did.

Thank you to all those who provided invaluable support throughout this project, especially Dan Jones, Beth Marshall, and Paige Martin. To my stepson, Woody, who has taught me all sorts of things about the world that you can only learn from a child. To Mike and Mandy Roe and

Francesca Fowler for providing space and time for both research and writing.

Thank you most of all to my family, my grandparents—Dina and Paul—for introducing me to the West and always telling me I could do anything I put my mind to. My brother, Daniel, for reading with an eye for detail I can only aspire to and for asking all the right questions. And to my parents, Gillian and Darren, who have supported me without question in all my endeavours and to whom I owe my curiosity and love of storytelling.

Last to my partner, Duncan—thank you for driving me all over America, for your numerous hours spent reading and rereading passages, and for always being there to talk me out of a rut. I can't wait to see what we do next.

Notes

The majority of sources key to the construction of this book are those held at the Kansas Historical Society State Archives. They include the boxes of Governor's Records, in which the unwieldy nature of the search for the Benders becomes apparent, as does the legacy of the crimes in the history of the state. Also inside these boxes are documents that provide the link between the McPherson brothers and the Bender family, most notably the statement written by Samuel Merrick in 1879.

Except for Kate's advertisement and the German inscriptions in the Bible and prayer book found on the property, the Benders left none of their own words after fleeing the state. As such, they are characterised through the eyewitness testimony of those who interacted with them, much of which comes from *Articles Prepared for the Kansas State Centennial Commission: Slayings, Bender Family of Southeast Kansas* (Unit ID: 40001 KSHS). Among the many sources that brought the people of south-east Kansas to life and provided insight into the myriad relationships formed among people on the frontier and the lasting impact of the crimes on the community *The Bender Tragedy*, Mary York's heartfelt account of the years 1873–5 and The *Bender Hills Mystery: The Story Behind the Infamous Murders from 1870s Kansas by Jean McEwen*, as told by Leroy Dick were of particular importance. *The Bender Hills Mystery* first appears in *The Parsons Sun* (9 June 1934), but page numbers here are taken from the printed copy held at the Kansas Historical Society State Archives in Topeka.

Introduction

For a comprehensive look at the Gunfight at the O.K. Corral and the way it affected the lives of those involved see Jeff Guinn's excellent book *The Last Gunfight: The Real Story of the Shootout at the O.K. Corral and How It Changed the American West*. For more on the legacy of the cowboy and ways of approaching the mythologisation of the West see Sharman Apt Russell's *Kill the Cowboy: A Battle of Mythology in the New West*. Richard Slotkin's *Gunfighter Nation: The Myth of the Frontier in Twentieth-Century America* is also a valuable resource for those interested in this topic.

An introduction to the topic of Wild West shows can be found in Paul Fees's "Wild West Shows: Buffalo Bill's Wild West" (https://centerofthewest.org/learn/western -essays/wild-west-shows/). The article's accompanying bibliography is a good place to start for those wanting to navigate the rich vein of literature on Buffalo Bill, his Wild West show, and its influence on American culture. See also Michelle Delaney's *Buffalo Bill's Wild West Warriors: A Photographic History* by Gertrude Käsebier. The advertisement for *History, Romance and Philosophy of Great American Crimes and Criminals of the Various Eras of Our Country* comes from *The Union*, 10 January 1885. A brief biography of Cullen Baker is available at the Texas State Historical Association's *Handbook of Texas* (https://www.tshaonline.org/handbook/entries/baker-cullen -montgomery).

More Infamous Crimes That Shocked the World is a treasure trove of well-known and obscure violent crimes. For an example of an article comparing Belle Gunness and H. H. Holmes to the Benders see "Bodies of Five Slain Unearthed in Yard" in *The New York Times*, 6 May 1908. The suggestion that the Benders be adapted for the screen comes from "Hollywood Material" in the *St. Louis Daily Globe-Democrat*, 5 August 1940. For the illustrated articles see "Murder Hotel: Guests Checked in but Seldom Out" in *The Odessa American*, 10 August 1958, and "Professor Miss Kate" in the *Brooklyn Daily*, 4 April 1956. For "The Bender Hills Mystery," see *The Parsons Sun* (9 June–11 August 1934). An interview with Jean Bailey appeared in *The Parsons Sun* under the headline "BENDER MYSTERY" AUTHOR SUCCESSFUL WOMAN WRITER (21 July 1934). In the interview she discusses her other published works and states that "there should be authentic acts for the basis of a story or poem interwoven with imagination."

Labette County, Kansas

One of the few incidents concerning the Bender crimes that accounts agree upon are the circumstances surrounding the discovery of Dr William York's body. Though the newspapers occasionally confuse Edward and Alexander York, Leroy Dick (*The Bender Hills Mystery*, 24–5), and Mary York (*The Bender Tragedy*, 95) both name Ed as the one to make the discovery in the orchard. A full-page spread dedicated to the crimes in the Thayer *Head-light* (14 May 1873) and several editions of the *Leavenworth Daily Commercial* (13 and 15 May 1873) inform the rest of this account.

Part I: The Theatre of a Nation's Struggle

A State Birthed in Violence

The discussion of life in Kansas Territory and early Kansas statehood is informed by "Borderlands of Memory" and "The Nastiest Bits" (1–43) in Matthew Christopher Hulbert's *The Ghosts of Guerrilla Memory: How Civil War Bushwhackers Became Gunslingers in the American West*, as well as Kristen Tegtmeier Oertel's *Bleeding Borders: Race, Gender and Violence in Pre-Civil War Kansas* and Jeremy Neely's *The Border Between Them: Violence and Reconciliation on the Kansas-Missouri Line.*

The minutes for the meeting of the Settlers of Kansas Territory were reprinted in *The Weekly Kansas Chief* (15 August 1883) and include the following resolutions: "10. That we will afford protection to no abolitionist as settler of Kansas Territory; 11. That we recognise the institution of Slavery as already existing in this Territory, and recommend to Slaveholders to introduce their property as early as practicable." The quote from *The Kansas Herald of Freedom* includes an incitement to violence: "He who cries Peace, Peace, is only waiting for stronger manacles to be placed upon his own limb . . . the freemen in Kansas will not permit the slave power to exterminate them from the Territory." *The Kansas Herald of Freedom* was based in Wakarusa, Kansas, a settlement that had existed in the territory long before it became a state.

James Montgomery's raid on Fort Scott to rescue Benjamin Rice was widely covered by the newspapers on both sides of the slavery debate. A number of free state newspapers condemned the violence, most notably the *Herald of Freedom* (18 January 1859), which stated "we wish to say that the pen that gives this hurried account of Free State ruffianism, is wielded by a Free State Hand." Sene Campbell's letter to James Montgomery (4 January 1859) is featured on a display board at the Fort Scott National Historic Site. The raid on Lawrence is one of the most famous incidents of guerrilla violence in the Civil War, and an entire room of the Watkins Museum of History in the town is dedicated to the massacre and its aftermath. Descriptions of the raid and the Bushwhackers are taken from the *White Cloud Kansas Chief* (27 August 1863) and *The Leavenworth Times* (30 August 1863). For the recent history of the state and how it continued to be a source of fascination for its inhabitants and the press, see "Interesting Historical Reminiscences" in the *Western Home Journal* (6 January 1870), which prefaces a short history of the state with the opening line, "A strange, romantic history has this prairie state of Kansas."

Details regarding the make-up of what was then known as Indian Territory are from *An Act to Regulate Trade and Intercourse with the Indian Tribes and to Preserve Peace on the Frontier,* Chap. CLXI. Statute I. 30 June 1834. Clara Sue Kidwell's essay "Indian Removal" from the *Encyclopedia of the Great Plains* (an online project by the University of Nebraska–Lincoln) provides a timeline of the removal treaties pushed on to Native Americans until 1854. Daniel Littlefield discusses the impact of the Reconstruction Treaties on Native Americans at length in his paper "The Treaties of 1866: Reconstruction or Re-Destruction" (in *Proceedings: War and Reconstruction in Indian Territory, A History Conference in Observance of the 130th Anniversary of the Fort Smith Council,* Fort Smith, AR, 1995). Information regarding the routes of railway companies through Indian Territory comes from Michael D. Green's essay "Indian Territory, 1866–1889" (*Historical Atlas of Oklahoma,* 98–9) and *Colton's New Map of the State of Texas and Adjoining Portions of New Mexico, Louisiana and Arkansas.*

An example of state-specific Black Codes is the "Mississippi Black Codes" (*Laws of Mississippi,* 1865, 82), which states that "any freedman, free Negro or mulatto . . . may be imprisoned at the discretion of the court" for a number of purposefully vague reasons such as being a "runaway" or "practicing unlawful games." Further discussion of the implementation of Black Codes in the South and its relation to the prison system can be found in Christopher Adamson's "Punishment After Slavery: Southern State Systems, 1865–1890" (*Social Problems* 30, no. 5, Thematic Issue on Justice, 1983). Information on the Black Codes also comes from an essay on the subject for the Texas

State Historical Association by Carl H. Moneyhon. Most of the settlements in Kansas occurred towards the latter half of the 1870s in what became known as the "Exoduster" movement. Kansas was a popular choice because of its association with the abolitionist movement in the lead-up to and throughout the Civil War.

The discussion of south-east Kansas in the aftermath of the Civil War is informed by time spent at the Fort Scott National Historic Site, along with William Fischer's "Fort Scott, Kansas," *Civil War on the Western Border: The Missouri-Kansas Conflict, 1854–1865*, Kansas City Public Library. The quote describing Independence is from *The Leavenworth Bulletin* (9 May 1870).

The Benders Come to Kansas

The story of the large skunk spotted by fur trappers is one traditionally told as the reason for the county's name, though other sources suggest it may also have been named after Pierre Bete, a fur trapper who married an Osage woman during the 1830s (Kansas Counties, Labette, Kansas Historical Society website). Nelson Case's *History of Labette County, Kansas, from the First Settlement to the Close of 1892* (90) states that the first murder was committed by Charles Van Alstine near a saloon in Oswego, before devoting an entire chapter to crimes committed in the county up to the volume's publication. For the report on the accident with the rifles, see "Fatal Accident—Elegant French Shirts" in *The Fort Scott Daily Monitor* (1 October 1870).

Numerous sources attest to the Bender men arriving in October 1870, including witnesses under oath in the winter of 1889, as recorded by defence attorney John T. James (*The Benders in Kansas*, 13). The bulk of the account of the Bender men's interactions with Edward Ern and Rudolph Brockman is derived from Leroy Dick's recollections (*The Bender Hills Mystery*). Rudolph Brockman and Edward Ern are registered to Dwelling Number 184, Osage, Labette, Kansas, on the U.S. Federal Census of 1870. George Hieronymus appears in the 1875 Kansas State Census as residing in Labette, Kansas. *The Chetopa Advance* lists the area where the Benders staked their claim in "Section 12, township 41, range 17, Osage Township, Near Timber Hill Creek" (14 May 1873). Details regarding the experience and prevalence of German settlers in Kansas come from *Peopling the Plains: Who Settled Where in Frontier Kansas* by James Shortridge.

Descriptions of the Bender men are taken from the Governor's Proclamation (Kansas Historical Society) along with eyewitness testimony from neighbours such as Maurice Sparks ("Light on Benders," *The Topeka State Journal*, 5 August 1911).

The Drum Creek Treaty came about from continued controversy regarding the Sturges Treaty that had been signed in 1868 (*Treaties and Laws of the Osage Nation as Passed to November 26th, 1890*, 28–44). Named for William Sturges, president of the Lawrence & Galveston Railroad, the treaty would have put a huge swath of Kansas under the private ownership of the railways. The treaty was never ratified by Congress and was instead altered to exclude the railway companies before being approved by all other parties. Details on the removal of the Osage and sale of tribal land come from Louis F. Burns's essay "Osage" (*The Encyclopedia of Oklahoma History and Culture*) and "Kansas Settlers on the Osage Diminished Reserve: A Study of Laura Ingalls Wilder's *Little House on the Prairie*" by Penny T. Linsenmayer. The quote from the *Labette Sentinel* can be found under the headline "What an Indian Thinks of It" (20 October 1870).

The northern lights were a source of great excitement in the region, particularly their unusual red colouring. The *Wyandotte Gazette* reported the event as "midnight Aurora Borealises of unparalleled splendor" (27 October 1870).

Descriptions of the Bender cabin itself as 16 x 24 feet (5 x 7 metres) are consistent across the majority of sources, give or take a few feet. Photographs of the cabin taken by Elkanah Tresslar of Fort Scott and George Gamble of Parsons verify this information (available online at Kansas Memory or at the Kansas State archives). A wagon found on the outskirts of Thayer recognised as belonging to the Bender family contained a plank of wood that had been the sign for the family's meagre dry goods selection. *The Head-light* reported the detail as follows: "'Grocry,' pulling this off we found on the other side in the same style 'groceries'" (16 April 1873).

An Ambitious Town Just Four Weeks Old

The U.S. Department of the Interior Bureau of Land Management records show that Dick was issued with a State Volume Patent on 1 July 1872, the required five years after first staking a claim in 1868. Details regarding his early life in Labette County come from an obituary published in *The Parsons Sun* (3 April 1839) and his own account. *The Lawrence Daily Journal* announced "trains begin running to Cherryvale" in its 12 July 1871, edition.

"Happy Jack" Reed of Cherryvale, as he appears in John T. James's account (*The Benders in Kansas*, 27–8), provides one of the more sensible recollections of an experience at the Bender cabin. James describes him as a familiar face in the region but does not expand beyond the man's relationship with the Benders. Descriptions of Ma Bender are sparse and she is often afforded little more than a sentence: "the oldest murderess is presumed to be about fifty five" (*The Head-light*, 14 May 1873). Though Ma would later be associated with the names Almira and Elvira, she is not named in any sources prior to 1889. Descriptions of Kate vary wildly, but confusion over her appearance tended to favour the more appealing descriptions, as in the *Leavenworth Daily Commercial*. "They tell different stories about the 'child of the devil' Miss. Katie Bender. 'Giff' of the *Parsons Herald* describes her from personal inspection as a buxom, good-looking country girl" (15 May 1873).

An example of a man who was harassed by Pa appears in the *The Republican Daily Journal* (17 May 1873): "The old man stepped up to him, having a hammer in his hand and asked him where he lived." Leroy Dick describes Edward Ern's unfortunate experience with the Bender family in great detail in *The Bender Hills Mystery* (9–11). In *The Benders in Kansas*, James recounts a story that matches the details, under the heading "German Guest" (29). Mary Hiltz and Rudolph Brockman's marriage licence confirms that they wed on 23 February 1871, several months after the arrival of the Bender women.

Matters Spiritual and Temporal

In George C. Cunningham's article for the Kansas Centenary he recalls his father's description of the cabin as "a box, one-story, made of native walnut lumber . . . They had a red calico curtain stretched across the center of the room in the front part"

(Centennial Commission Papers, KSHS). Mrs Newland, raised not far from the Bender cabin, shared memories related to her by her father that typified the general response to the family: "Father even danced with the Bender girl, he thought Kate Bender was very beautiful and so did everyone else. The Benders all were very odd behaving people though. Father remarked about this a great deal" (Centennial Commission Papers, KSHS).

The family's spiritualist beliefs are at the centre of what made them so famous at the time, and whether or not they were true adherents became a hotly contested topic, see: "the Bender family professed to be spiritualists" (*The Daily Phoenix* [Columbia, SC], 15 May 1873) and "Kate of the Evil Eye" (*Atchison Daily Globe*, 30 September 1873). Discussion of spiritualism is informed by Simone Natale's *Supernatural Entertainments: Victorian Spiritualism and the Rise of Modern Media Culture* and Keith Souter's *Medical Meddlers, Mediums and Magicians*. For the movement's relationship to the Civil War and radical thinking see *Free Spirits: Spiritualism, Republicanism, and Radicalism in the Civil War Era* by Mark Lause; and "'There Is No Death': Spiritualism and the Civil War" by Bridget Bennett in *Transatlantic Spiritualism and Nineteenth Century American Literature* (147–75). For the number of attendees at the First Society of Spiritualists see *The Weekly Commonwealth* (4 January 1870). Advertisements for Fannie Allyne's lectures in Kansas showing her tour across the state, starting in Topeka, "Miss Allyne at the Opera House" (*Daily Kansas State Record*, 29 January 1871), to Labette, "Miss Fannie Allyne" (*The Oswego Register*, 14 April 1871). In Labette, Allyne spoke at Perkins' Hall, the Methodist Church, and the general town hall, where she focused on the subject of "woman as she is and she should be." When local doctor Dr G. W. Gabriel recalled Kate Bender delivering lectures on spiritualism in the area, it is likely she would have spoken at similar venues as well as establishments like boarding houses (*The Benders in Kansas*, 76). *The Oswego Independent* makes reference to her lectures before stating that "she is represented in her own neighbourhood as a doctress" (10 May 1873).

Details exploring the duality of spiritualism come from "The Ghost of King Solomon" and "Deceive a Credulous Public by the Grossest Charlatanism," in the *Leavenworth Daily Commercial* (8 and 28 January 1870). For tragedies involving spiritualism see "They were firm Spiritualists" in the *Chicago Tribune* (7 March 1871) and "people will avoid them as they would a deadly pestilence" in *The Howard County Ledger* (30 March 1871). Despite the controversial nature of the belief, *The Weekly Commonwealth* reported that spiritualism was on the rise in Kansas (4 January 1870). In his book *Kate Bender, The Kansas Murderess: The Horrible History of an Arch Killer*, folklorist Vance Randolph notes that the following charm by Kate was recorded in an autograph album in 1873:

> *Dullix, ix, ux,*
> *You can't come over Pontio*
> *Pontio is above Pilatio*

Thomas Tyack and his family, Susanna, Hannah, Samuel, Christopher, and Thomas, are listed as residing at dwelling number 178, Osage, Labette, Kansas, in the U.S. Federal Census of 1870. Susanna appeared in a number of newspaper articles after her arrest, most notably in *The Weekly Commonwealth* (21 May 1873), where her inability to fix the man's leg using magnetic healing is referenced. The older woman who sought out Kate's assistance is not named in any sources that tell her story, but the particulars of the experience are consistent enough to warrant its inclusion. Leroy Dick notes that she "put up her side saddle as collateral" (*The Bender Hills Mystery*, 11). The *Lawrence Daily Journal* reported the incident and wondered why "no one seemed to attach any importance" to the woman's story (17 May 1873). Julia Hestler's account of her experience with the Benders appears in Dabney Taylor's essay "Underneath the Vine and Fig Tree" (*Frontier Times*, March 1966). Julia and her husband are listed in the U.S. Federal Census of 1880, where they are registered as residing in Harlan, Nebraska.

The First of Many

The body of the story of the Feerick family is taken from Mary York's memoir (*The Bender Tragedy*, 121–3). Mary Feerick appears in the Montgomery County Records in 1875 as marrying Alfred Campbell. According to Mary York's account she returned to Howard County in December 1874 and, having lost her child and her husband, remarried but chose to stay in the area. Howard County became defunct in 1875 after being split in two; the subsequent areas were named Elk County and Chautauqua County.

The weather was a favourite topic of the newspapers because it had such an impact on the lives of those on the frontier. Under the Local Items listing, *The Head-light* notes: "Our first snow fell last Saturday. Lake Richmond was frozen over on Monday morning. Nice moonlight nights" (22 November 1871). A history of the early settlement of Baxter Springs can be found in Nathaniel Allison's *History of Cherokee County, Kansas and Representative Citizens* (151–3). The complicated relationship between homesteaders and the railway companies in Kansas is covered extensively in John Mack's *Bucking the Railroads on the Kansas Frontier: The Struggle over Land Claims by Homesteading Civil War Veterans, 1867–1876*. Squatters arguments with the railway company in Fort Scott specifically are discussed in Harold Henderson's "The Building of the First Kansas Railroad" (*A Journal of the Central Plains* 15, no. 3, August 1947, 225–39).

An example of one such pamphlet reads "Are You Going West, if so, and if You Wish to Secure Good Homes in a Rich County, Please Read the Facts Herein Stated" (Southern Kansas Land Association, Ottawa, Journal Print, 1873.) The Watton family appears in the U.S. Federal Census of 1880, where they are listed as residing in La Fayette, Chautauqua, Kansas, in dwelling number 103. Jeremiah D. Watton filed the land claim for the property in Chautauqua on 1 October 1873 (U.S. General Land Office Records, document number 5439). As it took families five years to prove their claims, the Watton family listed in the census are Mary Feerick's companions and may have encouraged her to stay after the death of her husband.

An Invitation

David Dary's excellent book *Red Blood, Black Ink: Journalism in the Old West* gives a comprehensive analysis of the development and role of the newspapers on the frontier. Examples of articles given in the discussion of newspapers are: "Incendiaries and rascals of all kinds," *The Head-light* (18 May 1872), "Money," *The Osage County Chronicle* (21 February 1873), and "One or Two Citizens in Kansas City," in the *Leavenworth Daily Commercial* (17 June 1873). The full article on the mob that attacked the railway agent can be found under the headline "The Leaguers Mob at Parsons," in *The Fort Scott Daily Monitor* (28 November 1872). "One farmer kills another with a Butcher-Knife" is from the *Osage Mission Journal* (6 April 1872).

Once again the details of Happy Jack Reed's experience are derived from John T. James's *The Benders in Kansas* (27–29) along with an article in the *San Francisco Examiner* featuring an interview with Colonel Frank Triplett, who had been in Labette County at the time the crimes were discovered (18 November 1889). It includes a description of the supposed murder of a guest while Reed was on the property: "the old man went out and conducted the owner and his team to the barn, and soon after Reed heard a heavy blow followed by a scream, then a rain of blows in rapid succession."

Not Much Law in the Land

The *Leavenworth Daily Commercial* reported Kate's experience at the boarding house, lambasting Scroggs as "fully impressed with the belief that Professor Miss Katie Bender was a high muck-a-muck in the art of necromancy" (20 May 1873). Dr G. W. Gabriel reported that he "met both Mrs Bender and Kate at Neighbours during 1872 and 1873 when he was called there to treat patients . . . he met Kate at Parsons, also, when she was there on one of her lecture tours" (*The Benders in Kansas*, 23).

Ladore is now a ghost town, its post office having closed in 1901. Information about the settlement and the lynching of the five outlaws who assaulted the Talbott girls comes from David Beach's *How Did the Whiskey Go Down at Ladore?*, Christy Mog's *The Rough and Gone Town of Ladore, Kansas*, and the chapter "Deadly Day in Ladore: A Quintuple Lynching" in Larry Wood's *Murder & Mayhem in Southeast Kansas*. James Roach had a large extended family, several of whom are listed as residing with him at Dwelling No. 72, Ladore, Neosho, Kansas, in the U.S. Federal Census of 1870. The *Lawrence Daily Journal* had announced the formation of the "Fort Roach Town Company" in the spring of 1868 (21 May 1868). A comprehensive history of the Missouri-Kansas-Texas Railway Company in Kansas can be found in V. V. Masterson's *The Katy Railroad and the Last Frontier*. Information on the role of vigilance committees in the West comes from "Keeping Vigil: The Emergence of Vigilance Committees in Pre-Civil War America" by Jonathan Obert and Eleonora Mattiacci (*Perspectives on Politics* 16, no. 3, September 2018, 600–16). Further discussion on the use of lynching as a method of terrorising Black Americans can be found on the NAACP website; from 1882 to 1968, 4,743 recorded lynchings took place in America, with Black people accounting for 72.7 per cent of the number. The actions of the vigilance committee in Ladore were reported across the states; see *The New York Times* (14 May 1870).

The life of Fr Paul Ponziglione is covered at length in the article "Father Paul Mary Ponziglione—the Jesuit Trail Rider" for acatholicmission.org, and in Willard Rollings *Unaffected by the Gospel: Osage Resistance to the Christian Invasion* (149–52). Ponziglione's account of his experience with the Bender family was first reported in *The St. Paul Journal* (24 July 1902), where the article is reported as a transcribed account. *The Odessa Amer-*

ican featured a whole page on the priest, complete with illustrations of Kate, Ponziglione, and John Gebhardt (10 August 1858). An obituary for Ponziglione published in *The Parsons Weekly Eclipse* reported that he expressed it was his belief in God that warned him away from the family (14 December 1904).

Part II: A Nursery of Moral Monstrosities

So Foul a Murder

The account of the boys' discovery of the body of William Jones comes from several different sources. Edwin Durkholder recorded Bill Wright's memories of the incident for "Those Murdering Benders" (*True Western Adventure*, 2). Wright was a resident in the area who often regaled younger folk with stories of his time in the early days of the state. Newspaper articles that reported the murder include "Horrible Murder" in the *Osage Mission Transcript* (1 November 1872) and "The Spot Being out of the Way" in *The Atchison Daily Champion* (5 November 1872). The two papers that printed the autopsy did so under the following headlines: "Foul Murder!" in *The Kansas Democrat* (17 October 1872) and "A Man Killed for His Money" in the *Osage Mission Transcript*. Martha Jones's confirmation that the man was her husband was reported in the *Waubansee County News* (6 November 1872). *The Kansas Chief* contains the detail that "he was to have met [Martha] at Independence, but he never came" (7 November 1872). R. M. Bennett, the man unlucky enough to own the land on which the body was found, had registered the land in June 1870 (State Volume Patent, registered 6 June U.S. Department of the Interior, Bureau of Land Management). William Jones is the first man confirmed to have been murdered by the Benders, linked to their criminal activity by his mode of death and the location of the body. Where Jones was killed is uncertain, but it is likely that the Benders attacked him in the cabin, then dumped him in the creek. The presence of the woman's blouse suggests it was worn by one of the Bender women and soiled during the process of committing or cleaning up the crime. Jones's murder is sometimes erroneously reported as having taken place as early as the spring of 1871.

By Some Persons Unknown

Nearly all later stories surrounding the Bender family claim that two bodies that were never identified were found on the prairie at some point during 1872, having been dumped by the Bender family. Given the location and manner of death of the body discovered near Oswego, it is possible he was a victim of the Benders. As *The Fort Scott Daily Monitor* reported that "no one is missing from the neighbourhood," he would also fit the family's pattern of murdering single men who were not from the local area (27 March 1872). John Phipps, whose body was discovered in December 1872, also fits the Benders' victim type. Phipps appears in the 1870 State Census as living in Jackson, Missouri, the place the papers report he was travelling from at the time of his murder. He was aged thirty-one and married to a young woman named Harriet Broom. As his body was "mutilated by hogs as to be unrecognisable," his father had identified him from his clothing and other property found with the body (*The Head-light*, 21

December 1872). These two murders may account for the unidentified bodies on the prairie, as they unsettled the communities of south-east Kansas enough for *The Head-light* to acknowledge a trend of disappearances in the region: "Another horrible murder" (21 December 1872). Both also occurred within the year and time period when the Benders escalated their crimes.

Leroy Dick's reluctance to acknowledge that there was an issue with disappearances in the region is discussed at length by Edwin Durkholder in "Those Murdering Benders," describing the township trustee as "an easy-going type who didn't like anything that required work or responsibility," though he also admitted that "the settlers were too busy getting on with their farm work to become detectives" (*True Western Adventure*, 1960, 2).

Henry McKenzie and his wife, Nancy, are listed in the U.S. Federal Census of 1870 as residing in Hamilton, Indiana. McKenzie's Civil War "draft card" for inscription lists his enlistment as 20 July 1863 (U.S. Civil War Draft Registration Records, 1863–1865). His movements in the lead-up to his murder at the Bender cabin are drawn from *The Bender Hills Mystery*, in which Leroy Dick refers to his wife's cousin by the family nickname of "Hank" and makes specific reference to his chinchilla coat (28); and also from the full page dedicated to the murders in *The Head-light*, which describes McKenzie's status as a veteran of Chickamauga, as well as noting that he "was a strong and very athletic man" (14 May 1873). This specific edition of *The Head-light* provides the most verifiable information about the victims of the family, and as such, also provides details for Benjamin Brown and William McCrotty. McKenzie's intention to visit his sister and night spent at the house of J. H. Sperry are verified by *The Weekly Commonwealth* (21 May 1873) and the *Leavenworth Daily Commercial* (15 May 1873).

The Brown family had been living in Kansas since at least 1870, when Benjamin, Mary, and their children George and John were registered in the U.S. Federal Census of 1870 as residing in Humboldt in a tent while they decided on a piece of land on which to stake a claim. Benjamin was thirty-six at the time of his murder, his children fifteen and seven. The *Western Home Journal* named the man with whom he had exchanged horses as "Johnson," and reported Brown "is supposed to have had $53 with him" (15 May 1873). The detail regarding Mary Brown's search for her husband was reported in the *Leavenworth Daily Commercial*; "a painful circumstance attending this murder is that on his wife setting out in search of her husband, her horse fell sick, and she stayed three days at Bender's, lying within one hundred yards of her husband's mutilated body" (17 May 1873).

How William McCrotty came to be murdered by the Benders is drawn from an interview with resident George Burton in *The Parsons Sun* (7 March 1821). Burton was the one to identify his body in May 1873. The *Sun* reported that "McCrotty had a contestant and was understood to have gone after Burton for a witness when he met his death on the Bender farm." Details about his exchange with Dan Gardner come from *The Chanute Blade* (15 October 1891). Confusion about how much other victims had on them at the time they were murdered ran rampant in the press, with the *Lawrence Daily Journal* stating that McCrotty "was not supposed to have had any money with him. Another report is that he had sold his claim, horses, and wagon, and together with $400 sent him to make his payments on his claim, was possessed of about $1,900. We are not inclined to credit this later report" (11 May 1873).

A Man and a Little Girl

Of the victims of the Bender family, with the exception of William York, the most is known about George Longcor and his eighteen-month-old daughter, Mary Ann. The disappearance of the two on their way to Iowa is the tipping point in the story, as it led to the murder of William York. Mary Ann is also the only confirmed female victim of the family who does not adhere to their pattern of murdering men travelling alone. As Longcor was moving to Iowa indefinitely, he made an attractive target for the family as he was carrying the majority of his possessions. George is commonly referred to as moving to Iowa directly after the death of his wife, but a family memorial indicates that she died on 10 January 1871; this is consistent with Mary Ann being eighteen months old at the time of her murder (Gilmore Family Cemetery, Montgomery County, Kansas).

Mary York discusses the Longcor family and their relationship with the Yorks in *The Bender Tragedy* (42–5). George and Mary Jane Longcor are listed as residing in dwelling number 90, Rutland, Montgomery, Kansas, in the U.S. Federal Census of 1870, and his service in the Civil War is confirmed by his "draft card" for conscription, which puts his enlistment date as 9 August 1862 (U.S. Civil War Soldier Records and Profiles, 1861–1865). The debate over the total number of deaths during the war was reopened in 2012, when demographic historian J. David Hacker published a paper estimating that the number was likely to be as high as 750,000, nearly 20 per cent more than the previously accepted figure of 620,000. For the study, see "A Census-Based Count of the Civil War Dead" (*Civil War History* 57, no. 4, 307–48). Details on the number of maimed men come from "Maimed Men," Life and Limb: The Toll of the American Civil War, online at the U.S. National Library of Medicine (www.nlm.nih.gov).

The discussion of homesteading and mortality rates on the frontier is informed by an *Emigrant Life in Kansas* by Percy Ebbutt (London, 1886), "Pioneer Kitchen Gardens: How the Pioneers Planned and Planted" by Karen Atkins (4 April 2015), and Jim Kornberg's "An Awful Time for Children" in *True West* (October 2009). For a detailed breakdown on the impact of childbirth and infant mortality on the frontier, see "High-Risk Childbearing: Fertility and Infant Mortality on the American Frontier" by Lee Bean, Geraldine Mineau, and Douglas Anderton (*Social Science History* 16, no. 3, 337–63). Robert Longcor's cause of death was recorded as "Lung Fever" in the U.S. Federal Census Mortality Schedules Index (ID 197_199451).

Newspapers referenced in this section include *The Netawaka Chief* (4 December 1872); *The Star of the Valley*, which notes that Longcor "was on his way to place the child with her grandparents" (10 June 1873); and *The Portsmouth Daily Times* (24 May 1873).

Deeds of Blood

J. A. Handley's account comes from *The Benders in Kansas* by John T. James (23–4). Writing nearly forty years earlier in her own account of the crimes, Mary York recounts matching eyewitness testimony from two men and specifies that "they were accompanied by a large dog, which followed them into the house" and that "the young men, perceiving they were very unwelcome callers, started on, notwithstanding the severity of the weather" (*The Bender Tragedy*, 111–12). Her account contains specific references to a storm that is presumed to have driven Longcor and Mary Ann into the Bender cabin to seek refuge: "it was found . . . by comparing dates, that this storm, in which the young men were travelling, occurred the next day after Mr. Longcor and his little child had been travelling in the neighbourhood, and stopped at Bender's" (113). Newspaper reports from the time confirm the adverse weather, with *The Junction City Union* announcing the "lowest reading of the thermometer on our record of five years" (28 December 1872). Due to the freezing conditions, the Benders would have been unable to immediately dig a grave for Longcor and would have concealed the body in the cellar, which accounts for Pa Bender's aggressive behaviour towards Handley's dog. Dr Keables would later pronounce that Mary Ann had been buried alive, suggesting there was a period when her father was dead, but she remained in the cabin. With a corpse in the cellar and a little girl who didn't belong to them on the property, it is not surprising that the Benders were behaving in an inhospitable manner.

Various eyewitness accounts of Kate Bender have her wearing her hair in a coil that was both a practical and fashionable method of styling; see Mrs Elma Logan's testimony in "The Earth Seemed to Swallow Them, as It Had Their Victims," in *The Coffeyville Journal* (collected in the Centennial Commission Papers, Kansas City Historical Society).

A Man of Resolution and Nerve

Alexander York's personality is best described by his friend Lyman Humphrey in *History of Montgomery County, Kansas, By Its Own People* (248), which paints a picture of the man as a highly driven, talented public speaker who "lacked some of the necessary attributes to a successful life in the [legal profession]." During his Civil War career, he served with the 15th Regiment of the U.S. Colored Infantry, entering as a captain and leaving as a colonel (M589, Roll 98, U.S. Civil War Soldiers, 1861–1865). His actions on board the steamer *The Tempest* are relayed in *History of the Ninety-Second Infantry*.

The saga of the 1873 Senate race is covered in great depth in T. A. McNeal's *When Kansas Was Young* (1922). The chapter entitled "The Downfall of Pomeroy" provides further information on Pomeroy's earlier career in the state, as well as the names of all the politicians involved on both sides of the debate. It also includes a full transcript of Alexander York's famous speech to the legislature, as recorded by Colonel W. H. Rossington. McNeal concludes this chapter with the assertion that "if there was any need at this time for argument in favor of the election of United States senators by direct vote of the people it can be found by digging back into history." Further details on the Senate race are from "Götterdämmerung in Topeka: The Downfall of Senator Pomeroy" by Albert Kitzhaber (*Kansas Historical Quarterly*, August 1950). For a biography of Pomeroy, see "Samuel C. Pomeroy: A Featured Biography" (www.senate.gov/senators /FeaturedBios/Featured_Bio_Pomeroy) and "Samuel Clarke Pomeroy, 1816–1891" (www.territorialkansasonline.ku.edu). A write-up of the incident in the legislature in *Harper's Weekly* shows portraits of the two senators above an illustration of York producing the money in front of the house (*Harper's Weekly*, 1 March 1873).

For the dynamic of the relationship between Samuel Pomeroy and Alexander York, including the particulars of the removal of the land office to Independence, see

"Why Did Pomeroy Trust York" by H. W. Young in *History of Montgomery County, Kansas, By Its Own People* (24–7). Alice Caton's experience is also covered in Barbara Brackman's *Civil War Women: Their Quilts, Their Roles* (97). Alexander York gave an interview to *The Leavenworth Times* about the role of Caton's affidavit in securing the land office, in which his quote beginning "they were questionable" can be read in the context of an investigation into his behaviour both before and during the senate election (13 February 1873). The Ross letter (22 July 1862) can be read in full in Martha Caldwell's "Pomeroy's Ross Letter" (*Kansas Historical Quarterly* 13, no. 7, 1944).

Further newspapers informing the discussion of the election include the *Leavenworth Daily Commercial* (29 January 1873), *The Saline Country Journal* (21 March 1872), "Put up or Shut up" in *The Fort Scott Daily Monitor* (21 January 1873), *The Courier Tribune* (3 January 1873), "Pomeroy Played Out" in *The Olathe Mirror* (30 January 1873), and an extended article in the *Daily Kansas Tribune* entitled "The Senatorial Earthquake and How It Came About," in which the paper claimed Alexander's exposure of Pomeroy "fell like a bombshell in their midst. Strong men were appalled and stronger men grew pale and trembled at the unblushing audacity of the act" (30 January 1873).

No Traveller Is Safe

Alexander York became a favourite of the press. Newspapers on both sides of the Pomeroy affair frequently published updates as to York's whereabouts and endeavours. Alongside the politics, many of the newspapers in south-east Kansas carried advertisements for the York nursery and Alexander's law firm. See "Col. A.M. York, the most widely esteemed citizen of the State," *South Kansas Tribune* (2 April 1873) and "$1000, Blood Money," *Daily Kansas Tribune* (13 March 1873). Later letters from Alexander to Governor Glick show a man deeply devoted to his family and his children in particular (Letter from Alexander York to Governor Glick, 25 June 1884, Governor's Correspondence, Kansas Historical Society).

William's Civil War record lists him as an assistant surgeon for the 15th Regiment Colored Infantry (U.S. Colored Troops Military Service Records, 1863–1865). For an extended read on the siege of Vicksburg see *Vicksburg 1863* by Winston Groom (2010). Mary York details William's experience as a prisoner of war in *The Bender Tragedy* (18–19). Information about Camp Ford is derived from Leon Mitchell Junior's "Camp Ford, Confederate Military Prison" (*Southwestern Historical Quarterly* 66, 1962).

William's characterisation, early life, and relationship with his family is derived from Mary York's *The Bender Tragedy*, with details corroborated by articles in *The Topeka State Journal* (5 August 1911), "Disappearance of Dr WM. York," in *The Fort Scott Daily Monitor* (6 April 1873), "W. H. York Left Fort Scott March Tenth and Has Not Yet Returned to His Family," in *The Head-light* and "All Trace of Him Was Lost" in *The Daily Commonwealth* (9 April 1873).

An Anxious Heart

Mary York relays her experience of the days leading up to discovering her husband's disappearance in *The Bender Tragedy* (34–58). Her interaction with Mrs Preston and

Manasseh shows a woman already certain that her husband is dead: "They both tried to cheer me with all the suggestions that he would yet return. Oh! How my poor heart longed to believe it, but my better judgment, and my knowledge of his promptness in returning at any given time, bade me say—'No—he will never return'" (58).

A Match to a Powder Mill

Folklorist Vance Randolph discusses the growing suspicion around Kate Bender's spiritualism in his book *Kate Bender, The Kansas Murderess: The Horrible History of an Arch Killer* (1944). Susanna Tyack's ill-fated séance at the Bender cabin was reported in a number of papers after she became suspected of being involved in the crimes; see "Magnetic Healer," *The Weekly News-Democrat* (23 May 1873).

Prairie fires were an ongoing source of distress for white settlers. One particularly evocative example from *The Atchison Daily Champion* describes the fires as follows: "Desolation and Suffering Throughout our State. Daily we are in receipt of the sickening details of the ravages of the unmerciful prairie fires that have crept like demons over our fair young state, licking up with its tongues of flame, in almost an instant, the labored toils of years. Hundreds have lost their all, and thousands have, in an hour, lost their whole year's work" (25 November 1873). Further information on the ecological and cultural importance of prairie fires can be found at "Kansas Prairie Fires," *NASA Earth Observatory* (https://earthobservatory.nasa.gov/images/83477/kansas -prairie-fires).

The details of the Dienst family's struggle with Kate Bender come from testimony given by both Henrietta Dienst and Delilah Keck at trial in 1890, during which Henrietta reported telling Kate to "let my folks alone, alive or dead" (John T. James, *The Benders in Kansas*, 72, 76). John Dienst's headstone is at Harmony Grove Cemetery, Labette, Kansas. His death is listed as 8 March 1872.

The Trace of Him Is Lost

James Roach's letter is one of two sources that exist prior to the discovery of the bodies on the Bender homestead to explicitly name the missing men: "The first was by the name of Jones, the second by the name of McCarthy, the third by the name of Brown, the fourth is by the name of York." Its tone gives a good indication of the frustration of those in the area whose pleas for assistance had gone overlooked by local authorities such as Leroy Dick. In his conclusion, Roach explicitly accuses them of not caring about the welfare of the citizens under their protection (Letter from James Roach, 2 April 1873, Governor's Correspondence: Osborn, Kansas Historical Society). A letter expressing this sentiment, as well as accusing Alexander of "not acting as a gentleman should," later appeared in the *Parsons Weekly Herald*, possibly also written by Roach or a member of his family on behalf of the people of Ladore (3 July 1873). The letter describes the actions of the York brothers as "with fifty or sixty men, raked and scraped this country, threw down fences, tore open farms, tore down clothes lines, . . . and passed through the country similar to Price's Raiders." The *Waubansee County News* reported that the Roach family had been arrested "as being implicated in the numerous murders in the vicinity of Osage Mission," but this was later refuted by the letter published in July (30 April 1873). The disappearances of John Arbunkle and John Martin were reported in *The Tioga Herald* under the headline "Mysterious Disappearance of Men from Ladore" (16 September 1871).

Edward York was born in Illinois in 1852, making him twenty-one at the time of William's murder (U.S. Federal Census of 1870). His role in the search is confirmed by both Mary York (*The Bender Tragedy*, 85) and Leroy Dick (*The Bender Hills Mystery*, 10). *The Head-light* reported that William "fed his horse at Mr. J. C. White's residence" (9 April 1873) and Mary York recalls the detail that the Whites "asked the Doctor if he were acquainted with Senator York. He replied that he had seen him, but did not tell them of their relationship" (67). An obituary of Thomas Beers published in the *Emporia Weekly Gazette* (16 June 1904) provides the basis of Beers's characterisation, along with an interview he gave to the paper in 1901.

By 9 April, a consensus was forming that "there is an organised band of murderers, and that six or seven murders have been committed by them during the past six months" (*The Head-light*, 9 April 1873). This would prove to be an accurate prediction as, with the exception of James Feerick, all the confirmed victims of the family were murdered between October 1872 and March 1873.

The Mystery Still Unravelled

As addressed in the text, interactions in the chapter are based on Leroy Dick's account of the events leading up to the discovery of William's body at the Bender homestead (*The Bender Hills Mystery*, 10–4). Ed reads the note that is one of the key primary sources that represent the Benders' voice. In full it reads:

Prof. Miss KATIE BENDER.

Can heal all sorts of Diseases; can cure Blindness, Fits, Deafness and all such disease, also Deaf and Dumbness. Residence, 14 miles East of Independence, on the road from Independence to Osage Mission one and one half miles South East of Morehead Station.

Katie Bender, 18 June 1872 (Currently held at the Kansas Historical Society).

A Disguise of Hellish Cunning

The details of the search were reported at length in *The Fort Scott Daily Monitor*, which informed its readers that "the locality where he disappeared is a notorious one, this not being the first event of a similar kind that has transpired in the neighbourhood" (6 April 1873). Gebhardt's habit of sitting outside the cabin with a Bible on his knee also became a point of focus for the press after the fact; *The Weekly News-Democrat* described him as "sitting all day long apparently absorbed in God's Holy Word. It is more likely he was on guard watching the approach of victims" (23 May 1873). Alexander York's visit to the Bender cabin and the behaviour of the family while he was there is reported across all sources, likely because it occurred relatively close to when the bodies were discovered and a number of people in the area were aware of it. Both

Leroy Dick (*The Bender Hills Mystery*, 14–17) and Mary York (*The Bender Tragedy*, 74–6) deal with the matter in detail. Dick states that it was Jim Buster who was most suspicious of Kate's behaviour and told Alexander, "Your questions about Will were shooting so close to the mark that she got scared" (16). Alexander recalled his visit to the cabin over a decade later; "I saw the Benders when they were living in Labette Co." (Letter from Alexander York to Governor St. John, 13 December 1879, Governor's Correspondence: St. John, Kansas Historical Society). The newspapers were particularly enraptured by Kate's promise to Alexander that she would contact William's soul if he came back to the cabin on his own. As far as South Carolina, she was referred to as "the pretended sorceress and real fiend [who] told York privately that if he would come the next, Friday—when best she worked her spells" (*Yorkville Enquirer*, 29 May 1873).

The petition and accompanying letter are the first to explicitly name George Longcor as a suspected victim of the "organised band of outlaws." Interestingly, it narrows the place where the missing men had vanished to "Big Hill Creek or the crossing of Drum Creek in the eastern portions of Montgomery or in the Western portions of Labette and Neosho County," which makes Alexander York's hasty conclusion that the Benders were too stupid to commit such a series of crimes even more surprising (Letter from Citizens of Montgomery County to Governor Osborn, 2 April 1873, Governor's Correspondence: Osborn, KSHS). *The Daily Commonwealth* announced Osborn's reward several days later (9 April 1873).

The Night Express

That the Benders fled the night of 4 April, the same day Alexander visited the cabin, is corroborated by testimony from the ticket agent at Thayer. The escape of the family was included in early reports of the bodies at the cabin; see "About three weeks ago this family departed very suddenly, and left their cattle to starve on the farm, drove to Thayer and hitched their team close to the railroad depot, and bought tickets to Humboldt" (*The Daily Kansas Tribune*, 7 May 1873). The timetable for the "Night Express" shows that the last train out of Thayer headed towards Humboldt was at 9.03 p.m. and stopped at Chanute and then Humboldt (*The Daily Kansas Tribune*, 4 April 1873). An advertisement for the Missouri-Kansas-Texas Railway published in *The Kansas Democrat* the same day as the Benders fled the state announces the railway as "now finished to Denison," with coaches running from Humboldt, but only during the day (4 April 1873). Taken with an article from the *Leavenworth Daily Commercial* that reports the entire family had been seen at Chanute eating breakfast "at the Sherman house" (15 May 1873), it is clear the Benders left the train on the fourth and reboarded, headed for Humboldt on the morning of the fifth, where they then separated. Information on the crash at Crush comes from Lorraine Boissoneault's "A Train Company Crash" (*Smithsonian*, 28 July 2017).

Conjectures of Robbery and Murder

Mary York's account devotes entire passages to her mental state in the weeks leading up to the discovery of William's murder. She discusses her need for "active labor to crowd out the fearful pantomimes which tormented my overtaxed brain" (*The Bender Tragedy*, 80) and refers to the period as "a wearing interval of suspense" (82). *The Daily Commonwealth* reported that "there is no longer any doubt that he has been murdered" (9 April 1873); two days earlier *The Fort Scott Daily Monitor* had come to a similar conclusion that "he was foully murdered to get possession of his horse" (6 April 1873). Mary states that after reading the news that "it was my constant prayer that reality might be made known, and terminate these terrible imaginations of death in the most fearful manner" (83). Leroy Dick recalls the meeting at Harmony Grove schoolhouse in great detail, after which he expresses regret that they waited until the twelfth to finalise the details of the search: "Our mistake was our failure to instigate a speedy and drastic search" (*The Bender Hills Mystery*, 9). *The Head-light* reported the "Meeting of Osage Township" on the twelfth and published the following resolutions:

> Resolved: That a committee be appointed to investigate and report at our next meeting.

> Resolved: That we heartily sympathise with the friends of those who have been slain, and that the citizens of Osage Township will make every effort in our powers to detect and bring to justice the murderers.

> Resolved: That the Independence, Parsons, Oswego, Chetopa, Thayer and Osage Mission newspapers be requested to publish the foregoing resolutions (23 April 1873).

The two articles on the discovery of the wagon at Thayer can be found under "Mysterious" (9 April 1873) and "Foul Play" (*The Head-light*, 16 April 1873). The governor's reward was widely circulated in the region, along with the names of the men who were missing along with William. *The Kansas Democrat* listed "William H. York, George Longcor, Benjamin Brown and William Jones" below the notice of a "five hundred dollars reward" (25 April 1873). Alexander's reward was printed in *The Head-light*; "Col. York offers a reward of one hundred dollars to any person who will give any information that will lead to the recovery of his brother's person" (9 April 1873).

The weather during April was sporadic and unpredictable and caused the search party to struggle. *The Fort Scott Daily Monitor* provides a good indicator of the weather over the month, printing that "the stormy weather of the past few days has greatly interfered with telegraphic communication" (10 April 1873). Several days later the paper reports a combination of snow and "the wrathful red glare" of a prairie fire (16 April 1873). The weather affected trade across the state, with *The Kansas Daily Commonwealth* noticing the trend between lively and dull retail "as the weather was bright or stormy" (30 April 1873). In its article announcing the discovery of the wagon, *The Head-light* also reported that "search for the owner was almost entirely prevented by the heavy rain and snow storm of Monday and yesterday" (9 April 1873).

Sources vary as to which of the Tole brothers was the first to discover the claim had been abandoned, but the circumstances themselves are consistent. *The Chetopa Advance* names Silas (11 May 1873), but Leroy Dick attributes the discovery to Billy (*The Bender Hills Mystery*, 18).

Part III: A Revolting Spectacle of Crime Made Public

A Veil of Mystery

In *The Bender Hills Mystery*, Leroy Dick devotes several pages to Sunday, 4 May, and Monday, 5 May (18–20), in which he relays his initial investigation of the Bender property and the reaction of the Harmony Grove schoolhouse community. Also informing the discussion of the initial discovery of the abandonment of the homestead is the Maurice Sparks interview, "Light on Benders" (*The Topeka State Journal*, 5 August, 1911). Sparks was a well-known resident who remained in the area for most of his life and is frequently referenced by Leroy Dick and the papers. "Light on Benders" also includes a diagram of the layout of the cabin in relation to the road from Osage Mission to Independence. Sparks recalls that "one of the Toles took occasion to ride by the Bender place" and "evidences of the desertion of the place were immediately noticed as he approached the house." He also corroborates Dick's testimony that Sparks went to "Thayer on Monday to look at the team and wagon" and that the link was thus made between the Bender family and the disappearance of William York. The *Western Home Journal* printed a diagram of the interior of the cabin and describes the decision to "fully search the premises" (15 May 1873). The hammers discovered in the cabin are now on display at the Cherryvale Historical Museum, where they are presented alongside a certificate of authenticity. A description of the hammers in *The New York Times* confirms that "in the house were found two shoemaker's hammers" (13 May 1873). *The Daily Capital* reported that investigation had revealed the body of William Jones was "hauled to the creek in Bender's wagon, which was easy to track, as one wheel was dished and wabbled" (2 August 1880).

What the Benders Have to Answer For

As the circumstances surrounding the discovery of the bodies at the Bender homestead were the most widely reported event in the narrative of the case, this discussion draws from myriad different newspapers. *The Fort Scott Daily Monitor*, *The Head-light*, *The Weekly News-Democrat*, and *The Daily Commonwealth* had all been following the story of William's disappearance since mid-March and as such were quick to report on the discovery of his body. A concise article in *The Weekly Commonwealth* gives the best overview of the state of William's corpse:

> The back of the skull was found to have been broken, and both temples crushed in, as if by blows with a shoe hammer. One eye had been driven from its socket, and the victims throat had been cut. A shoe hammer found in the house fitted the indentations in the back of the head. An attempt had been made to conceal the grave by plowing over it . . . The remains were not so far decomposed as to prevent their easy recognition by Mr. Ed. York" (14 May 1873).

Newspapers differ on whether Ed discovered a bridle or a pair of glasses belonging to his brother; the *Daily Kansas Tribune* says bridle (8 May 1873), *The Weekly Commonwealth* says glasses (14 May 1873). For further details surrounding William's identification of his brother see the same issue of the *Daily Kansas Tribune*. The *Republican Valley Empire* reported that the discovery of William York "solved, we think, among other mysteries, the disappearance of a stone mason named Jones, who started to go from Osage Mission to Independence last fall" (16 May 1873). Other newspapers consulted are *The Atchison Daily Champion* (10 May 1873), *The Kansas Chief* (15 May 1873), and *The Oswego Independent* (25 August 1877).

Also informing this chapter are *The Bender Hills Mystery* (23–8) and Mary York's *The Bender Tragedy* (84–8). Leroy Dick's account of the removal of William's head can be found on page 26, though this particular series of events does not occur in any other source. An example of how cabins were commonly moved on the frontier can be found opposite page 83 of Percy Ebbutt's *Emigrant Life in Kansas*. Alexander's inability to recognise the Benders for the monsters they were became a point of contention for many people besides the man himself. See the *Parsons Weekly Herald* (3 July 1873) as an example. Members and friends of the York family defend Alexander by saying that the Benders put on such a convincing show of stupidity that it was impossible to believe they were intelligent criminals.

An advertisement for George Gamble's photography studio can be found in *The Parsons Weekly Sun* (14 March 1874). He took several photographs of the crime scene, all of which are available online through Kansas Memory (www.kansasmemory.org) or at the Kansas Historical Society Archives. In Gamble's photograph of the grave of William York, a man likely to be Leroy Dick is wearing a very light tan suit. Gamble also returned the following day, as seen in his photographs containing several excavated graves and coffins on the property. The engravings done from his images were published in *Harper's Weekly* (7 June 1873). Gamble's role as "Photographer, Bertillon Dept." at the Ohio Penitentiary comes from his entry in the U.S. Federal Census of 1910.

The Burying Ground

Mary York describes learning of the discovery of her husband's body (*The Bender Tragedy*, 85–7), noting that "the messenger was very merciful to me; he kept back the worst details." She also dedicates an entire chapter of her account to the story of James Feerick and his family (119–26). Leroy Dick covers the unearthing of the rest of the graves in *The Bender Hills Mystery* (28–32). During Maurice Sparks's recollection of the events he expresses the opinion that the family varied their method of attack and likely just struck when people were least expecting it (*The Topeka State Journal*, 5 August 1873). Newspapers informing the discussion of 7 May are "Another Horror" in *The Leavenworth Times* (8 May 1873), the *Lawrence Daily Journal* (11 and 17 May 1873), the *Leavenworth Daily Commercial* (15 May 1873), *The Weekly News-Democrat* (23 May 1873), *The Girard Press* (15 May 1873), and *The Osage Mission Journal* (7 May 1873). The full-page spread entitled "Most Horrible Crimes on Record" was published in *The Head-light* on 14 May 1873, with its earliest coverage appearing under "Horrible Discovery" (7 May). Elkanah Tresslar's stereoscopic images are held at the Kansas Historical Society Archives.

Names associated with the man in the well are Peter Boyle, William Boyle, and John Geary. As Leroy Dick refers to him as Johnny Boyle, that is the name I have chosen to use here (*The Bender Hills Mystery*, 30). For Henry McKenzie's defensive wounds, see "he was a strong and athletic man, and from the number of wounds evidently showed fight before he was murdered" in *The Weekly News-Democrat* (23 May 1873). The paper also lists the full text of William McCrotty's tattoo as: "W.F. McCrotty—Born 1843" [an American flag] 123 Ills. Infantry, Co. D." His identification by Dan Gardner appears in "Never Knew His Fate" in *The Chanute Blade* (15 October 1891). Opinion differs largely on the amount each man had with them when they were travelling. Those who were en route to the land office were more likely to be carrying cash; but the fact that McCrotty had to borrow money for dinner suggests he had little of value on his person save his clothes. The identification of Benjamin Brown by his widow appears in the *Leavenworth Daily Commercial* under "A Painful Circumstance" (17 May 1873). The attempted hanging of Rudolph Brockman is covered most vividly in *The Atchison Daily Champion* (10 May 1873).

Facts and Theories of the Crimes

Newspapers referenced in the opening discussion are "Death's Wayside Inn" in the *San Francisco Chronicle* (27 May 1873), "The Kansas Murderers" in *The New York Times* (13 May 1873), and "Butchery in Kansas" in *The Courier* (22 May 1873). Over the course of his career as a private detective, Thomas Beers frequently spoke to the newspapers about his pursuit of the family and often embellished his exploits.

Examples of covers from *The Illustrated Police News* can be seen online at the British Library: https://www.bl.uk/collection-items/front-page-of-the-illustrated-police-news -25-june-1870. Examples of cheap "dime" novels (an American dime is a coin worth ten cents, similar to a sixpence) are available on the Stanford University online archive: http://web.stanford.edu/dept/SUL/library/prod/depts/dp/pennies/home.html. Further information about the role of the mug shot in the nineteenth century can be found in Samantha Rae Long's thesis "The Mug Shot, Wanted Poster, and Rogues Galleries: The Societal Impact of Criminal Photography in England, France, and the United States from 1839 to 1900." An example of an album of mugshots designed for the consumption of the general public is *Professional Criminals of America* by Thomas Byrnes.

Due to the fast and often loose nature of frontier reporting, the difficulty of corroborating names and places, and the reliance on gossip, the names of the Benders' victims are frequently misspelled or jumbled up. Henry McKenzie is reported as "McKinzey," William McCrotty as "McCarthy," and Benjamin Brown as "L. G. Brown." Before the positive identification of James Feerick as the eighth body buried in the orchard, the man was reported as Alonzo Sconce, Joe Sowers, Leigh Mitchell, and Jack Bogart. Through hyperbolic reporting in the newspapers at the time and in the years following, the number of victims attributed to the Benders during their time in south-east Kansas sometimes ranges as high as 150 (supposed confession of Bender accomplice Nicholas Minon in *The Chetopa Advance*, 4 June 1873). In the direct aftermath of the discovery of the murders, the consensus was that, regardless of names, eight bodies had been found on the Benders' property. Taken with William Jones, John Phipps, and the unidentified man found in the campsite in March 1872, this puts the confirmable number of victims at eleven. It is quite possible that the number was indeed higher, as Leroy Dick himself notes, "but from the many enquiries about missing men . . . we were certain the number of victims must have greatly exceeded that figure" (*The Bender Hills Mystery*, 30). The quote from *The Fort Scott Daily Monitor* was reprinted in *The Western Spirit* (30 May 1873).

Discussion of Kate and the overall dynamic in the family is informed by *The Topeka Weekly Times* (17 August 1873) and the *Leavenworth Daily Commercial* (15 May 1873). Julia Hestler's story appeared in several different forms as more people came forward about the story, but all focus on a woman who fled the cabin after being threatened under supernatural circumstances; see the *Yorkville Enquirer* (29 May 1873) and the *Lawrence Daily Journal* (17 May 1873). Mary York's comments on the family are from *The Bender Tragedy* (107–8, 128). Descriptions of Kate in the press are from the "Pistols and Knives for Supper" in *The Wichita Eagle* (22 May 1873) and the *San Francisco Examiner* (1 August 1873).

It seems that "Hell's Half-Acre" as a name for the Bender homestead was first used in *The Kansas Democrat*, though it is hard to know who first came up with the name (16 May 1873). Leroy Dick's statement to the *Leavenworth Daily Commercial* appeared on 20 May. Articles that contain supposed first-hand experiences of the Bender family can be found in *The Girard Press* (22 May 1873), the *Lawrence Daily Journal* (17 May 1873), and the *San Francisco Examiner* (1 August 1873). The quote regarding the family's materialism disguised as spiritualism is from *The Daily Phoenix* (15 May 1873).

Intense Excitement in the Neighbourhood

An announcement in *The Kansas Tribune* reported that people in the surrounding areas "are so excited about the Bender horror, that they have prevailed upon the L., L. & G. Railroad Company to run excursion trains to-day from those towns to Morehead . . . to enable them to visit the 'slaughter pen'" (15 May 1873). Further details about the deluge of visitors the site received come from *The Kansas Democrat* (16 May 1873), *The Head-light* (14 May 1873), *The Western Spirit* (16 May 1873), and *The Kansas Chief* (15 May 1873). Leroy Dick's exhibition of the hammers was spotted by a reporter for *The Kansas Democrat*.

Provoking much interest was a Bible and a Catholic prayer book found in the cabin on the day that William York's body was discovered. Both were unremarkable books in bad condition, but what really intrigued people was a series of notes written in German on the inside covers. The exact content of the inscriptions varies among newspapers, but most report the following notations:

"Jo—Bender, born July, 1848

Twenty-second of January, 1873. Hell went off!

Nineteenth of January is a *slaugh* day."

Most considered "slaugh" to be a shortened form of "slaughter," indicating that a murder took place on the named date. Variations in the reports likely derive from issues translating the writing from German, or from newspapers that chose to embellish the content to better suit their stories. In her account of the crimes, Mary York offers a different translation altogether, supposedly done by an old German man at the scene: "Katie has left The Slaughter House, and gone to superintend the Department of Hell" (*The Bender Tragedy*, 135). Bible inscriptions are taken from *The Weekly Commonwealth* 14 May 1873), *The Head-light* (14 May 1873), and *The Weekly News-Democrat* (23 May 1873).

Alexander York's heavy-handed attempt to catch potential accomplices of the Bender family is best documented in the letter to the *Parsons Weekly Herald* from the citizens of Ladore (3 July 1873), which accuses York, District Attorney E. C. Ward, and Detective Thomas Beers of failing to apologise for the mass arrests conducted in the wake of the murders. It contains details of all those arrested, as well as their poor treatment in prison and the attempt by authorities to bribe people into testifying against their neighbours. Articles supporting the details of those arrested are "A Magnetic Healer" in *The Head-light* (14 May 1873), "The Neighbours Kindly Cared for It" in *The Weekly News-Democrat* (23 May 1873), and "Suspected Confederates" in *The Girard Press* (15 May 1873). Major Mefford received specific attention because he had arrived from out of state: "Meffort discharged" (*The Fort Scott Daily Monitor*, 14 May 1873).

Part IV: In Pursuit of Murderers

Texas Is the Place

John Gebhardt relayed the story of his and Kate's journey down through Indian Territory to Samuel Merrick; Merrick names the Arkansas River, the Creek Agency, and Stonewall, he also states that "in coming down through the Nation they all wore men's clothes" (statement of Samuel Merrick, enclosed in a letter from Superintendent Joseph Nicholson to Governor St. John, 14 December 1879, Governor's Correspondence: St. John, Kansas Historical Society, 2). For information on the problems with policing white outlaws in Indian Territory see "Indian Territory, 1866–1889" by Michael Green (*Historical Atlas of Oklahoma*, 98–9) and Larry Ball's "Before the Hanging Judge: The Origins of the United States District Court for the Western District of Arkansas" (*Arkansas Historical Quarterly* 49, Autumn 1990). Information on Stonewall comes from Martha E. Rhynes, "Stonewall" (*The Encyclopedia of Oklahoma History and Culture*). Further information on American Indian boarding schools and their devastating impact on Indigenous peoples can be found in *Stringing Rosaries: The History, the Unforgivable, and the Healing of Northern Plains American Indian Boarding School Survivors* by Denise K. Lajimodiere and "History and Culture: Boarding Schools" on Northern Plains Reservation Aid (http://www.nativepartnership.org/site/PageServer?page name=airc_hist_boardingschools). Since Merrick reports that Kate and John crossed the river at a safe place and the couple was next seen in Denison, it is likely they used Colbert's ferry as a means of crossing into Texas. More information about the ferry and Benjamin Colbert himself can be found in Ruth Ann Overbeck's "Colbert's Ferry" (*Chronicles of Oklahoma* 57, Summer 1979).

The discussion of Denison is informed by "Memorial Sketch of Denison" in *The Denison News* (27 December 1872) along with David Minor's "Denison, TX" (*Handbook of Texas Online*, www.tshaonline.org/handbook/entries/denison-tx). The layout of the city can be seen in "The Bird's Eye View of the City of Denison" made on 23 May

1873 (Library of Congress: http://hdl.loc.gov/loc.gmd/g4034d.pm020519). Editor B. C. Murray's quote can be found in "Ho! For Texas" (27 December 1872).

Albert Owens's account of the Benders and their time in Denison is found in Leroy Dick's account (*The Bender Hills Mystery*, 33–4) and supported by an article in the *Denison Daily News* entitled "The Benders in Denison" (20 May 1873). The article notes that Owens had given an interview to *The Parsons Sun* in which he stated "a party, old man and woman, young man and young woman, answering exactly the description of the Bender family, were camped two weeks ago last Sunday, at the spring in the north part of Denison. The young man told Mr. Owens that his name was Bender." The article informed its readers that the Benders left the town and headed west on 5 May. *The Fort Scott Daily Monitor* also reported that the family had been seen in Denison (21 May 1873). Owens told Dick that the young couple had arrived alone and were later joined by an older couple (33).

A detailed physical description of Frank McPherson lists the man as "twenty three years old, weighs 175 pounds [twelve and a half stone/seventy-nine kilograms], has chronic sore eyes, short upper lip, dark hazel eyes and is about five feet ten and one half inches high [179 centimetres]" (*The Head-light*, 14 May 1873). *The Fort Scott Daily Monitor* included more details: "slight mustache, upper lip short, revealing prominently upper row of front teeth . . . of morose disposition, sullen appearance, and has been a railroad hand" (13 May 1873). Frank's attack on Lucas Eigensatz appeared in numerous papers in south-east Kansas because of the brutal nature of the attack and his subsequent escape. See "Arrest and Escape of a Desperado" in *The Girard Press* (1 May 1873), "A murderous affray took place in Parsons' in the *Osage Mission Transcript* (2 May 1873), and "McPherson's money was used in bribing the official" in *The Sedalia Democrat* (24 April 1873).

Ironically while in Labette to report on the Bender crimes, a correspondent for the *Leavenworth Daily Commercial* encountered Annie Eigensatz on a train, where she told him of the murder of her husband and "the conductor corroborated this statement, and added that [Frank] has been guilty of two or three other causeless murders" (20 May 1873).

Go Out and Lay Hands on 'Em

Along with Detective Thomas Beers, Charles Peckham is one of the most consistently represented members of the search party in the Governor's Correspondence held at the Kansas Historical Society Archive. When he is not writing to Governor Osborn personally, he is referenced by B. W. Perkins, a Labette County attorney responsible for overseeing the financial element of the search (Governor's Correspondence: Osborn, Kansas Historical Society). An issue of the *South Kansas Tribune* shows advertisements for both Peckham's and York's legal practices listed next to each other on the first page (12 May 1873). *The Girard Press* announced Peckham's involvement in the search: "Col. Peckham is at Parsons and in communication with the Detective and pursuing forces, which he is directing" (15 May 1873). The article attacking Alexander York can be found in *The Kansas Chief* (22 May 1873).

The movement of Peckham and Beers is discussed in Dick's account, though Dick makes the claim that he was the one directing the search (*The Bender Hills Mystery*,

32–6). This is unlikely, as he is not referenced by anyone else involved, although it is likely that as township trustee he was involved in dealing with claims relating to the family at a local level, and he certainly spoke to Albert Owens when the man arrived in Labette County. For sources supporting the movement of the Benders in fleeing Kansas, see notes for "The Night Express." *The Head-light* reported that before fleeing, Kate had often spoken of "a house of ill fame at Lafayette Park (*Daily Kansas Tribune*, 7 May 1873). Peckham's travels in Missouri were reported in the expenses sheet sent to B. W. Perkins, as are telegrams sent between parties involved in the search (Exhibit A, Letter and Expense Report from B. W. Perkins to Governor Osborn, 30 December 1873, Governor's Correspondence: Osborn, Kansas Historical Society).

The Atchison Daily Patriot's article on sightings of the family referred to them as "The Kansas Grave Diggers" (28 May 1873). The governor's proclamation announcing a reward for the apprehension of the family as well as descriptions of its members is stored at the Kansas Historical Society. *The Girard Press* "low opinion of the amount offered" is from the article "Crimes, Catastrophes, Casualties and Calamities" (29 May 1873).

Where Horse Thieves Do Congregate

Like many other settlements that were once frontier boom towns, Red River Station is now a ghost town, indicated by a historical waypoint by the river. The description of the town here is largely informed by Glen O. Wilson's "Old Red River Station" (*Southwestern Historical Quarterly* 61, no. 3, January 1958, 350–8), along with "Life at Red River Station" in the *Leavenworth Daily Commercial* (20 July 1873) and "Items from the Cattle Trail" in *The Weekly Democrat Statesman* (26 June 1873). The latter gives a good indication of the dangers of life in the area, stating that "it has been raining constantly for eight or ten days . . . it is estimated there are about 30,000 cattle in this vicinity waiting to cross the river . . . it rained and stormed every night and the cattle 'stampeded' every time it rained." The *Wyandotte Gazette* later reported that the Benders were known to have been in the area around Red River Station throughout the summer of 1873 (5 December 1873).

The characterisation of William McPherson, alias "Missouri Bill," comes from obituaries published in both the *Denison Daily News* (4 March 1875) and *The Sedalia Democrat* (6 March 1875), which described him as a "man of great size and strength, and known to be desperate and reckless when aroused." The detail about him leaving Sedalia in his late teens comes from the same issue of the *Democrat*. Frank McPherson's attempt to use counterfeit currency also appears in the *Democrat* (24 January 1872), as does his attack on the police officer (5 July 1872). The entire McPherson family is listed as residing in Sedalia in 1870 (U.S. Federal Census of 1870), and many of Frank and Bill's siblings remained in Parsons or the surrounding area for the rest of their lives. Their tendency to roam among Texas, Indian Territory, and Colorado was noted by both Merrick (statement of Samuel Merrick, enclosed in a letter from Superintendent Joseph Nicholson to Governor St. John, 14 December 1879, Governor's Correspondence: St. John, 1, 6) and letters from James Sullivan (letter from James Sullivan to Governor Osborn, 3 November 1874, Governor's Correspondence: Osborn, Kansas Historical Society). Sullivan also links Missouri Bill and Frank to the family. Beers wrote of his frustration with law enforcement in the region in a letter to Osborn: "the Sheriff of Montague is considered implicated with them and it is known that he advised them to leave the station for the present" (Beers to Osborn, 20 August 1873, Governor's Correspondence: Osborn, Kansas Historical Society). A resource of immeasurable assistance in tracking the Benders through the region is *Colton's New Map of the State of Texas: The Indian Territory and Adjoining Portions of New Mexico, Louisiana and Arkansas, 1873* (online at: https://texashistory.unt.edu/ark:/67531 /metapth231414/m1/1/?q=map%20of%20texas%201873).

In his statement of 1879, Samuel Merrick states that he lived with the Slimps and Missouri Bill in 1872 and names members of the Slimp family as Floyd and Clint. A combination of U.S. Federal Census records (1850–1880) indicate that the Slimp family was very large and, in the years 1870–1880, moved between various regions in Texas, Kansas, and Missouri. The full names of the Slimp children referenced by Merrick are John Floyd Slimp and Sebastian Clinton Slimp (see the Slimp Family in Precinct 8, Collin, Texas, U.S. Federal Census of 1860). Merrick states explicitly that, prior to him meeting the Benders himself, Floyd often talked about his second cousins: "They said their sister would come down in the fall in winter with their cousins the Benders that lived in Labette co. Kansas. Floyd that was the second son said their mother and old Mrs Bender was cousins. Their mother was dead" (Merrick, 1, Kansas Historical Society). The Slimps provide the common link between the Benders and the McPhersons and, as the McPherson brothers ran a loosely organised criminal racket, the rest of the outlaw colony. The Benders' move to Mud Creek is reported by Beers (Beers to Osborn, 20 August 1873) as well as the *Wyandotte Gazette* (5 December 1873).

Some Blundering Detective

This stage in the pursuit of the family is largely informed by the letters of Thomas Beers, B. W. Perkins, Governor Osborn, and Colonel Peckham. A letter from Osborn to Perkins informing the men that they would at last be granted funds for the search indicates that it was taking a long time for the hunt to truly get off the ground (Osborn to Perkins, 24 May 1873). Leroy Dick describes Peckham and Beers arriving in Texas to continue the investigation, along with their journey westwards and frustration at the lack of funds in *The Bender Hills Mystery* (34–5).

In June, after the two men arrived at Red River, B. W. Perkins forwarded a letter from Peckham to Osborn with the following note: "enclosed I send you for your information a letter just received from Col. Peckham which speaks for itself. If you can issue a requisition upon the Gov of Texas, prior to the arrest of the offenders please do as requested by Col. Peckham," and concluded by saying he felt considerably encouraged by the developments (20 June 1873). A later letter from Thomas Beers indicates that they had made a deal with Missouri Bill that the latter evidently had no intent of seeing through. Writing of hiring a second man to help track the Benders, Beers states that "I have no fear of his playing the same game that Missouri Bill played" (20 August 1873). Taken with a letter from James Sullivan that states Bill had agreed to take him to the Benders for "a deed of money," it is reasonable to assume that he made a similar deal with Peckham and Beers (Sullivan to Osborn, 3 November 1873).

An Organised and Extensive Gang

For more information about Indian raiders in the territory and their influence on the settlement of Clay County see *"Border Land*: The Struggle for Texas" (University of Texas, online at: https://library.uta.edu/borderland/tribe/kiowa?page=1). Information on the attack on Gottlieb Koozer and his family comes from *American Indian Wars: A Chronology of Confrontations Between Native Peoples and Settlers and the United States Military* by Michael L. Nunnally (125) and J. J. Methvin's *Andele: Or, The Mexican-Kiowa Captive. A Story of Real Life Among the Indians* (137–9).

Floyd and his father, Granville Slimp, appeared at the United States District Court for the Western District of Arkansas at Fort Smith accused of stealing "two mules to the value of three hundred dollars" (Fort Smith, Arkansas, U.S. Criminal Case Files Index, 1872). Merrick noted that the Slimps "had some corn growing and used to run off Caddo and Wichita Indians from the Wichita Agency on the Washita River" (statement of Samuel Merrick, enclosed in a letter from Superintendent Joseph Nicholson to Governor St. John, 14 December 1879, Governor's Correspondence: St. John, 1).

The movements of the Benders and their interactions with members of the gang come from details in Merrick's statement. He arrived three days after the Bender family and was "made acquainted with the old woman and John and Kate that went by the name of Gardener. John was called Bill Gardener. Kate was called Jennie Gardener" (Merrick, 2). Merrick's prison records indicate that he was born in New York and was about twenty-nine at the time he first met the Benders (Samuel Merrick, Detroit House of Correction, Michigan, U.S. Federal Census of 1880). Beyond his age and eyewitness accounts of his horsemanship and athletic ability, there are no available descriptions of his physical appearance.

Be Sure Your Sins Will Find You Out

Beers recalled his interaction with the man on the Little Wichita in his August letter to Osborn: "I talked with a good reliable man in that country that told me that Bill came to him and wanted to borrow some money. He told him that there was some German people come to this country with Frank his brother and that they had got in trouble in the open country and that he wanted the money to help them" (Beers to Osborn, 20 August 1873). His quote about public opinion pointing to the Wichita River basin as a location for the family is included in the above letter. Peckham wrote his letter to Osborn requesting he be allowed to return to the search in early September and urged the governor to consider the "embarrassing position of failing after all that has been done." But he also informed him that he would "transmit through Perkins my final account of expenditure" if Osborn decided the search no longer warranted funds (1 September 1873). Perkins and York both expressed the desire that the money taken from Pomeroy should be used to hunt the family. "Would it not be wise for our legislature to appropriate by retribution the $7000 turned over to the State Treasurer . . . to continue the search and secure the capture of these ghouls in human form," wrote Perkins to Osborn (30 December 1873). *The Leavenworth Times* reported that "York suggests the money be devoted to ferreting out the Benders" (28 August

1873). For *The Texas Democrat*'s damning assessment of Thomas Beers, see "The Benders" (*The Wyandotte Gazette*, 5 December 1873). Leroy Dick discusses his attempt to contact Texas authorities in *The Bender Hills Mystery* (36).

The examples cited in this chapter are a few of the thousands of words printed about the Bender family in the year following the discovery of the murders alone. Newspapers referenced are the *South Kansas Tribune* (30 September 1874), the *Indiana Weekly Messenger* (29 April 1874), *The Topeka Weekly Times* (16 July 1874), and for the man's subsequent arrest see the *Weekly Kansas State Journal* (10 May 1877). Nathan J. Pierce appears in the Chicago City Directory as an agent (Illinois, 1873), and the report on his visit to Labette comes from the *Atchison Daily Globe* (30 September 1873).

James Sullivan wrote two letters to Osborn in June 1874, both from Las Animas. In the first he expresses thanks for the governor's help: "thanking you for your magnanimous aid and hoping you will never regret having aided me" (Sullivan to Osborn, 1 June 1874, Governor's Correspondence: Osborn, Kansas Historical Society). In the second he states that "I have not enough means to buy me enough horses so I have asked York to help me," along with his request for funds from Osborn (20 June 1873). Alexander recalled Sullivan's visit some years later: "Sullivan mentioned in Merrick's statement visited me at Independence and went from there to Texas in search of them" (Alexander York to Governor St. John, 3 December 1879, Governor's Correspondence: St. John, Kansas Historical Society).

Make This Sacrifice and All Will Be Right

For a timeline of settlement in Henrietta see "Timeline for Clay County's Early Years" by Lucille Glasgow (online at https://www.co.clay.tx.us/timeline). Sam Satterfield's dry goods shop can be seen in a photograph of the town taken by J. A. Caldwell in 1882 (Lawrence T. Jones III Texas Photography Collection, DeGolyer Library, Southern Methodist University). *The Galveston Daily News* reported that "Clay County is filling up rapidly with industrious immigrants" (16 July 1874). This discussion of the Red River War is informed by "The Southern Plains Indians" in *Battles of the Red River War* by J. Brett Cruse (9–20). For a detailed look at the history of the Comanches in the region, including a chapter dedicated to the Red River War, see S. C. Gwynne's *Empire of the Summer Moon: Quanah Parker and the Rise and Fall of the Comanches, the Most Powerful Indian Tribe in American History.* I am indebted to John Bird of the Eastland Historic Hotel for providing me with first-hand descriptions and photographs of the area, as the pandemic prevented me from visiting it.

Informing the movements of the Bender family is Merrick's account: "they had moved to Prairie Dog River in what was called Prairie Dog Corner." (statement of Samuel Merrick, enclosed in a letter from Superintendent Joseph Nicholson to Governor St. John, 14 December 1879, Governor's Correspondence: St. John). On the same page Merrick also notes that "there had been quite a congregation to Clay Co." Missouri Bill's criminal record states that he was frequently indicted on the charge of selling spirits without paying the correct tax (United States District Court for the Western District of Arkansas, 14 October 1873). A pencil annotation to a court document relating to the selling of untaxed spirits reads: "In jail Gainesville, Missouri Bill, Several cases of larceny against him, Red River Station."

The interaction between Missouri Bill and James Sullivan comes from Sullivan's letters to Governor Osborn in November and December 1874. The first outlines his interaction with Bill: "I received an answer from Missouri Bill confessing he knew where they were and telling me that he would be co-operative to get a pardon for his brother and for a deed of money" and requests that Osborn "grant the pardon of this Frank McPherson" (Sullivan to Osborn, 3 November 1874, Governor's Correspondence: Osborn, Kansas Historical Society). In the second letter, Sullivan confirms that he and Missouri Bill are in pursuit of the Benders and that "there will be no trouble in making the capture." After his request to be allowed to tour with the family, he requests that if the letter is published, McPherson's name be omitted (Sullivan to Osborn, 11 December 1874, Governor's Correspondence: Osborn, Kansas Historical Society).

Satterfield's

Samuel Merrick recalls being present at the time of the events at Satterfield's: "While I was there, there was a Detective called Sullivan come to Henrietta that got wind of it and Bill Gardener came down and saw him in Satterfield's Store. At that place he told Floyd Slimp he was not afraid of that man, he was to [*sic*] stylish." Floyd was less convinced and told Merrick he thought there might be others with him (statement of Samuel Merrick, enclosed in a letter from Superintendent Joseph Nicholson to Governor St. John, 14 December 1879, Governor's Correspondence: St. John, 4). For Gebhardt to have seen Sullivan in the dry goods shop, Bill had to have taken the man at least as far as Henrietta, and it is unlikely he would have purposefully informed the Benders that he had pretended to make a deal with the detective that included a pardon for his brother. A letter written by Governor St. John in 1879 indicates that there was no record of a reward offered for Frank McPherson, implying that Osborn had, in fact, sent Sullivan into Texas with a pardon (letter from St. John to J. S. Waters, 3 September 1879, Governor's Correspondence: St. John, Kansas Historical Society). Alexander York later wrote that after he saw Sullivan in November 1874 he "never heard from him since" (Alexander York to Governor St. John, 3 December 1879, Governor's Correspondence: St. John).

Information Wanted

Mary Feerick's identification of her husband is covered by Mary York in *The Bender Tragedy* (124–6). The articles in the *South Kansas Tribune* were published on 2 and 9 December 1873. The marriage of Mary Feerick to Alfred Campbell appears in the Montgomery County Marriage Records (10 February 1875); the children, Alfred and Frank, appear in the U.S. Federal Census of 1880.

Alexander is most commonly referred to in the press as Colonel York and the fallout of the Pomeroy incident remained in the papers until 1875. The quote from the *Manhattan Beacon* comes from a discussion of the impact of the ongoing legal proceedings on both men's careers (3 June 1874). The settlement of the civil suits appeared in the *South Kansas Tribune* (17 March 1875), among others, and Juliette's death was reported in *The Coffeyville Courier* (15 April 1875). The moonlight social was advertised in the *South Kansas Tribune*, the profits of which were "to be used in purchasing new singing books" for the Sunday school (14 July 1875). A week later *The Workingman's Courier* reported a "pleasant time at the Sunday School social at Col. York's residence" (29 July 1875). Ed's marriage to Elizabeth Carter appeared in the same paper (30 September 1875), which often commented on the comings and goings of the York family. The baseball game between the "Hoppers" and the "Athletics," in which Ed played for the latter drew a decent crowd according to the *South Kansas Tribune*. The debate that featured Ed and Mary was organised by the *Literary* paper and advertised in the *South Kansas Tribune* (3 February 1875).

Mary covers the aftermath of William's death in the final chapter of her account (*The Bender Tragedy*, 141–4), including the loss of Lulu and the transferal of her sons to Manasseh's care. In the spring of 1875, she was still listed as residing in Independence along with Bertha (Kansas State Census, 1875), but by 1880 the two were living in Illinois (U.S. Federal Census of 1880). *The Topeka Weekly Times* (19 November 1875) and *The Junction City Union* (20 November 1875) are among the papers that advertised her coming account of the crimes. Mary's marriage to James M. Jackson occurred in the spring of 1881 (30 March 1881, Illinois Marriage Index).

The Bold Front of the Plains

Samuel Merrick's final encounter with the Benders is the most detailed, as is reflected in this chapter. His description of the Caprock Escarpment comes from page 4 of his statement (statement of Samuel Merrick, enclosed in a letter from Superintendent Joseph Nicholson to Governor St. John, 14 December 1879, Governor's Correspondence: St. John, Kansas Historical Society). For John's joke to Kate see "Kate dressed like a man most of the time. She was complaining how poor they were and how they had to live. John said they would always be worth at least a thousand dollars apiece no matter how poor they got" (5). Merrick lists a number of Native Americans as interacting with the outlaw colony during their time in the Panhandle (5–6). His recommendation of the camp on the Colorado is taken verbatim from the text: "I told them of a good place on the head of the Colorado River of Texas, where no one would ever look for anyone. It is a place a person might pass close to and never know it. I was there with some Indians. There is two stone corners laying near the spring" (6). Frank's request for more guns and ammunition appears on page 5.

Missouri Bill's death was reported in several papers, none of which presented a flattering picture of the man beyond his "good looking" physical appearance. According to the *Denison Daily News*, Bill "was arrested by two U.S. Marshalls, assisted by U.S. troops at his home in Elm Spring, Chickasaw Nation. He was sick with pneumonia at the time" (4 March 1875). Bill's last words also come from this paper. *The Sedalia Democrat* called Bill's life "a reckless and wandering one" (6 March 1875). *The State Journal* out of Missouri took a more abrupt tone in its announcement: "'Missouri Bill' a native of Pettis county, and a notorious bad man, 'passed in his checks' last week, at Fort Sill I.T." (12 March 1875).

Restless Spirits

The letter from B. W. Simmons reporting that Kate was in league with an accomplice of the James-Younger Gang can be found in the Kansas State Archives (28 January 1876, Blue Earth Co. Minnesota, Governors Correspondence: Osborn). Osborn's correspondence about the Bender family is comprised of over a hundred documents from all over the states, many of which simply request descriptions of the family and confirmation of the reward money.

In *The Bender Hills Mystery*, Dick states that he believes the family went as far as El Paso and that he was certain they were still alive. As the point of contact for Osage Township, where many of the people who could identify the family lived, he would have been aware of developments in the search. The medium's interaction with the spirit of Nathaniel Green is from "What the Spirits Say" in the *Western Home Journal* (27 April 1876). The *Daily Kansas Tribune* took a less positive approach and printed the announcement under the headline "Not Reliable," informing its readers that "Murderers cannot be captured in that way" (1 May 1876).

Hell on the Border

More information on the history of Native American slave owners can be found in Barbara Krauthamer's *Black Slaves, Indian Masters: Slavery, Emancipation and Citizenship in the Native American South*, and Claudio Saunt's *Black, White and Indian: Race and the Unmaking of an American Family*. This discussion of life for freedmen in Indian Territory is derived from Linda Reese's "Freedmen" in *The Encyclopedia of Oklahoma History and Culture* (online at: https://www.okhistory.org/publications/enc/entry.php?entry =FR016); *The Civil War and Reconstruction in Indian Territory*, edited by Bradley R. Clampitt, specifically "Who Defines a Nation? Reconstruction in Indian Territory" by Christopher B. Bean (110–31); and "Boley, Indian Territory: Exercising Freedom in the All-Black Town" by Melissa N. Stuckey (*Journal of African American History* 102, no. 4, 492–516).

The capture of Samuel Merrick was described in great detail during his time in court and is corroborated by Lieutenant James Parker's memoirs, which refer to Merrick by his alias Limber Jim (*The Old Army* from the *Frontier Classics Series*, 70). A Robert Pettis appears in the military records of Fort Sill in 1872. Given the name, the proximity of the fort to Arbuckle, and the knowledge Pettis displays of the area in the court records, it is reasonable to assume these are the same man (Roll 95, M744, U.S., Buffalo Soldiers, Returns from Regular Army Cavalry Regiments, 1866–1916). Further information about the role of buffalo soldiers in the West can be found at "Buffalo Soldiers: Legend and Legacy" (National Museum of African American History and Culture, https:// nmaahc.si.edu/explore/manylenses/buffalosoldiers). The legacy and role of the Black regiments has been widely explored by historian Frank Schubert, an example of which can be found under "The Myth of the Buffalo Soldiers" on *Black Past* (https://www .blackpast.org/african-american-history/myth-buffalo-soldiers/).

Samuel Merrick was charged both for the theft of the horses and the assault on Robert Pettus. In his statement to the court, Pettus stated: "the man was the defendant, he got into a house and we could not get him out. Finally he came to the door and fired at me but only hit me once, he then fired at another man but did not [hit] him" (Samuel Merrick, 1877, 139, Defendant Jacket, Fort Smith, Arkansas, U.S., Criminal Case Files, 1866–1900). Pettus also noted that "there were some children in the house and we could not shoot without danger of hurting the children." Pettus's testimony is incredibly detailed, down to the movement of the group in pursuit; "we ran him out of the timbers onto the open prairie, we did not fire at him until he got onto the open prairie."

Details of Samuel Merrick's sentencing come from the court records associated with the district court (Samuel Merrick, 1877). Pettus specifically recalled that "when the defendant was under arrest he asked me to let him look where he shot me and said he was sorry he done it." Merrick's statement in his own defence also comes from this account. For the state of the jailhouse at Fort Smith see "Congressman John Rogers of Arkansas reading from the Attorney General's report on the jail at Fort Smith, Arkansas" (S. 610, 49th Cong., 1st sess., Congressional Record, 1 March 1886). For the influence and legacy of Judge Isaac Parker see Mary M. Stolberg's "Politician, Populist, Reformer: A Reexamination of 'Hanging Judge' Isaac C. Parker" (*Arkansas Historical Quarterly* 46, no. 1, 1988, 3–28). For Parker's opinions on the prison system see "Parker's Letter to Attorney General Garland, 1885" via the National Park Service (https://www.nps.gov/fosm/learn/historyculture/letter-to-attorney-general-garland 1885.htm).

   Bass Reeves and his role on the frontier is a topic receiving increasing attention in recent years, both academically and in popular culture. The most comprehensive study on Reeves remains Art Burton's *Black Gun, Silver Star: The Life and Legend of Frontier Marshal Bass Reeves* (University of Nebraska Press, 2008).

Part V: Bender or Bust

Office of the Superintendent

The letter is taken verbatim from the correspondence of Governor St. John (Nicholson to St. John, 20 September 1879, Governor's Correspondence: St. John, Kansas Historical Society).

The Way I Became Acquainted with the Bender Family Is This

Prison Superintendent Joseph Nicholson wrote four letters to Governor St. John during the autumn and winter of 1879, all of which can be found at the Kansas State Archives in Topeka. Nicholson references his letter to the Pinkertons as follows: "I wrote Pinkerton but he replies he had positive information of the death of the Benders and further information was of no use now. Yet he wished this death information kept very secret" (6 October 1879). The progress of Nicholson's letters and the two separate statements written by Merrick show St. John's reluctance to entertain the man as a possible lead until enough information was provided. Nicholson urged the governor repeatedly to "send a trusty man here" (6 October 1879), believing that Merrick "has not the ability of writing such things as comprehensively as he can talk them" (14 December 1879).

The quote from Nicholson about Merrick's intimate connection with the gang comes from the letter written on 14 December 1879. Merrick's statement about the soldiers in the region is adapted from his statement: "The soldiers are no account, they never try to see anything and won't fight. When they do if they can get away without. I know this to be so for I have been with them on more than one scout and have tried to get them to fight" (statement of Samuel Merrick, enclosed in a letter from Superintendent Joseph Nicholson to Governor St. John, Governor's Correspondence, 10 November 1879, 1). His assertion "a man's life wouldn't be worth more than a cartridge" comes from the same statement. The extended discussion about where the family was likely to have gone can be found on page 6 of the statement written on 14 December 1879.

Strife and Agitation

The letter reporting the sighting of Frank McPherson and requesting financial aid in bringing him back to Kansas to stand trial came from the Labette County Clerk's office, written by Deputy County Clerk W. A. Starr. It stated that "our officers are in possession of positive evidence of his whereabouts" and that steps would be taken to arrest him if the governor confirmed the reward money (W. A. Starr to Governor St. John, 22 August 1879, Governor's Correspondence: St. John). A second letter from County Attorney Vaters reported that "his whereabouts has just been learned and he is a long distance from here and it will be quite expensive to get him here and I feel that he ought to be brought to trial" (1 September 1879).

Alexander York's response to the letter provides us with a detailed overview of the movements of Colonel Peckham and Detective Beers during their time in Texas in 1873; it also alludes to a report by Beers that Alexander may have sent to the Pinkertons himself at a later date, as it is not contained in the Governor's Records at the State Archives in Topeka. His letter reports that "Merrick's statement corresponds exactly with the report of Detective Beers" and that the Benders were known to have gone to "the frontier of Texas in a camp with ten other white persons, making fourteen in all" (13 December 1879, Governor's Correspondence: St. John).

Charles Morris's interview with *The Emporia Ledger* went largely unnoticed at the time and the paper itself stated that it believed the Benders had in fact been hanged by an angry mob (19 August 1880). The arrest and confession of the McGregor couple was covered extensively by the papers; see the *Fremont Weekly Herald* (29 July 1880), *The Kansas City Times* (1 August 1880), and *The Leavenworth Times* (11, 12, and 17 August 1880), to name but a few.

Nicholson's last letter to St. John was sent several weeks before Merrick's release (27 November 1880). The report of Kate joining the vigilance committee in pursuit of the family is from *The Evening Visitor* (Raleigh, NC: 28 December 1880).

Dreams and Detective Work

For a description of a typical county fair, including the racehorse named Kate Bender, see "The Fair a Success!" in the *Sumner County Standard* (5 September 1889).

The newspapers, even those that believed her story, struggled to make sense of Frances McCann but were impressed with the tenacity with which she had pursued Sarah and Almira. The physical description of Frances comes from the *San Francisco Examiner* 31 October 1889). Frances gives some of the history of her upbringing, including the supposed murder of her father, John Sanford, in a letter to Governor Humphrey (20 October 1889, Governor's Correspondence: Governor Humphrey, Kansas Historical Society). Frances first appears in the U.S. Federal Census of 1870, where she is listed as residing with Albert McCann in Iowa. By 1880, they were residing in McPherson with their five children, Nettie, Alberta, Frank, Minton, and Roy (U.S. Federal Census of 1880). The quote describing Sarah's reaction to Frances's dream is from "Benders, The Latest Sensation in Reference to the Atrocious Murders" in *The Oswego Courant* (2 November 1889) and the newspaper also gives a good history of the circumstances that led Frances to believe the women were the Benders. *The Oswego Independent* has a retelling of the events that echoes Dick's sentiment that Sarah became delirious with fever, thought she was going to die, and confided in Frances to assuage her guilt (20 September 1889).

Leroy Dick covers the arrest of 1889 extensively in *The Bender Hills Mystery*, in which he assigns himself a leading role in the events (26–58). His description of the interactions between Frances and Sarah, when the latter was ill, appear on pages 37–8. Dick claims to have met Frances before the autumn of 1889, at which time he told her, "I don't believe the Benders ever left the Texas Colony," when she asked him to visit Niles and see Sarah and Almira for himself, though no other sources mention this previous interaction. His identification of the tintype of Almira as Ma Bender come from pages 40–1. Dick's subsequent role in the proceedings was well reported in the newspapers and in John T. James's *The Benders in Kansas*.

County attorney Morrison was evidently exasperated by the entire proceedings, writing to Governor Humphrey that "it would take a volume to give in detail the work of this, as I think, misled woman" and warning him of her ability to "work on the feelings" of law enforcement until they entertained her perspective (letter from County Attorney Morrison to Governor Humphrey, 7 October 1889, Governor's Correspondence: Humphrey).

A Siege of Examination

The discussion of Leroy Dick's time in Niles before the larceny trial and his positive identification of Almira as Ma Bender comes from John T. James's *The Benders in Kansas* (61–4), noting that "in his opinion they were, beyond doubt, the guilty parties . . . upon the strength of Mr. Dick's positive identification the papers for requisition were prepared" (64). Dick covers the matter in *The Bender Hills Mystery* (41–3), and his theory about how the Bender women ended up in Niles is outlined on page 36. Both Dick and James make frequent mention of the women's near-constant attempts to accuse the other of being involved in the Bender crimes. *The Sedan-Times Journal* informed its readers of this fact, noting that "Dick says that the mother and daughter quarrel bitterly at intervals when left to themselves and each accuses the other of being responsible for the position in which they are placed at present" (8 November 1889). For

Frances McCann's imploring the governor to believe she has the right women see the letter written on 20 October 1889 (Governor's Correspondence: Governor Humphrey, Kansas Historical Society).

The larceny trial itself is also covered in the above accounts (*The Bender Hills Mystery*, 44–8; *The Bender Tragedy*, 65–7) and in a variety of newspapers, though rumour resulted in all manner of crimes being reported as unearthed. For papers consulted in this section see "Mrs Eliza Davis Discharged" in *The Evening News* (30 October 1889), "Keeping a Secret" in *The Pittsburg Dispatch* (1 November 1889), and "Mrs Eliza Davis" in *The Parsons Daily Journal* (14 November 1889), which also contains a description of the excitement surrounding John Flickinger. In an interview with the reporter from the paper, Sarah is recorded as stating that "old man Flickinger who was old man Bender, put Kate and John Bender out of the way in the Indian Territory, because they had threatened to give them up to justice . . . he shot them both and buried them in a buffalo wallow," a story that conveniently extracted her from the possibility of being Kate Bender. For examples of crimes supposedly committed by Almira see the *Chicago Tribune* (31 October 1889) and *The Head-light* (6 December 1889). The quote from the *Wichita Daily Journal* can be found under "The Benders Again" (1 November 1889).

Evidence Against Them

The theory that the Bender family was lynched still prevails in south-east Kansas today. Examples of stories of the execution of the Benders appear in the *Walnut Valley Times* (20 August 1880), *The Leavenworth Times* (17 August 1880), and "The Benders Blood!," a florid, evocative, and baseless account first published in the *Chicago Times* and then reprinted in *The Osage Mission Journal* (18 August 1880). For a letter implicating the Yorks in the crimes see Detective James Dingman of the Southwestern Detective Association's letter to Governor St. John (17 August 1880). For the York family's response to the accusations see Alexander's letter to Governor Glick, reprinted under the headline "Denies the Deed" in the *Leavenworth Daily Commercial* (25 September 1884). The notice from Labette County authorities was reprinted in *The Daily Commonwealth* (5 September 1880).

The arrest of Sarah and Almira was nearly as widely covered as the discovery of the bodies themselves over a decade earlier. Descriptions of the train journey and Frances McCann's courting of the press are informed by *The Scottsboro Citizen* (Alabama, 7 November 1889), *The Fort Scott Daily Monitor* (1 November 1889), and *The Pittsburg Dispatch* (1 November 1889). *The Oswego Courant*'s article on the supposed Bender women covered half the front page of the newspaper, with the subheading "Two unfortunate and helpless women dragged from their homes in Michigan to Oswego, KS., by the strong arm of the law, under the hideous charge of being old Mrs Bender and her wayward daughter Kate" (2 November 1889). The article in *The Oswego Independent* that informs this section is entitled "Hope Gone" and makes reference to the women's defence attorney, John T. James, as well Silas Tole's assertion that the women were not the Benders (8 November 1889). James gives his reasons for agreeing to represent the women at trial in *The Benders in Kansas* (69).

The contents of the preliminary hearing were covered daily in the newspapers and corroborate the accounts given by Leroy Dick (*The Bender Hills Mystery*, 54–55) and

John T. James. Interestingly, though Dick devotes a lot of time to the women in Niles and his own investigations into their backstory, he does not afford the same amount of detail to the hearing in Oswego. James provides a transcript of each of the witnesses with page references as follows: Charles Booth (71), John Handley (72), Delilah Keck (72), Henrietta Dienst (75), and Maurice Sparks (77–9), whose testimony is a good example of the confusion surrounding the case. He states that he "was not much acquainted with the Benders, especially the women" . . . "and could not say that seeing scar on this defendant's eye does enable me to say more definitely where Kate's scar was" (78). Rudolph Brockman's testimony (73–4) is among the longest. The attempts to reignite suspicion of his involvement are detailed on page 74, as well as in an anonymous letter published in *The Bronson Pilot* (6 December 1889).

For newspapers covering the case see *The Mound Valley Herald* (22 November 1889), the *Labette County Democrat* (21 November 1889), *The Daily Mail* (20 November 1889), and the *Evening Gazette*, which announced with confidence that "They Are the Real Benders" and bulldozed over the minutiae of the hearing, claiming that "County Attorney Morrison and his associate are confident they have the Benders" (Pennsylvania, 21 November 1889).

Bound Over

As this chapter covers the second half of the hearing, it draws its information from the aforementioned sources. James's criticism of Leroy Dick is quoted from *The Benders in Kansas* (96), along with his concern that "the state might get a verdict convicting the clients of that murder." James's unflattering description of his clients comes from page 96, where he states his belief that Frances McCann had "unearthed a family some of whom were criminals, guilty of crimes almost as atrocious as those which were committed by the Benders," though it is not clear exactly what these crimes were.

Hope Gone

Newspapers referenced in the section pertaining to the women's time in custody are *The Oswego Independent* (27 December 1889), *The Oswego Courant* (27 December 1889), *The Parsons Weekly Sun* (16 January 1890), and the *Parsons Daily Eclipse* (16 January 1890). The *Sun* reported that "she may not be the veritable Kate Bender, but she is a 'gay deceiver' all the same."

A detailed breakdown of the affidavits supplied by James can also be found under "The Alleged Benders Again" in *The Parsons Weekly Sun* (16 January 1890), examples of which include "In the case of Mrs Griffith I will show by the wife and daughter of the man Daniel Perry, in whose house she formerly resided, that she was in Concord Township, Berrien County, Michigan during the years 1870–1871 . . . As to Mrs Davis, Mr. and Mrs Snell of Bay Port Michigan swear to her residence in that city during the years 1871 and 1872 with her husband Hiram Johnson," etc. *The Sedalia Weekly Bazoo* also covered the probable release of the two women (Missouri, 14 January 1890), along with *The Oswego Independent* (18 April 1890). John T. James outlines the details of Almira Griffith's record at the House of Correction at Detroit as follows:

"They secured official information by certified copies of records of the arrest, trial, conviction, sentence and commitment of Mrs Almira Griffith, under the name of Almira Shearer, to the House of Correction at Detroit Michigan, in April 1872, and her receipt at that institution in May 1872, and her discharge from it in March 1873" (*The Benders in Kansas*, 104). Almira's marriage to Shearer is recorded in the Jackson County Michigan Marriage Records (Record No. 768, Michigan, U.S. Marriage Records, 1867–1952). For the death of Sarah's daughter see "Belle Johnson, Deceased November 2, 1873" (Huron County, Michigan, U.S., Death Records, 1867–1852).

The quote from *The Lawrence Journal* concluded, "As it is they only serve as examples of what the modern detective system can do" (16 April 1890). Frances's visit to Oswego was reported in the *Labette County Democrat*, which made certain to point out that Sarah's assertions that "she has caused the arrest of Detective McCann" were not true "as that lady was in the city this week" (17 April 1890). Leroy Dick reports his encounter with Sarah on page 55 of *The Bender Hills Mystery*. Sarah's intent to "make it hot" to the tune of ten thousand dollars was also reported in the *Labette County Democrat*, as well as *The Oswego Independent* (18 April 1890). Frances's letter to the editor appears in the *Parsons Palladium* (7 August 1901), and *The Lindsborg Record*'s assessment of the situation appeared as follows: "of course the Benders were not unearthed and the private opinion of the people who knew Mrs McCann was that her trolley was off" (2 August 1901). For Frances's death certificate, see "Missouri, U.S., Death Certificates" (No. 30710, September 1946). She is buried in Fairview Cemetery, Joplin, Missouri.

Almira married Dolphus Skinner in November 1892 before marrying Charles Eaton in March 1896; the record of her marriage to Eaton can be found in the Michigan Marriage Index (No. 872, 16 March 1896). The U.S. Federal Census of 1910 records her as living at the Muskegon Alms House, and her death certificate is available in the Michigan Deaths and Burials Index (FHL Film Number 1320185). Sarah was married to Hardy Colburn in September 1891 (Michigan, County Marriages, FN 001017877), and George Freeman in June 1904 (Michigan Marriage Records, No. 39), from whom she was divorced in 1905 on the grounds of "extreme cruelty" (Michigan, Divorce Records). Sarah's death certificate is in the Michigan Death Records, 1867–1952 (FN 1135). The community's reaction to the case is from *The Oswego Independent* (18 April 1890). Alexander York talked about his feelings on the matter in "Col. York Is Confident" in the *Chicago Tribune* (3 November 1889).

As to the Benders

Alexander York's interview was often reprinted in a manner that suggested he put his full confidence behind the arrest of Sarah and Almira, but this is not the actual content of the *Chicago Tribune* interview (3 November 1889). Correspondence relating to the sighting by Thomas Gates can be found in the Governor's Correspondence for George Glick. The letters quoted here are as follows: Gates to Glick (9 October 1883), Alexander to Glick (2 May 1884), and Gates to Glick (17 April 1884). Alexander's response to the sighting in Colorado comes from a letter to the governor (June 25 1884).

In a letter to Glick during his correspondence regarding the sighting in Arizona, Alexander wrote that the Benders were "in the camp of a party of fourteen men &

women engaged in gathering up mules and horses for the Colorado trade" (21 May 1883). Frank's murder of Romero was covered in the most detail in *The Gunnison Daily News-Democrat* under a segment on crime in New Mexico (Colorado, 29 July 1881) but also appeared in the Kansas newspapers (see *The Daily Commonwealth*, 22 July 1881). Frank is referred to as living in Gunnison in *The Kansas City Times* article "Stabbed in the Back" (17 March 1887); supporting this is a notice in *The Gunnison Daily Review-Press* announcing Frank McPherson's visit to Crested Butte with his siblings from Kansas City (10 August 1883). The attack on Edward was widely reported at the time and prompted several articles also accusing Frank of murdering the sheriff of Bourbon County back in the 1870s. For articles covering the crime see "The Knife Was Ready" in *The Kansas City Star* (17 March 1887) and "Stabbed in the Back" in *The Kansas City Times*. For articles accusing him of the murder in Fort Scott see "McPherson again" in *The Sedalia Weekly Bazoo* (29 March 1887).

Frank's movements throughout the rest of his life are drawn from the sources as follows: For the assault on him at the Cañon City Penitentiary see "May Be a Fatal Wound" in *The Sedalia Weekly Democrat* (25 March 1898). For his appearance in the labour wars see "Threatened Trouble Did Not Materialize" in *The Cañon City Record* (10 November 1904), in which Frank is described as "a Peabody worker," after James Peabody, the unpopular governor of Colorado whose campaign of violence against union workers made him infamous. McPherson and Springer appear as business partners in the city directory consecutively from 1902 to 1907. The saloon is first listed in the 1907 directory (U.S. City Directories 1822–1995, Trinidad, Colorado, 1907, 205). As Frank's obituary was printed in *The Kansas City Star*, it is plausible that his family simply lied to the paper about his past (11 May 1917).

A census record from 1880 perhaps supports this theory, listing a Katie and Joseph Bender as residing at the mountain town of Buena Vista, Colorado (U.S. Federal Census of 1880). Both are reported as being born in Germany, though their age gap is just under ten years (twenty-eight and thirty-seven, respectively). Rudolph Brockman told a newspaper in 1880 that he thought Kate was in her late teens when the family first arrived, with John in his mid-twenties, which would align better with the ages listed in the census than those on the Governor's Proclamation (*Arkansas Valley Democrat*, 14 August 1880). In her book *Death for Dinner: The Benders of (Old) Kansas*, author Phyllis de la Garza subscribes to this theory, suggesting that Kate went on to run a successful tavern in Colorado. However, there is little available on the movements of either of these people before 1880 and, as such, I would be hesitant to state it as fact. I also believe that the Benders were evidently capable of committing such cruel, premeditated crimes, that they would find it hard to live out the rest of their lives on the right side of the law.

From the Old Century into the New

Statistics regarding the expansion of Cherryvale's population are compiled from census data between the listed dates. Mary Louise Brooks is better known by her stage name Louise Brooks, and a comprehensive history of her life in Cherryvale can be found on display in the Cherryvale Historical Museum. Further information on the minutiae of the natural gas and oil boom in Independence can be found in the chapter "Gas and Oil Developments in Montgomery County" by H. W. Young in *History of Montgomery County* (1903). Information on the Oklahoma Land Run is from "1889 Oklahoma Land Run: The Settlement of Payne County" by Karen Maguire and Branton Wiederholt (*Journal of Family History* 44, no. 1, 2019, 52–69). The tensions in Oklahoma would eventually culminate in the Tulsa Race Massacre of 1921, when white residents attacked Black residents, homes, and businesses, burning the wealthy Greenwood District to the ground.

Ed York frequently came back to visit the people of Fort Scott after his initial move to Denver, as noted in *The Fort Scott Daily Monitor* (27 December 1890). Mary York's passing was noted in a number of newspapers in the area, including *The Fort Scott Weekly Monitor* (9 March 1898), but most notably in the Christian newspaper *The Weekly Star and Kansan* (15 April 1898). The interview with Thomas Beers in which he claimed he was weeks away from catching the Benders appeared under the headline "He Caught the Benders" (*Emporia Weekly Gazette*, 18 July 1901). His obituary was printed in the same newspaper three years later (23 June 1904). Details of the later life of Charles Peckham are from "Judge Peckham" in *The Evening Journal* (10 January 1900) and *The Williamstown Mail* (10 December 1901). The deathbed confession of Katha Peters is taken from *The Buffalo Enquirer* (5 May 1910) and the response of the justice of the peace from the *Chanute Weekly Herald* (13 May 1910). Leroy Dick remained active in the community up until his death and was often found playing cards with other older citizens and reminiscing about their younger years. *The Parsons Sun*, which had also first published *The Bender Hills Mystery*, is where the details of his obituary come from (3 April 1939). The speech by Laura Ingalls Wilder was given at the Detroit Book Fair and reprinted in *The Saturday Evening Post*, 1978. More on the relationship between Wilder and her daughter can be found in Caroline Fraser's article "The Strange Case of the Bloody Benders: Laura Ingalls Wilder, Rose Wilder Lane, and Yellow Journalism." Census records put the Longcors in the township of Rutland, Montgomery County, Kansas, at the same time as the Ingalls family, but there is no evidence to suggest to suggest that the two groups ever interacted (U.S. Federal Census of 1870).

Alexander's interview features only a short paragraph about the Benders, as had become typical of his response to questions about the family (*The Wichita Eagle*, 20 January 1911). The quote from his obituary in *The Centreville Press* is included in the article "Col. York's Death Seals Old Secret" (5 April 1928). The discussion of his importance in the outcome of the Senate election was printed under the headline "Colonel York Elected Young John Ingalls" in *The Parsons Daily Sun* (8 March 1928). Buster Keaton was inspired to make *The General* (1926) after reading *The Great Locomotive Chase* by William Pittenger (1863). Ed's obituary in *The Eugene Daily Guard* noted that he had resided in Cottage Grove for ten years (29 September 1936). Ed's body was shipped to Denver, where he was buried next to his brother at the family plot in Fairmount, Colorado.

Epilogue

Fern Morrow Wood's *The Benders: Keepers of the Devil's Inn* was the first account of the Bender crimes to try to separate the fact from the folklore and, as such, I am hugely indebted to her work on the subject.

The quote from the *Burns Mirror* concluded with the sentiment "this is a grateful relief in these dull times to the overworked newspaper man" (15 November 1889).

Articles written in 2020 about the Benders are as follows:

"Kansas Land etc." by Rachel Sharp for *The Daily Mail* (online at: https://www.dailymail.co.uk/news/article-7929989/Kansas-land-Bloody-Benders-slayed-11-people-1870s-auction.html).

"The Kansas Homestead" by Brigit Katz for *Smithsonian Magazine* (online at: https://www.smithsonianmag.com/smart-news/sale-kansas-land-where-bloody-benders-committed-their-crimes-180974121/).

"A Property That Once Belonged to a Family of Serial Killers" by Allen Kim for CNN (online at: https://edition.cnn.com/2020/02/06/us/bloody-bender-house-trnd/index.html).

"The Kansas Land" by Michele Debczak for *Mental Floss* (online at: https://www.mentalfloss.com/article/616255/kansas-land-once-belonged-bloody-benders-americas-first-serial-killer-family-auction).

"Property Belonging to the 'Bloody Benders'" by Robyn Merrett for *People* (online at: https://people.com/crime/property-belonging-to-the-bloody-benders-americas-first-family-of-serial-killers-up-for-sale/).

"Kansas Site of 1870's 'Bloody Benders' Serial Killings Is on the Auction Block" by Amy Renee Leiker for *The Wichita Eagle* (online at: https://www.kansas.com/news/local/crime/article239501418.html).

Bibliography

Archival Sources

An Act to Regulate Trade and Intercourse with the Indian Tribes and to Preserve Peace on the Frontier, Chap. CLXI. Statute I. 30 June 1842; https://www.loc.gov/law/help/statutesat large/23rdcongress/Session% 201/c23s1ch161.pdf.

"Are You Going West, if so, and if You Wish to Secure Good Homes in a Rich County, Please Read the Facts Herein Stated." Southern Kansas Land Association: Ottawa: Ottawa Journal Print, 1873.

Articles Prepared for the Kansas State Centennial Commission: Slayings, Bender Family of Southeast Kansas (Unit ID: 40001 KSHS).

"Bird's Eye View of the City of Denison." 23 May 1873; http://hdl.loc.gov/loc.gmd /g4034d.pm020519.

Caldwell, J. A. *Bridge St., Henrietta Tex., Looking South, 1882*. DeGolyer Library, Southern Methodist University Digital Collections.

Campbell, Sene. *Letter to James Montgomery*, 4 January 1859. Kansas Historical Society; online at Kansas Memory: https://www.kshs.org/km/items/view/90110.

Colton's New Map of the State of Texas and Adjoining Portions of New Mexico, Louisiana and Arkansas. Library of Congress. New York: G.W. & C.B Colton & Co., 1872.

Defendant Jacket Files for U.S. District Court Western Division of Arkansas, Fort Smith Division, 1866–1900. National Archives.

Kansas. Governor (1873–1877: Osborn) Correspondence Files, Correspondence Received, Subject Files, Box 2 Folder 47.

Kansas. Governor (1879–1883: St. John) Correspondence Files, Correspondence Received, Subject Files, Box 12 Folder 2.

Kansas. Governor (1883–1885: Glick) Correspondence Files, Correspondence Received, Subject Files, Box 7 Folder 1.

Kansas. Governor (1885–1889: Martin) Correspondence Files, Correspondence Received, Subject Files, Box 21 Folder 4.

Kansas. Governor (1889–1893: Humphrey) Correspondence Files, Correspondence Received Subject Files Box 9.

McEwen, Jean, as dictated to by Leroy Dick. "The Bender Hills Mystery: The Story Behind the Infamous Murders from 1870s Kansas." *The Parsons Daily Sun*, 23 June 1934.

Articles

Adamson, Christopher. "Punishment After Slavery: Southern State Systems, 1865–1890." *Social Problems* 30, no.5, 1983.

Atkins, Karen. "Pioneer Kitchen Gardens: How the Pioneers Planned and Planted." *Little House on the Prairie*; https://littlehouseontheprairie.com/pioneer-kitchen-gardens-how-the-pioneers-planned-and-planted/?hilite=%27pioneer%27%2C%27gardens%27.

Ball, Larry. "Before the Hanging Judge: The Origins of the United States District Court for the Western District of Arkansas." *Arkansas Historical Quarterly* 49, Autumn 1990.

Beach, David. *How Did the Whiskey Go Down at Ladore?* CreateSpace, 2014.

Bean, Lee, et al. "High-Risk Childbearing: Fertility and Infant Mortality on the American Frontier." *Social Science History* 16, no.3, 1985.

Boissoneault, Lorraine. "A Train Company Crash." *Smithsonian*, July 2017.

"Border Land: The Struggle for Texas." University of Texas; https://library.uta.edu/borderland/tribe/kiowa? page= 1.

"Buffalo Soldiers: Legend and Legacy." National Museum of African American History and Culture; https://nmaahc.si.edu/explore/manylenses/buffalosoldiers.

Caldwell, Martha. "Pomeroy's Ross Letter." *Kansas Historical Quarterly* 13, no.7, 1944.

Crouch, Barry A. "Baker, Cullen Montgomery." Handbook of Texas Online; https://www.tshaonline.org/handbook/entries/baker-cullen-Montgomery.

Debczak, Michele. "The Kansas Land That Once Belonged to the Bloody Benders, America's First Serial Killer Family, Is Up for Auction." *Mental Floss*; https://www.mentalfloss.com/ article/616255/kansas-land-once-belonged-bloody-benders-americas-first-serial-killer-family-auction.

Durkholder, Edwin. "Those Murdering Benders." *True Western Adventure*, 1960.

"Father Paul Mary Ponziglione—The Jesuit Trail Rider." A Catholic Mission; http://www.acatholicmission.org/frpaul-ponziglione.html.

Fischer, William E., Jr. "Fort Scott, Kansas." *Civil War on the Western Border: The Missouri-Kansas Conflict, 1854–1865*. The Kansas Public Library; https://civil waronthewestern border.org/encyclopedia/fort-scott-Kansas.

Fraser, Caroline. "The Strange Case of the Bloody Benders: Laura Ingalls Wilder, Rose Wilder Lane, and Yellow Journalism," in *Pioneer Girl Perspectives: Exploring Laura Ingalls Wilder*, Nancy Tystad Koupal, ed. Rapid City, South Dakota Historical Society, 2017: 20–52.

"Frontier Fantasies: Imagining the American West in the Dime Novel." Rauner Special Collections Library, Dartmouth College.

Glasgow, Lucille. "Timeline for Clay County's Early Years." https://www.co.clay.tx.us/timeline.

Hacker, J. David. "A Census-Based Count of the Civil War Dead." *Civil War History* 57, no.4, 2012.

Henderson, Harold. "The Building of the First Kansas Railroad." *A Journal of the Central Plains* 15, no.3, August 1947.

Katz, Brigit. "The Kansas Homestead Where America's First Serial Killer Family Committed Its Crimes Is Up for Sale." *Smithsonian*; https://www.smithsonianmag.com/smart-news/sale-Kansas-land-where-bloody-benders-committed-their-crimes-180974121/.

Kim, Allen. "A Property That Once Belonged to a Family of Serial Killers." CNN Online; https://edition.cnn.com/2020/02/06/us/bloody-bender-house-trnd/index.html.

Kitzhaber, Albert. "Götterdämmerung in Topeka: The Downfall of Senator Pomeroy." *Kansas History Quarterly*, August 1950.

Kornberg, Jim. "An Awful Time for Children." *True West*; https://truewestmagazine.com/article/an-awful-time-for-children/.

Leiker, Amy Renee. "Kansas Site of 1870s 'Bloody Benders' Serial Killings is on the Auction Block." *The Witchita Eagle*; https://www.kansas.com/news/local/crime/article239501418.html.

Linsenmayer, Penny T. "Kansas Settlers on the Osage Diminished Reserve: A Study of Laura Ingalls Wilder's *Little House on the Prairie*." *Kansas History* 24, no.3, Autumn 2001.

Littlefield, Daniel. "The Treaties of 1866: Reconstruction of Re-Destruction." *Proceedings: War and Reconstruction in Indian Territory, A History Conference in Observance of the 130th Anniversary of the Fort Smith Council*. Fort Smith, AR, 1995.

"Maimed Men." *Life and Limb: The Toll of the American Civil War*. U.S. National Library of Medicine; https://www.nlm.nih.gov/exhibition/lifeandlimb/maimedmen.html.

Maguire, Karen, and Branton Wiederholt. "1889 Oklahoma Land Run: The Settlement of Payne County." *Journal of Family History* 44, no.1, 2019.

Merrett, Robyn. "Property Belonging to the 'Bloody Benders.'" *People* Online; https://people.com/crime/property-belonging-to-the-bloody-benders-americas-first-family-of-serial-killers-up-for-sale/.

Minor, David. "Denison, TX." *Handbook of Texas Online*; https://www.tshaonline.org/handbook/entries/denison-tx.

Mitchell, Leon Junior. "Camp Ford, Confederate Military Prison." *Southwestern Historical Quarterly* 66, 1962.

Obert, Jonathan, and Eleanor Mattiacci. "Keeping Vigil: The Emergence of Vigilance Committees in Pre-Civil War America." *Perspectives in Politics* 16 no.3, September 2018.

Overbeck, Ruth Ann. "Colbert's Ferry." *Chronicles of Oklahoma* 57, no. 2, Summer 1979.

Palmer, Ernest J. "Trees Used by the Pioneers." *Arnoldia Arboretum*; http://arnoldia.arboretum.harvard.edu/pdf/ articles/1933-1--trees-usedbythe-pioneers.pdf.

Reese, Linda. "Freedmen." *The Encyclopaedia of Oklahoma History and Culture*; https://www.okhistory.org/publications/enc/entry.php?entry= FR016.

Rhynes, Matha E. "Stonewall." *The Encyclopaedia of Oklahoma History and Culture*; https://www.okhistory.org/publications/enc/entry.php?entry= ST042.

"Samuel Pomeroy: A Featured Biography." www.senate.gov/senators/FeaturedBios /Featured_ Bio_ Pomeroy.

"Samuel Clarke Pomeroy, 1816–1891." www.territorialkansasonline.ku.edu.

Scott, Robert F. "What Happened to the Benders." *Western Folklore* 9, no.4, 1950.

Schindler, Harold, "Rogues Gallery: A Page from Police History," in Harold Schindler, ed., *In Another Time.* Logan: Utah State University Press, 1998.

Schubert, Frank. "The Myth of the Buffalo Soliders." *Black Past*; https://www.black past.org/ african-american-history/myth-buffalo-soldiers/.

Sharp, Rachel. "Land Owned by America's First Family of Serial Killers Goes on Sale Where 'The Bloody Benders' Bashed the Heads of 11 Victims with a Hammer, Slit Their Throats and Dropped Them Through a Trapdoor in 1870s." *Daily Mail*; https://www.dailymail.co.uk/news/ article-7929989/Kansas-land-Bloody-Benders -slayed-11-people-1870s-auction.html.

Stolberg, Mary M. "Politician, Populist, Reformer: A Re-examination of 'Hanging Judge' Isaac C. Parker." *Arkansas Historical Quarterly* 7, no.1, 1988.

Stuckey, Melissa. "Boley, Indian Territory: Exercising Freedom in the All-Black Town." *Journal of African American History* 102, no.4, 2017.

Taylor, Dabney. "Underneath the Vine and Fig Tree." *Frontier Times*, March 1966.

Walker, David. "The Humbug in American Religion: Ritual Theories of Nineteenth-Century Spiritualism." *Religion and American Culture: A Journal of Interpretation* 23 no.1, 2013.

Wilson, Glen O. "Old Red River Station." *Southwestern Historical Quarterly* 61 no.3. 1958.

Books

Allison, Nathaniel. *History of Cherokee County, Kansas and Representative Citizens.* Chicago, IL: Biographical Publishing Co., 1904.

Baughman, Robert. *Kansas in Maps.* Topeka: Kansas Historical Society, 1961.

Bennett, Bridget. *Transatlantic Spiritualism and Nineteenth-Century American Literature.* New York: Palgrave Macmillan, 2007.

Brackman, Barbara. *Civil War Women: Their Quilts, Their Roles.* Concord, CA: C&T Publishing, 2000.

Burns, Louis F. *A History of the Osage People.* Tuscaloosa: University of Alabama Press, 1989.

Burton, Art. *Black Gun, Silver Star: The Life and Legend of Frontier Marshal Bass Reeves.* Lincoln: University of Nebraska Press, 2008.

Butler, Anne, and Wendy Wolff. *United States Senate Election, Expulsion, and Censure Cases, 1793–1900.* Washington, DC., 1995.

Byrnes, Thomas. *Professional Criminals of America.* London: Cassell & Co, 1886.

Case, Nelson. *History of Labette County, Kansas, from the First Settlement to the Close of 1892.* Topeka, Kansas: Crane & Company, 1893.

Clampitt, Bradley R. *The Civil War and Reconstruction in Indian Territory.* Lincoln: University of Nebraska Press, 2015.

Courtwright, Julie. *Prairie Fire: A Great Plains History.* Lawrence: University Press of Kansas, 2011.

Cruse, J. Brett. *Battles of the Red River War.* College Station: Texas A&M University Press, 2017.

Dary, David. *Red Blood, Black Ink: Journalism in the Old West*. Lawrence: University Press of Kansas, 1999.

de la Garza, Phyllis. *Death for Dinner: The Benders of (Old) Kansas*. Talei Publishers /Amazon, 2003.

Delaney, Michelle. *Buffalo Bill's Wild West Warriors: A Photographic History by Gertrude Käsebier*. New York: Harper Collins, 2007.

Ebbutt, Percy. *Emigrant Life in Kansas*. London: Swan Sonnenschein, 1886.

Finn, Jonathan. *Capturing the Criminal: From Mugshot to Surveillance Society*. University of Minnesota Press, 2009.

Fitzpatrick, W. S. *Treaties and Laws of the Osage Nation, as Passed to November 26, 1890*. Cedar Vale, Kansas: Press of the Cedar Wale Commercial, 1895.

Goins, Charles Robert, et al. *The Historical Atlas of Oklahoma*. Fourth Edition. Norman: University of Oklahoma Press, 2012.

Guinn, Jeff. *The Last Gunfight: The Real Story of the Shootout at the O.K. Corral and How It Changed the American West*. London: The Robson Press, 2012.

Groom, Winston. *Vicksburg 1863*. New York: Vintage, 2010.

Grossman, James, ed. *The Frontier in America Culture*. Berkeley: University of California Press, 1994.

Gwynne, S. C. *Empire of the Summer Moon: Quanah Parker and the Rise and Fall of the Comanches, the Most Powerful Indian Tribe in American History*. London: Constable, 2011.

Hulbert, Matthew Christopher. *The Ghosts of Guerrilla Memory: How Civil War Bushwhackers Became Gunslingers in the American West*. Athens: University of Georgia Press, 2016.

Humphrey, Lyman. *History of Montgomery County Kansas By Its Own People*. Kansas: Press of Iola Register, 1903.

James, T. John. *The Benders in Kansas*. Witchita: The Kan-Okla Publishing Company, 1913.

Krauthamer, Barbara. *Black Slaves, Indian Masters: Slavery, Emancipation and Citizenship in the Native American South*. Chapel Hill: University of North Carolina Press, 2015.

Lajimodiere, Denise K. *Stringing Rosaries: The History, the Unforgivable, and the Healing of Northern Plains American Indian Boarding School Survivors*. Fargo: North Dakota State University Press, 2019.

Lause, Mark. *Free Spirits: Spiritualism, Republicanism, and Radicalism in the Civil War Era*. Champaign: University of Illinois Press, 2016.

Laws of the State of Mississippi, Passed at a Regular Session of the Mississippi Legislature, Held in the City of Jackson, October, November and December. Shannon & Co. State Printers, 1865.

Limerick, Patricia Nelson. *The Legacy of Conquest: The Unbroken Past of the American West*. New York: W.W. Norton & Company, 1988.

Mack, John. *Bucking the Railroads on the Kansas Frontier: The Struggle over Land Claim by Homesteading Civil War Veterans, 1867–1876*. Jefferson, NC: McFarland & Co., 2012.

Masterson, V. V. *The Katy Railroad and the Last Frontier*. Columbia: University of Missouri Press, 1988.

McNeal, T. A. *When Kansas Was Young*. New York: Macmillan, 1922.

Methvin, J. J. *Andele: Or, The Mexican-Kiowa Captive. A Story of Real Life Among the Indians*. Albuquerque: University of New Mexico Press, 1996.

Mog, Christy. *The Rough and Gone Town of Ladore, Kansas*. Manhattan: Kansas State University, Chapman Centre for Rural Studies, 2010.

Moore, Charles. *Portions of a Book About Pioneer Narratives, Family Papers, 1832–1917.* Denton: University of North Texas.

More Infamous Crimes That Shocked the World. London: Macdonald & Co., 1990.

Natale, Simone. *Supernatural Entertainments: Victorian Spiritualism and the Rise of Modern Media Culture.* University Park: Pennsylvania State University Press, 2017.

Neely, Jeremy. *The Border Between Them. Violence and Reconciliation on the Kansas-Missouri Line.* Columbia: University of Missouri Press, 2007.

Nunnally, Michael L. *American Indian Wars: A Chronology of Confrontations Between Native Peoples and Settlers and the United States Military, 1500–1901.* Jefferson NC: McFarland & Co, 2007.

Oertel, Kristen. *Bleeding Borders: Race, Gender and Violence in Pre-Civil War Kansas.* Baton Rouge: LSU Press, 2009.

O'Reilly, Harrington. *Fifty Years on the Trail: A True Story of Western Life.* London: Chatto and Windus, 1889.

Parker, James. *The Old Army: Memories, 1872–1918.* Frontier Classics Series. Mechanicsburg, PA: Stackpole Books, 2003.

Randolph, Vance. *Kate Bender, the Kansas Murderess: The Horrible History of an Arch Killer.* Girard, KS: Haldeman-Julius Publications, 1944.

Rollings, Willard. *Unaffected by the Gospel: Osage Resistance to the Christian Invasion.* Albuquerque: University of New Mexico Press, 2004.

Russell, Don. *The Wild West: A History of the Wild West Shows.* Fort Worth, TX: 1970.

Russell, Sharman Apt. *Kill the Cowboy: A Battle of Mythology in the New West.* Boston: Addison Wesley, 1993.

Shortridge, James. *Peopling the Plains: Who Settled Where in Frontier Kansas.* Lawrence: University Press of Kansas, 1995.

Slotkin, Richard. *Gunfighter Nation: The Myth of the Frontier in Twentieth Century America.* New York: Atheneum, 1992.

Socolofsky, Homer. *Kansas History: An Annotated Bibliography.* New York: Greenwood Press, 1992.

Souter, Keith. *Medical Meddlers, Mediums and Magicians: The Victorian Age of Credulity.* Cheltenham, UK: The History Press, 2011.

Stratmann, Linda. *The Illustrated Police News: The Shocks, Scandals and Sensations of the Week, 1864–1938.* London: British Library Publishing, 2019.

Warren, Louis S. *Buffalo Bill's America: William Cody and the Wild West Show.* New York: Alfred A. Knopf, 2005.

Wilson, Theodore B. *The Black Codes of the South.* Tuscaloosa: University of Alabama Press, 1965.

Wishart, David J., ed. *Encyclopaedia of the Great Plains Indians.* Lincoln: University of Nebraska Press, 2007.

Walter, John. *The Guns that Won the West: Firearms on the American Frontier, 1848–1898.* London: Greenhill Books, 1999.

Wood, Fern Morrow. *The Benders: Keepers of the Devil's Inn.* Self- published, 1992.

Wood, Larry. *Murder & Mayhem in Southeast Kansas.* Cheltenham, UK: The History Press, 2019.

York, Mary. *The Bender Tragedy.* Independence, KS: Geo. W. Neff Book and Job Printer, 1875.

Index